THE STORYTELLER

Also by Anna Porter

Hidden Agenda
Mortal Sins
The Bookfair Murders

THE STORYTELLER

MEMORY, SECRETS, MAGIC AND LIES

ANNA PORTER

Anchor Canada

National Library of Canada Cataloguing in Publication Data

Porter, Anna

   The storyteller : memory, secrets, magic and lies : a memoir of Hungary

ISBN 0-385-25957-3

1. Rácz, Vilmos – Family. 2. World War, 1939-1945 – Hungary.
3. Hungary – History – Revolution, 1956. 4. Hungary – History – 20th century. I. Title.

DB955.6.R33P67 2001   943.905   C2001-930562-1

Cover and insert photographs courtesy the author
Text design by Susan Thomas/Digital Zone
Map by CS Richardson
Printed and bound in Canada

Published in Canada by
Anchor Canada, a division of
Random House of Canada Limited

Visit Random House of Canada Limited's website:
www.randomhouse.ca

TRANS   10 9   8   7   6   5   4   3   2   1

For Catherine and Julia,
in memory of Vili Rácz,
the Storyteller.

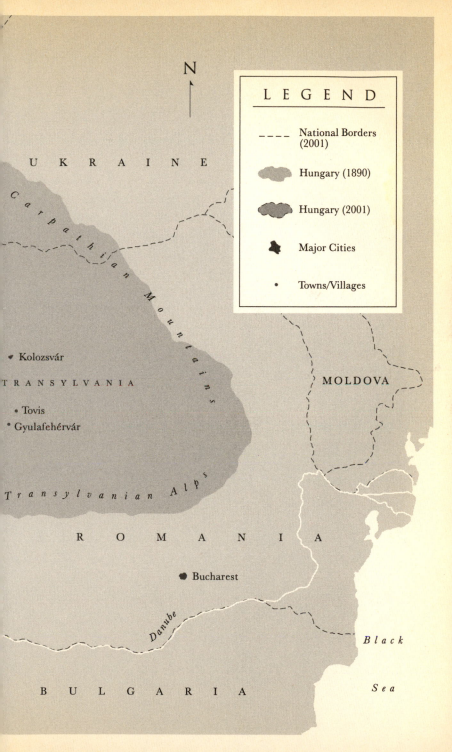

ACKNOWLEDGEMENTS

ONE WAY OR ANOTHER I have been writing this book for forty years, most of a lifetime. It is impossible to thank everyone who has added to the stories I have set down here. Nevertheless I'd like to acknowledge the extraordinary memories of Maria des Tombe, my mother, and her formidable friends, Anna Gellert, Bora Pallay, Magda Szenttamasi, Margit Csepeli, Martha Fairfield, Ivan Vassey, Lorand Wanke, George Nagy; the kindness of Kati Balogh in sending me the Hungarian Chronicles — *A Magyarok Krönikája* — and the book of Hungarian kings — *A Magyar Kiralyok Könyve;* and my friend Istvan Bart who waded through an early draft and took the trouble to correct names and spellings, and to argue with me over Vili's interpretations of Hungarian history.

It was Andy Sarlos's great enthusiasms for things Hungarian that took me back to Budapest to revisit some of our shared memories. Andy helped erect a statue of Imre Nagy close to the place I had hid during the '56 Revolution, in front of Parliament Square. On a hot summer day in 1996 we stood around the lifesize bronze Nagy, listening to speeches about those times past, then the haunting sounds of *Va, Pensiero* from Verdi's Nabucco, and everyone was crying. Thanks, also, to Hal Jones, Andy's partner back then, for helping me get to Transylvania.

I am grateful to George Jonas for his encouragement and for sharing his insights; to the librarians at the Magyar Ház on St Clair Avenue in Toronto for allowing me access to a range of their more obscure books; for *The Tragic Fate of Hungary* by Yves de Daruvar, *A Short History of Hungary* by Zoltan Halasz, *Memoir of Hungary* by Sandor Marai, *Magyar Mult, Magyar Sorsok* by Laszlo Pusztaszeri, *A Ket Hunyadi* by Dezso Dummerth.

Most of all, I thank my husband, Julian — he of English heritage — for being moved by these ancient tales of another culture; and my daughters for listening to the stories and coming on my strange journeys.

PROLOGUE

MY GRANDFATHER VILI had a particular weakness for the "Gerbaud girls." The Gerbaud was then, much as it is now, a wonderful place to meet. It was a glittery, overproduced spot on Budapest's Vörösmarty Square, where you went to be seen as much as to see who else was there. Around the turn of the century it was already a Baroque period piece, a coffeehouse in the Viennese tradition with touches of Turkish influence, and it was one of Vili's favourite spots as a young man. The Gerbaud girls had been a challenge for his amorous advances. Though young and inexperienced, they had been well-trained by Madame Gerbaud in the art of evading the eager hands of pushy customers. Vili succeeded in charming them with silk stockings — a rare luxury even among the wealthy and unknown in the countryside where most of the girls had come from.

Years later, in 1949, when he took me to the Gerbaud for the first time, he told me that once he had fallen in love there.

The three high-ceilinged rooms had been restored, except for the crystal chandeliers (smashed by the Germans, the pieces taken home by the Russians), and there were the blood-red drapes, the lion-footed tables, the discreet murmur of grown-up conversation, the hand-painted counter, the glass-enclosed confections, chocolate tarts with whipped

cream caps, tortes with marzipan, vanilla swirls, candy-
covered cakes — it was the pinnacle of all my best dreams.

Vili pulled the chair out for me to sit on — "It's how gentlemen do it," he told me — and when I couldn't slither up or hop
onto it, he lifted me into the whooshing, soft, maroon velvet
cushion. The sound of magic.

For me, he ordered chestnut purée over vanilla whipped
cream with drizzled chocolate topping. For himself, espresso.
The woman who wrote this down onto her cream-coloured
notepad was slender and her smile was warm, her lips like wilt-
ed rose petals. Her face flushed when Vili spoke to her. She
tried to tuck her auburn wisps of hair under her white cap as
she turned to him and asked how he had been.

In those times, a simple question like that carried the
weight of other unasked questions. I knew he would sigh
when he answered. "What can you expect in these times," he
said and didn't disappoint me about the sigh. And I knew
that "these times" meant the bad times we were all enduring,
the times when the streets were full of rubble and our old
house on the other side of the Danube, Buda, had been
taken from our family by a government that had no use for
people like my grandfather and me.

The Gerbaud waitress's name was Klara and she came
from Kolozsvár (now called Cluj), one of the oldest
Hungarian cities in Transylvania. She rested her hand on
Vili's shoulder while she put the small coffee cup in front of
him, and I thought perhaps he hadn't noticed when she ran
her red-nailed fingers lightly through the little tuft of hair on
the back of his neck.

He soaked sugar cubes in his coffee and offered them to
me on his silver coffee spoon. "I've known her for some
years," he told me. "She was just seventeen when she came up
to Budapest. Slip of a girl. Hoping for a good man."

"Did she find one?" I asked through a mouthful of chestnut purée and whipped cream. Though I was only five, I

knew Vili didn't think finding a good man was quite the solution to a girl's problems, but I was cautious enough not to say so and risk spoiling the moment.

"Some. But they weren't good in the right way." Leaning over the white tablecloth, his massive elbows heavy on the rim of the table, he said with great seriousness, "Now, you" — offering me the coffee-soaked sugar cube — "you must get an education."

I

MY CHILDHOOD WAS FILLED with my grandfather's stories. Some I remember so clearly that I still hear his voice in their telling and still see the pictures I saw when I first heard them. My whole family told stories — many true, a few imagined, others invented so long ago they had become true — but none were as full of life as my grandfather's.

There were wise witches and wily giants, magic horses and soothsayers who commanded ancient spells; there were princes and heroes who did battle against the powers of evil; there were grand viziers and turbaned armies of merciless Turks; and there were our Hungarian ancestors, who never tired of wielding their broadswords in defense of our ancient lands. He told stories about glittering dances in bygone courts and poets whose words could move more people than military commands ever had. There were stories about his three beautiful daughters and their gallant admirers, about his mother who told him her tales until late into the Bácska nights, about his grandfather who held court in Transylvania and was murdered at his own dinner table and about his grandmother, the dark-eyed Petronella who escaped with her young son, then drove her wagon for three days and four nights to arrive at dawn in the tiny village of Kula in the southern Hungarian region of Bácska where my grandfather was born some fifty years later.

He was my childhood hero.

His name was Vili. Actually, his name was Vilmos, but everyone called him Vili. He was a big, raw-boned man, and even when I came along, and he was well into his fifties, he was extraordinarily strong. He used to demonstrate his strength by doing crazy things like lifting chairs with people sitting on them. To prove that both his arms were equally strong, he sometimes lifted two chairs and two people at once.

He would crouch down between the two chairs, grab one leg in each hand, take a deep breath, puffing up his chest and his cheeks, then lift. His back straight, his eyes focused on some midpoint over our heads, he would slowly stand up. The veins on the sides of his neck and down the centre of his forehead stood out like ropes. All the while, the people on the chairs — usually his daughters or their rather temporary boyfriends or husbands — were stiff as statues. Everyone else applauded, and Vili's bald head took an almost imperceptible bow. After that he'd quickly deposit his charges, rub his big palms together and wink at his most appreciative audience — me.

He could stop ice carts by stepping in front of the horses, grabbing the pole between them and pushing back on it till their front hoofs clawed the air; then he'd let them down gently, because he did not want to hurt the horses or let the ice blocks slide off and break. Back in the early fifties, ice still came by horse and cart to Budapest in the summer. On hot days my friends and I would run behind the carts, picking up bits of fallen ice and rubbing them over our faces or trying to stuff ice shards down each other's shirt fronts. We wrestled and shoved to get the best spots nearest the back wheels so we could soak in a freezing-cold shower when the cart stopped for its deliveries. We got the best showers when my grandfather lifted the front of the cart.

When my grandfather was nineteen, he represented Hungary in four events at the European Games. One of them was the shot-put, another the épée. I could never figure how he could shine at both events, since one required a heavy step while carrying something that weighed over sixteen pounds and for the other you had to be light on your feet. For a decade he held the European record in the one-hundred-yard dash. At the 1908 London Olympics, he finished fourth behind three Americans in that event, but he also took part in the pentathlon.

He became, quite accidentally, Hungarian heavyweight wrestling champion for a year. He had been sauntering past the elevated rink in the University Club gym when the try-outs ended. The guys were shouting, "Why don't you get up there, Vili, don't you have the courage to face the champ?" Vili was not from Budapest. He was a landowner's son from the South, a brawny boy. He needed to show that he was bet-ter than anyone else. That was the only reason he won. The champion didn't have anything to prove.

He played soccer on the Budapest University team and impressed his colleagues with his ability to make the opposing team members laugh. He did magic tricks with the ball and with his kerchief and socks. Sometimes he made white pigeons appear from his pockets and let them fly away while his team scored a goal. He was an amateur magician. At my fourth birth-day party, he conjured up a white rabbit, a turtle and two minia-ture pinschers who started yelping and chasing the rabbit around the apartment, much to the delight of my friends and the distress of my grandmother, who told him he would have to return all the animals to wherever he'd found them. She told him we were no longer in our own house and could not afford to feed a menagerie.

Sometimes when we travelled on the Rákóczi Street street-car, he'd make forints disappear. Or if there were children in the seats across from ours, he'd take the coins out of his pockets — those of a very respectable, well-dressed, elderly gentleman — examine them, pretend to taste them, then eat them. On our way to the exit, he'd make them reappear from the children's ears and look most disapproving, surprised that they had somehow taken his repast of coins and hidden them so well. I remember the children's faces, at first embarrassed, then fascinated, then amazed, finally released into laughter when my grandfather stepped off the streetcar, adjusted his pocket handkerchief and headed toward one of his favourite coffeehouses.

Of all his talents, I think he was proudest of his prowess with the sword. He had been, arguably, the best sword dueller in Budapest. His duels were mostly fought in the early hours, at five or six in the morning, somewhere in a park — Városliget (City Park), for example, where you could barely see your opponent in the dawn fog. Yet a crowd gathered when Vili Rácz fought. "Vili was a reprobate," his brother, Béla, told me, pursing his lips as he gazed off into his *palinka*-induced stillness. "A skirt chaser. He should never have fought, knowing he was an Olympic champion and the others backyard swordsmen. They didn't have a chance."

Young Vili barely attended his classes, spending his time perfecting his sporting skills both in the field and, Béla told me, in the bedroom. Once he moved to Budapest, he became one of the city's star bachelors. His apartment, on the Buda side overlooking the river, was a party centre for all his young friends. He had his own icebox, replenished each day with both ice and champagne. At least once a week he sent a dozen red roses to a woman. Most weeks there was a new woman. Each bouquet indicated another conquest.

Fortunately, the duels usually ended after first blood had been drawn. No one in my home liked to talk about my grandfather's duels. "It's because they were all about women," Béla told me. My first memory of Béla is of him smoking foul-smelling cigars in a tiny apartment full of dark furniture that was not to be sat on or touched. It was hung with dusty velvet curtains, slimy to my fingers and musty with

age and perspiration, as were his ancient-looking clothes.
Béla had small, refined hands, a high forehead and a very red
face. He was shorter than my grandfather and drank *palinka*
— Hungarian plum brandy — because nothing else was avail-
able. He preferred Calvados. His breath was rancid with gar-
lic, nicotine and alcohol. He said he had once been a very
important person in Parliament.

When I relayed this information to my grandfather, he
said, "Of course," which in my grandfather's language meant,
"bullshit." But Vili never swore.

Béla was his youngest brother, the boy who leans over his
mother's knee in the old photograph Vili had of his parents'
young family. All the boys wear the same round-necked white
shirts, knee socks and short pants. Vili, the eldest, has his right
hand on his hip and looks directly into the camera. Gyula,
who later stopped speaking to Vili after their Turkish bath
venture, is gazing at his father. Béla is playing with his fingers.
Later, he was the one who stayed behind on the family estate,
trying to command the farm hands after his father died.

Because I spent most of my childhood trying to impress
my grandfather, I took up fencing. I won no medals, and my
fondest memory of my fencing days is of a dank, yellow-lit
gymnasium and a dozen of us pretending we were audition-
ing for *The Three Musketeers*. Dumas's book had been a huge
hit in Hungarian, and we all knew the stories. We were taught
by a Jesuit friend of my grandfather who was somewhat portly and tended to fall asleep during much of the thrust and
parry. Unfortunately, he was fully awake the day I discovered
I was going to have breasts. I was wearing a white shirt that
hung over a pair of loose, black shorts down to my knees,
more or less like the ones I had seen Vili wear in those old
brown and yellow photographs with serrated edges that
showed him winning medals against Swedes or Greeks. With
the enthusiastic leaping about that I had come to associate
with my fencing efforts, I had worked up quite a sweat.

Suddenly I realized that the other kids had begun to giggle and fidget. I became distracted, dropped my épée and faced the old Jesuit's épée about an inch from my nose. He had missed his chance to pretend-stab me, as he usually did when I missed a step. "Well," he said with not much of a smile on his face, "there are many reasons why girls are no good at this stuff. Two of them are staring at me, and they're not the sort of thing priests are supposed to see. So, how about putting on a sweater?"

The other kids were all boys whose fathers had been in the cavalry during the Second World War — or so they claimed. I put on my sweater and swore all the way home. For sons of cavalrymen, I thought, they had seemed rather lacking in chivalry.

Chivalry was an art much discussed in our home. Vili was a gentleman of the old ways, with a great fondness for Spenser, Shakespeare, Vörösmarty, Petöfi, Gárdonyi, Dumas, Jókai, Stendhal, Madách, Dickens, Tolstoy, Arany and a range of Hungarian poets who celebrated chivalry and the sadness of our history in long narrative poems with ringing rhymes and galloping rhythms.

I had dreamed of becoming a great poet-swordsman, and it seemed dreadfully unfair that my ambitions should be dashed by something as insignificant as nipples.

I took up running but showed about as much talent for that as I had shown for fencing. Sometime during the second lap of my first real race, I lost my footing and fell headlong, tripping the runner behind. Vili spared us both by not coming to see me in action.

My mother thought my big, flapping 1920s bloomers were to blame. They had slid down and the rubber had snagged my knees.

My grandfather loved women but knew nothing about women's clothes.

By that time he had already fathered three daughters with my grandmother and, though I didn't find out till much later, some sixteen other children by an assortment of women who had found him irresistible.

His "gallivanting," as his daughter Leah used to call it, created little rivulets of tension around our dinner table. Now and then my grandmother, whose name was Therese, would throw some hot and soggy food at him and they would both leave the table to shout at each other in their (and my) bedroom.

Most of the time, though, my grandmother adored him. She called him "Papa" and always served his food first. He got the biggest helpings.

My grandmother had once been a stunningly beautiful girl, with lush, black hair, a small, oval face, a high forehead and big, olive-black eyes. She was slender and small, maybe five foot one to his six foot two, her head reaching my grandfather's chest "around heart level," as he'd tell us. When the two of them walked together, she seemed fragile and insubstantial.

She came from a village in what is now Slovakia, but back then, and for hundreds of years before, it was called Felvidék, Upper Danubia. She and Vili met in one of the few spaces in Hungarian history when the country wasn't at war or occupied by marauding armies, or just marauding citizens, from elsewhere.

For centuries, Hungary had provided a barrier of live folk between opposing factions of Slavs and Germans, a major accomplishment that helped focus the German tribes into one coherent nation and stopped the westward expansion of unwanted easterners, such as the the Tatars and the Turks, each of whom slaughtered Hungarians for sport over several centuries.

We had a photograph of Therese taken when she was sixteen and almost a bride. A formal portrait, it was commissioned by her parents just before she was carried off by the Transylvanian giant. The picture is tinted light brown. She has glowing eyes in a pale face. Her nose is small and there is a tiny dimple in her chin. She has an uncertain smile. Her long hair is gathered at the nape of her neck and fastened with a white ribbon. Her shoulders are bare. When I asked if that was not too daring for the times, she told me the dress had been painted out by the photographer, but I didn't believe her.

2

THERE ARE VARIOUS STORIES about how they met.

In one of them, she is walking home by the side of the road, carrying a basket of flowers. ("Why is she carrying flowers?" "Shhh ... it's the way the story goes.") He passes by in an open carriage. He has just arrived by train from Budapest for a week-end shooting party at a friend's country estate, and he is in a hurry — he wants to be there for the festive dinner. But he tells the coachman to stop when he sees her. He thinks her waist is impossibly small, her ankles exquisite, her hair too thick and unruly for the ribbons. She is wearing a blue and red skirt and a white embroidered blouse. The air is heavy with the scent of white acacia blossoms.

"We are going in the same direction," he tells her. "I would be deeply honoured if you would allow me to take you." Hungarian was a very formal language back then.

At first she demurs. "How do you know it's the same direction?" Her eyes are lowered, but through the dark fringes of her lashes, she sees his smile.

He jumps from the carriage into the dust of the road and she notices for the first time how tall he is. His shoulders strain against the fine wool fibre of his black jacket. The collar of his white linen shirt is hand-stitched. Everything he wears is expensive, down to the soft, black leather boots gleaming with spit and polish.

"Wherever you go is the right direction," he says.

When he lifts her into the carriage, the tips of his fingers touch at her back as his big hands encircle her slender waist. She blushes when he tells her she's the prettiest girl in Upper Danubia.

Forty years later he was still telling her she was the prettiest woman in Upper Danubia, and she still believed him.

In my Aunt Sari's version, my grandmother is helping to serve the guests in a huge house close to my great-grandfather's ancestral home in Erdély. She is a friend of the host's young daughter. When she ladles the stag broth into his Herendi porcelain bowl, Vili catches her hand.

My great-great-grandfather had sat in a similar room, at another long oak dining table, dressed for the evening in a maroon velvet jacket with gold braid, when he was shot through the window by an unhappy Wallach. My great-great-grandfather's blood soaked into the floorboards at the head of the oak table where he sat for his evening meals, and it is still there — according to Vili.

In this story, Vili holds my grandmother's hand gently, turns it to kiss the first knuckle of her little finger, then returns it as if it were a gift. She hesitates, feels herself blush, her lips tremble. There is laughter around the table.

She is sure they are laughing at her embarrassment. Years later, he still insists they were laughing at a joke about a Wallachian hunting party where the only one left standing at the end of the day is the stag. No one had noticed Vili holding her hand.

He told the joke again to his friends at the Százéves, where he often took me for pretzels and beer. There were cardboard squares under the fluted glasses, and the long, dark wood tables were stained with beer. Men in black suits with white shirts played gypsy music. No one had money to tip them. And he told the story again in the Emke coffeehouse, where he played chess in the window with other friends and sometimes by himself. A crowd gathered wherever he went. The head waiter bowed, though he only gave him a forint, not enough for a pack of cigarettes. Even that he was reluctant to accept, and he often slipped it into my hand.

His friends exchanged gossip about politics using chess codewords that even I could understand. "Don't let the pawns get your knight, Vili."

"Watch your back when you cross the rook."

Every time he told the stag story everybody laughed.

Later, when he told the story in New Zealand in too-formal English, nobody did.

In my Aunt Leah's version of my grandparents' courtship, Vili met Therese at the Pozsony ball. She was poor gentry, but her parents had saved for a gown of white muslin and silk so their youngest daughter could one day attend the debutantes' ball. It was the beginning of the season, and the girls wore long, white gloves, silk-covered shoes, rosebuds in their hair. The sons of the gentry would come to the first ball to see the new crop of girls. Vili chose the best of the lot, my grandmother.

"Like a goose market?" I asked.

Leah gave this some thought. "A little," she agreed, smiling.

When Vili and Therese married, they moved into a house on the classy side of the river Danube, Buda. He spoiled her with expensive jewellery, flowers that came in giant Chinese vases and servants to attend to her wishes. He had promised her family he would care for her always.

But by the time of my first clear memories, we lived on the other side of the Danube in a cramped apartment overlooking the streetcar tracks and the flashing neon lights of Pest's biggest department store. There were no more servants, and my grandmother had taught herself to cook and wash dishes.

My grandmother rarely complained about what she had lost. She kept a few mementos, pretty things in a box under her bed that she rarely opened. She missed her garden, her spacious house, but, I think, she grieved only over my grandfather's insatiable appetite for other women.

3

IN HUNGARY, TRANSYLVANIA is called Erdély.

It's where my grandfather's people were born.

It's where the Carpathian mountain range arcs westward, protecting the plains that were the earliest home of the Hun and later of the Magyar tribes. "They were horsemen," Vili told me, "tall, fine-featured, their clothes made of spun wool and softened leather, their weapons cased in silver and inlaid with pearls. They wore beaten gold bracelets, rings on their fingers, necklaces adorned with rubies. Their horses' necks were decorated with precious stones, gold fibula on the saddles. They so loved their horses, they were usually buried with them."

("Somebody killed the horses when the people died?"

"They didn't want to live anyway once their masters were buried."

"Oh.")

"They crossed the mountains under the cover of night, over steep, treacherous passes, carrying all their goods on their backs — they never had more than they could carry — fleeing from the Bulgars, or the Avars, or the Pechenegs, or perhaps all three. They settled in a lush, wooded land they called Erdély. With the mountains behind them, they felt protected from their enemies."

I first heard about Attila the Hun from Vili. We were hanging over the balcony of our apartment trying out my new bow and arrow, which Vili had found in an old curiosity shop in the Óbuda section of the city. He said the bow was made of the finest spruce, shaped like an eagle, dipped in red dye with a leather handle and sinew string, just like the ones Attila used when he laid waste to the Roman Empire. Laid waste, Vili said, meant he destroyed it. "It was an old empire, bloody, corrupt and bloated with the blood of its victims. All empires reach that stage, even this one." "This one," meant the Soviet empire, and that we were part of it. "Only Hungarians," he added, "would name their sons Attila."

Stories of the great plains and river valleys the Huns had found were told by their storytellers, who travelled throughout the nations talking about the exploits of the brave and the demise of the mighty, the wisdom of those who learn to listen to the advice of the elders and those who carry magic in their pockets, and sometimes in their souls.

("What kind of magic?" "The kind that keeps you out of trouble.")

When the Magyars, who were still fighting the Pechenegs, Avars and everybody else somewhere in deepest Asia, heard of the beautiful lands their cousins, the Huns, had found, they grabbed their children and animals and followed over the same passes.

There were seven tribes with seven chiefs, said Vili. Rather than fight over who was going to be leader, the seven elected one superchief. His name was Árpád. He was the strongest and wisest. His thick leather vest repulsed the arrows of his enemies, and he wore leather britches and deer-hide boots that rarely touched the ground because he spent most of his life on his stallion. Vili promised to take me to Heroes' Square to visit him one day.

The chiefs assembled under a deer-pelt tent and invited their people to witness a ceremony of blood that would unite them forever. Each chief in turn slit his forearm with a jewel-inlaid dagger and let his blood drip into an earthenware cup.

When the cup was almost full, the shaman, known as the *tál-tos*, mixed the blood with red wine, poured some onto the ground to appease the spirits of the earth, then handed it to each chief in turn, while uttering secrets in a language no one understood but that they all knew was more ancient even than the Magyars'. One by one, they drank from the cup. When it was empty, the *táltos* declared they were now united in blood and would act as one nation, not as seven separate tribes.

Vili now turned back to the arrows. They were gold-painted with black and white feathers at one end. He had tied strings to the feathery ends so we wouldn't lose them. We could shoot them over the side or up into the air so they would fall back onto the balcony. The trick was to get out of their way when they came back.

"There is an old tale about the first Hungarians," Vili said. "Do you want to hear it?"

"Does it have something to do with arrows?"

"Old tales about Hungarians always have something to do with arrows."

It was a tale about the two handsome sons of King Menrot, Hunor and Magor, who go deer hunting in the forests between the rivers Volga and Don, just to the west of the Ural Mountains. Being both handsome and clever, they are successful in their endeavours. Their arrows hit straight into the hearts of their prey. One would not expect less of them — at least not in this tale. As they turn for home with the fresh meat tied to their horses, they catch sight of a fabulous pair of antlers, a stag bigger and statelier than those they've already killed. Being the best in their kingdom, these two princes have no choice but to add this stag to their trophy collection. They chase it over land and water, night and day, over marshes, through forests so thick their horses must slow to a walk, through the domains of the black bear, the wild boar, even the stealthy tiger, and past the shores of the Black Sea, over steep passes and rocky ravines. Sometimes they lose sight of the prey and it reappears as if to mock them. They must go on because, being sons of King Menrot, they will not be mocked. They are determined to nail the stag's antlers to their castle wall. Ignoring their evil intent, the stag leads them into a land so mild and lovely, they forget their original plan, lay down their bows and arrows and begin to enjoy themselves.

The sun is warm, their horses are getting fat eating all the green grass, the brook water is sweet. To make matters perfect, they come upon a party of young girls disporting themselves with a gaggle of fairies. It was thought in those days that young girls could turn themselves into fairies if they were not grabbed first by men. No chance of that for these young sprites. Hunor and Magor take themselves a couple of brides and settle in this beautiful place.

There is no further mention of the miraculous stag, though the tale makes it clear that my ancestors would never have found Erdély had it not been for its leadership.

Most Hungarians still think of this land as their own, despite the fact that it is now part of Romania.

When I think of it as Erdély, it is a deceptively pastoral place with straw-roofed houses and warlike people, the birthplace of heroes like János Hunyadi, who beat back Sultan Mohammed's armies from the gates of Europe and whose castle is in Erdély. At noon, when church bells ring throughout Europe, it is to celebrate his victory over the "infidel."

When I was very young, I thought Kula was in Erdély because it made sense for my grandfather's people to have lived in the same place for all those hundreds of years. But it isn't. It's several hundred kilometres southwest, in Bácska, and it was a baffling accident of fate that landed Vili's grandmother so far from where she was born.

4

In Vili's stories, Kula also takes on mythic proportions. It is a vast, cloudless place where stars hug the horizon at night and a boy can hold the wind in his lungs and run as far as his legs will take him. It's flat, working land, black earth, wheatfields, chicken coops, vineyards; an apple orchard, stands of yew trees, willows by the brook; dogs barking, roosters crowing at the dawn, rolling grass for the horses, wheat so tall in the summer you could be lost and not found till harvest. In the early spring when the shoots are young, it's verdant, smelling of manure, and you are the tallest thing as far as the eye can see.

In the summer the family lives far from the village in a sprawling house surrounded by plane trees.

In the winter they live in a long, white house across from the church, which takes pride of place in the village. Twenty rooms, each with its own hearth, each covered in different coloured tiles. There are parquet floors and chandeliers in every room. Vili's mother, Jolán, planted oleanders all around the house and along the path leading to the front door; man-size oleander plants in wooden pots line the corridors and hug the windows. Jolán is tall and stately: she carries her shoulders squared, her arms folded in front of her: she wears long, flowing gowns with white collars, and white gloves when she mothers her plants. Oleanders are her favourite flowers.

There are high ceilings with frescoes and windows with double panes, shimmering red-yellow-blue Persian carpets, paintings in fat, gold frames on the whitewashed walls. The paintings are pastoral, showing galloping horses and young men in white shirts wielding long whips. There are a few with fighting men and one where a man is slitting his wife's throat rather than let her fall prey to the pursuing Turkish janissaries.

The first room off the entrance is his father's study. The one rule in the house is that the boys must be quiet when they enter lest they disturb him. György's study is the one room in the house without a carpet. When he walks from his desk to the bookcase, his heels pound on the floor. There is only one picture in his room, the painting of his old house in Erdély, surrounded by poplars. On his desk there is a small, framed, black and white drawing of a young girl in a white dress with flowers in her hair.

György is a quiet man, he never raises his voice with the children. When the boys play in the black marble pool where the fountain spouts coloured water on special days, he watches from the window of his study. He has always been solitary, an outsider in this village, respected and feared, though he never raises his voice with anyone.

Vili told me the fountain rose like a willow from its black marble pool. It was wide at the base, softened into a long narrow waist and sprouted water through furled scrolls held aloft by naked angels. The water sprayed in an arc, higher than the roof of the house, higher even than the fountain at the Városliget amusement park, where he took me once (Vili formally dressed in a three-piece suit, watch chain dangling from his vest pocket, hat tucked under his arm, gloves held firmly) to ride the gigantic, rattling roller coaster, our arms held high, his laughter louder than the wooden cart careening around the last giant bend before lining up for the last great plunge.

Even on Sundays, when the family trooped off to church in Kula, Vili's father stayed behind. Once, when he had given the church a new painting, the bishop came to the house to thank him. When the bishop asked if he would accept the congregation's thanks in person, he declined. The closest he had gone to the church was its steps.

The painting was of St. George and the dragon. It was the fiercest, greenest dragon Vili had ever seen: its green eyes followed you wherever you went; it was the kind of dragon Vili and his brothers were sure had lived in Erdély a long time ago and might still be hiding up in the mountains. When they were too noisy in church, Jolán sometimes told them the dragon might come to take them to his lair.

Jolán, Vili was sure, could have married any man she wished to marry, or none at all. She chose György because he was a dark prince in that small southern town, the only man who wasn't born there, one who remained a mystery to his neighbours. In the brown and white photograph my grandfather left me, his mother sits as straight as her husband, wearing lacy white that flows down her neck, spreads around her broad hips and settles in an arc at her feet. Her hair is piled on top of her head, her eyes look directly into the camera, her throat is exposed.

The chair is the photographer's, fancy wooden curlicues on the arms and the tips of the back. She had wanted something simpler, but that was all the photographer could offer. The picture was taken in his studio in Budapest, booked by her husband weeks before. They were giving one to György's mother, Petronella, for her birthday.

When Vili was little, Jolán told him bedtime stories about heroes and dragons and old women who always gave you three chances to succeed. Some of the stories featured turbaned Turks who took children and kept them captive so long they forgot who they were. Most dangerous of all, they forgot their language. They stopped being Magyar.

For over a thousand years, what had defined the tribe, she told Vili, was its language. Though they had journeyed far, fought with everybody, endured wars and servitude and absorbed many others into their thinning ranks, they still passed on their stories. Each generation added some words and other words had been forgotten, but the language had endured. Vili's mother insisted he learn the language well. She hired tutors for the boys, and though she was anxious that they also learn Latin and German, the stories she told were all Hungarian.

The marble for the pool, she told him, had come from the Carpathian Mountains, near his ancestral home. It had been a gift for his grandmother, Petronella Rácz. She had been a tiny woman, but fearless. It was Petronella who had taught Vili's father, György, to fence. She had been fast on her feet, quick with her blade, and her eyes never wavered. She rode a horse like a man. Her dark hair fanned out behind her, her skirts rode up to her knees, she held the horse so tight between her legs that she could let go of the reins and still control him. "It's how Hungarians ride, effortless, light, always in control."

In 1914 Vili rode his horse into the First World War with the confidence of a hussar officer, resplendent in his short, red wool tunic with the gold braid, blue pantaloons with white stripes down the sides, spit-polished leather boots, and the jaunty, visored hat that had been worn by millions of Hungarian fighting men over seven centuries of strife. He was proud of coming through officers' school stronger than the effete Viennese he had enjoyed beating in hand-to-hand combat. He had won his white horse from an Austrian captain late one night in a game of poker.

In 1914 war seemed like an opportunity to do something grand and heroic, to have a chance at the Russians, to pay them back for their 1849 intervention in Erdély.

("But you were fighting on the side of the Austrians."

"In a way. But that's another story.")

There was little room for heroes on the Russian front. Hungarians were the sorry rump of the Kaiser's armies. They were dispensable. As the war went on, they were sent, swords aloft, into enemy fire or were left to starve in snowbound camps.

Vili had few war stories to tell me. One was from the early days. It was a dawn excursion. Vili's one hundred hussars were patrolling an area outside Kiev. They encountered a group of Cossacks on horseback. "They, too, were beautifully attired, in furry hats and billowing britches. Cossacks, as everyone knows, are the only other horsemen in the world worthy of riding fine horses into battle." The Cossacks and the Hungarians fought one another valiantly for many hours, but neither could claim victory. Finally, after a brief rest, Vili suggested to the Cossack officer that they should settle the matter by a duel between the captains. The choice of weapon would be the Cossacks'. The winner would carry the day for his side.

The Cossacks, equally weary, agreed. Their leader chose the sword.

The two captains charged, their swords clashed, their horses bucked and heaved under them. The Cossack fell, unseated by Vili's ducking his powerful attack. Vili dismounted, and now they fought hand to hand on the frozen ground. When the sword flew from the Cossack's hand, Vili flicked it back to him, just as they do in *The Three Musketeers*. The Russian was good, but only one of the two men was an Olympic champion.

Vili won. He extended his hand to the defeated Cossack captain, who shook it with a smile. In that moment, Vili said, "we both realized we had been fighting somebody else's war. There were no prisoners that day."

In October 1918 Vili and his one hundred hussars were awaiting instructions in Odessa on the Black Sea. Early on the morning of the twenty-third of October they were told to abandon their horses and board a train. There were emotional scenes at the temporary paddocks where the hussars said goodbye to their mounts. The boys were young, some not yet twenty. They had survived fierce battles on horses they felt knew them better now than any relative at home.

Of the one hundred men, only one knew where they were going — the captain. Vili was handed the orders by an Austrian major, they saluted and that was the end of the war for my grandfather. By the time they crossed the border into Hungary, everyone had figured out the orders, and even those who had gone into formal mourning for their horses shouted and yelled with delight. The train went, with only a few stops to load coal, directly to the Eastern Railway Station in Budapest.

Vili had no idea that the war had already been lost. He didn't know that what would greet him at home was a world in disarray.

The much-unlamented Austro-Hungarian dual monarchy was over. The head of a new National Council, Mihály Károlyi, ordered the soldiers to lay down their arms and disperse. Károlyi then went to Belgrade to try to negotiate a separate peace for his countrymen. He thought the French commander of the southern Allied armies would be greatly impressed with his precipitate actions, which now included the assassination of the former prime minister, who had been arguing for peace for a couple of years and had sought out both the Americans and the British.

To Károlyi's dismay, the French commander, General D'Esperay, treated him with utter contempt. D'Esperay consulted his Romanian and Serbian liaison officers and, without discussing the matter with the other Allied commanders, handed Károlyi Hungary's fate.

Meanwhile, Romanian troops poured over the Eastern borders and found only sporadic resistance as they made their way toward the capital. Budapest was in ruins as mobs of angry citizens fought one another, some demanding peace, some a semblance of justice, most wanting to lynch Károlyi and his government. The Romanians entered the undefended city, looted what little they found, blew up a couple of Catholic churches and hanged a few citizens they caught in the after hours.

The confusion was so great no one could ever successfully explain how the Communist Party grabbed the government or how they managed to hang or shoot a further two or three thousand Hungarians before they were through with their brief reign of what became known as the "Red terror."

Vili remembered the bodies, some still dressed in their army uniforms, some in evening clothes, some in peasant dress, hanging from the ornate wrought-iron lampstands of Budapest and from ancient gibbets in the countryside. In a few short months in power, Béla Kun and his crowd executed as many of their perceived enemies as they could. When it was over, they escaped — perhaps surprisingly — toward the West. Only Kun himself made it to Russia.

When the First World War ended, Hungary lost two-thirds of its land and three million of its people to Romania, Serbia and the newish state of Czechoslovakia. While the war had raged on, the Czech leader Tomás Masaryk lobbied both sides of the Atlantic for a new homeland to be carved out of Hungary and shared with the Slovaks. The Serbs, delighted with the successful results of the assassination of the heir to the Austrian throne and observing that Hungary was, once again, on its knees, had invaded southwest Hungary and fully expected to keep it when the war was over. They were prescient in their expectations. Even the Austrians ended up with a piece of the Hungarian pie.

The Treaty of Trianon was signed on June 4, 1920, at 4 p.m. in the Trianon Palace at Versailles. In a fit of pique, a French general had declared that Hungary would be made to pay for the war. No one mentioned that the war had been a Russian/German war among feuding cousins. ("Cousins?"

"All those royals were related. They should have settled the matter in Városliget with épées, or in Vienna with gold-plated pistols at dawn.") Or that Serbia had provoked it in order to end up with a chunk of its neighbour. The biggest loser was Hungary.

Vili had a theory about the French role in the Treaty of Trianon. In 1889, when the French staged their grand World's Fair and built the Eiffel Tower to commemorate their own greatness, the Hungarian government had refused to attend with its own pavilion because they thought this would please Austria. When I was growing up, there was a little verse I learned from my aunts:

> *Once Hungary was a big country,*
> *Now it's a tiny little country,*
> *Nasty people robbed it of its heart,*
> *Poor little land of ours.*

Well, it suffers somewhat in the translation, but the sentiment is clear. Even in the 1950s, when it wasn't safe to suggest that other hard-working socialists were occupying our heartlands, most children knew this verse.

Though peace and government returned to Hungary some time after 1920, no one ever gave up hope that the lost pieces of land would one day return.

My cousin Edy, at seventy-five a knight in the revived Hungarian order of St. Michael, shows me a book when I meet her in 1998. It is a simply bound, white paperback with blue lettering. It purports to tell you everything about Trianon. For old times' sake, she invites me for coffee and cakes at the Gerbaud café. Her hair has turned white since I last saw her in early October 1956. She had long, dark brown, unruly hair back then. She had spent ten years in the infamous Szeged jail for helping the British embassy staff escape from Budapest before the return of the Russian Army in November 1956.

"Trianon is the shame of the whole Western world," she tells me in urgent whispers. "More than seventy percent of the country, sixty-five percent of our people, handed over like cattle. And the reparations: all the salt we could produce, iron, silver and the gold mines. Our trees for timber, our coal to fuel others' industries ... Can you imagine what that did to us?" She rubs her hands together as if to cleanse them and runs her fingers through her coarse, white hair. They are fine, long fingers, shaking as they come to rest above her eyes, shutting out the early afternoon sun. "Over three million people ... Can you imagine that?"

I bring the book home to Toronto, where it sits, somewhat incongruously, next to Paul Johnson's *History of Europe*, a book that mentions Hungary only once in its discussion of the Treaty of Versailles. Trianon, so important in Vili's story, barely deserved a paragraph. "Victors write history," Vili had said.

"Uncle Vili never got over Trianon," Edy confides about my grandfather.

She is probably right.

5

WHEN MY GRANDPARENTS referred to "peacetime," they meant the undefined time after the terrible end of the First World War and into the creeping beginning of the Second, when there was a semblance of peace in Budapest. "Peacetime" meant trying to forget, to get on with life. There were dances and debutante balls again, and the restaurants opened, Madame Ritz built a grand hotel on the bank of the Danube, the Olympic team won the gold in fencing, the theatres were packed with people and you had to reserve your table at the Gerbaud if you wanted to eat there on a Saturday night. Vili bought his first magazine, invested in a theatre company that performed musicals by Lehár and Strauss, bought a half share of one of the Turkish steam baths in Buda and acquired his first car — a yellow Studebaker — his country house and a vacation home on the Mediterranean close to Trieste, where there were civilized coffeehouses on the main square overlooking the harbour.

He and Therese had three daughters.

Leah was the middle one. She was the tallest and slimmest of the three Rácz sisters. She was the belle of the balls, her beauty celebrated in social columns from Budapest to Vienna, her dresses imitated by others whose fathers could not afford expensive new creations for every occasion. Her favourite colour was lilac. Her dresses cascaded to the ground and swished around the dance floor, swivelling her narrow hips so very unselfconsciously, so innocently that even the older men turned to look. She tilted her long, pale neck up toward her partners' faces as she danced. An elegant lilac orchid nestled precariously just above her small breasts where the dress divided and reached upward in an arc to meet in a bow behind her neck. The bow was tied so gently that some guessed it would not hold till the end of the night — and the night ended at around four in the morning.

Though it was only Leah's first season, the young Count Esterházy had heard of her beauty, and one night he came to the ball in his officer's dress uniform, white with gold braid, the ceremonial sword of the nobility by his side. He rode his horse up the carpeted steps to the grand ballroom and past the footman whose job it was to announce the guests. He needed no introduction, because the Esterházys were the grandest of Hungarian aristocrats. When his prancing white stallion entered the ballroom — the first time anyone had ridden a horse there — the crowd parted to clear a path. It was around one in the morning, the traditional rest period, when people ate ("sumptuous feasts of pheasant and wild boar, golden goose pâté, Persian caviar, black Viennese chocolate cakes") and replenished their champagne glasses.

The horse highstepped toward Leah, and the count dismounted ("Yes, there were a few broken glasses") and asked her if her next dance was taken.

It was. All her dances were taken. But her next partner offered her hand to the dashing young Esterházy. The horse was led off the dance floor. ("No, he hadn't messed the floor.") And the orchestra played another Strauss waltz. The two swept round and round in dizzy circles, and everyone was clapping. When the music stopped, she gave him her lilac orchid. He walked her to where her parents waited.

Vili had risen to acknowledge the presence of the count.

"I once served with your father on the Russian front," Vili told him. "He used his horse for battle. Never took him dancing."

There was embarrassed laughter.

"After that, he didn't come calling," Leah remembered sadly. She would have enjoyed being a countess.

Vili was proud of all three of his daughters. But he was particularly proud of Leah's beauty, her fragility, her ability to attract men. She had the darkest hair of all the sisters. At a ball, it rolled down her back, the silk ribbons barely holding it in check, her narrow waist — just like her mother's — disappearing in her partners' palms. She had a tinkling laugh, skin as white as a fairy's, big, wet, vulnerable eyes with long, black lashes, and ankles so slender they drove men wild.

Leah first married in 1940. He was a lawyer, but only in the sense that a gentleman might pick a profession he never really means to take seriously. A gentleman was not supposed to have a job. He came from a fine old family, he was an accomplished dancer, he had exemplary manners, a soft voice and soft, brown eyes. Leah confessed to her sisters that she didn't love him, but the Germans were glowering at the border, maybe there wouldn't be another season, and everyone knew what it meant if the season ended and you hadn't found a husband. She couldn't bear the embarrassment of failure.

When he left her to go to the front not quite two years later, he left her a good name and a daughter with soft, brown eyes.

Leah learned to drive in 1946. The war was over. People were coming out of the rubble, glad to be alive, hopeful, with nothing left to lose, and they figured there was a chance that life might come back to normal. Normal in Hungary meant no obvious sign of an occupying army. For a few shining months, so Vili told me, there were American soldiers in the city. "It's not that we loved the Americans, it's that we disliked the Russians."

Leah's American beau had a Chevrolet convertible. It had white tires and a white canvas top that rolled back. It was the perfect car for my aunt. Her hair could fly in the wind; everyone climbing out of their cellars could see her parade past the bomb craters in the shiny white car, itself careless of the mud and grime of what was left of the streets. Her slender arm and white-gloved hand rested casually along the frame. She seemed to be from another world.

They didn't envy her, Vili said. You can't envy something so unattainable. She was part of the moment of hope.

Leah was twenty-four, the American a year older. He had enlisted in the air force against his mother's wishes. He could have sat out the war as a medical student with high-level connections in Washington, a father who made cars in Detroit, a mother who had been born into the Boston set.

His name was something like Warren. Vili didn't remember it. He had been so much in love with Leah, he had flowers brought in from Paris. Mostly, they were lilacs and hothouse pink roses wrapped in wet French newspapers, their stems soaking in moss. Sometimes he brought them himself; sometimes the army Jeep delivered them, the driver waiting patiently at the door till he could hand them to her personally. Her fame had spread.

Nightclubs had opened in the inner city, and a few played jazz late into the nights. Warren took her dancing to show her off to his friends. There were Marlene Dietrich lookalikes displaying painted-on, black-stockinged legs, singing in husky voices in taverns. He took her there, Leah wearing her newly acquired black American silk hose attached to lace garters, the short skirts he brought her, high-heeled sandals, her hair piled on top of her head — the very height of fashion. He taught her to drive the Chevrolet because he wanted her to be able to drive when they were living in Detroit. Everyone in Detroit knew how to drive.

Along with his good looks, Warren had inherited his mother's manners and his father's confidence. One evening in early June, he surprised Vili by following him to the terrace of our old Buda house — the terrace was the only part of the house that hadn't been bombed — to ask for his daughter's hand in marriage.

Vili sat on a stone bench under an oak tree. He was facing the sunset from which Warren had come, his back to the east where he knew Russia waited, and he thought for a while that it would be just fine for Leah to leave for America while she could. Though there had been much talk of Russian-American friendship, Vili had seen the Russians and he was looking at the Americans. The friendship wouldn't last, he thought, and Truman would leave Hungary in the Russians' care. It was, the Russians maintained, their backyard.

Warren's speech had been short and to the point. He would be a good husband, and Leah would learn English and raise amazing children in Detroit. She would have a nice house in the suburbs, where there were good schools. They could visit Budapest once a year. This was a very practical proposition.

Vili wondered why Warren hadn't mentioned Leah's daughter, Kati, when he described the idyllic life in Detroit, and why he seemed unconcerned that Leah hadn't quite got around to divorcing her first husband, but he didn't say so. What Vili did say was that he had read too much Gárdonyi and Arany. He was a romantic about Hungary. He could not face his daughter leaving her country behind. He told Warren that Leah would wait for the man she loved. He was sorry that Warren was not the right one.

Leah's second husband was a wounded Hungarian Army captain. He had been on the Russian front somewhere near Volgagorod. His unit had spent most of the war in short skirmishes ahead of the German Army. A piece of shrapnel had hit him. He had a hollow in his forehead where the hair started. He allowed me to put my finger in it. I imagined I could feel his brain pulsating under my touch.

Vili said he had a good family name. That was all he brought to the marriage. My beautiful aunt Leah learned to drive trucks to support them.

In the summer of 1950, at a truckstop café some forty miles south of Budapest on the way to Szeged, she was raped and beaten in the cab of her four-ton, diesel-engined distance hauler and left by the roadside. The three men climbed back into their trucks, still laughing at her bourgeois ways. It seemed, they said later, that Comrade Leah Rácz hadn't understood the new spirit of sharing. They had shared their apricot brandy as sweetener for her coffee, and that was all they had. Afterwards, it was her turn to share what she had.

I had just started school in 1950 and already knew that "bourgeois" was a bad word, almost as bad as *kulak*, (landowner) — landowners were ticks on the backs of the peasants.

When my grandfather took me to see Leah in the hospital, his feet hammered the hard-shined floors in the all-white corridors, the tiny bottles on nurses's carts shaking with his every step. I had never seen him angry before that day. At her bedside, he took her shattered face between his large hands as gently as if he were holding an injured bird.

Some weeks later, when Leah was home again, she told me that her father had run two of her attackers through with his 1908 sword. The third one he threw out of the window of his second-storey apartment in Budakesz.

6

My aunt Sari, her second husband, Kálmán, and little Sari left for Vienna before we moved across the river to Pest. For years after we were told not to talk about them in public and certainly never to strangers or in front of strangers, even if we believed them to be our friends, because Sari had gone to "the West."

Sari was the oldest of the Rácz sisters. She wore her silky, blonde hair swept back into a chignon at the nape of her neck. She was proudest of her broad forehead, her strongly carved chin and high cheekbones, all denoting character, she told me. She had been the first of the sisters to be presented at the Vigadó's Hussar Ball, a year before anyone had heard of Leah. That year Sari was the most talked-about young lady in Budapest. For her first official portrait, she directed the photographer to take her in silhouette, her magnificent chin pointing slightly upwards, the clear lines of her forehead exposed, her lips gently parted.

Her first husband was an actor. Before he married Sari, he played small parts in cabaret theatres, sometimes not even in Budapest but in the provincial cities of Debrecen and Pécs. He had gone where the work was. Once he married Vili Rácz's daughter, he was featured in colour on the covers of theatre magazines, made two movies, became the romantic lead on the Budapest stage; there were interviews in *Woman's*

Journal, he was importuned by autograph seekers and he became the darling of the nightclub scene.

"He left her then?" I asked Vili.

"No. She left him. She met Kálmán at the officers' ball, and she couldn't remember why she had ever married the actor."

"Did the first husband look like my cousin?"

"He was just as pretty. Too pretty for a man, I think, but about right for a romantic lead. He was happier without Sari. He never had to try sharing himself again."

When Sari and Kálmán married, an honour guard of hussars lined the entrance to the cathedral, their drawn swords forming a bower over the heads of the young couple. They shouted "hurrah" when the ceremony was over and threw pink rose petals under Sari's feet as she passed. That was in 1943, while the war raged on.

Before Sari and Kálmán left for Vienna, there was much whispering and arguing. Everyone would clam up when Kati and I went by, making it a lot of fun to linger as the family waited, smoked and gave one another meaningful glances. Inevitably, someone would say in German, "Nicht vor dem Kind." That was about the only German I knew. It meant that Kati and I were on the prowl and whatever subject was being discussed had to be left till we were gone.

I have only hazy memories of our old house in Buda. There was a garden with sprinklers that we ran through in the summer, and Kati and I had rooms all to ourselves. There was a great deal of furniture, including some large, low-slung, velvety couches to hide behind, and there were doors opening in all directions.

I remember Aunt Sari sitting with her legs together, the fingers of her white gloves interlaced over her knees, her short blue and white spotted skirt riding up her thighs, and Kati peering from under the couch, her face squished into the carpet to see if Aunt Sari's panties were the lace ones we had seen drying on the line in the back of the house. They weren't. They were blue and white like her skirt. Even her shoes had a blue and white striped leather bow on the front.

Kálmán was a big, dark-haired man with a square face and a leather jacket. He had bandages on his knuckles. He sat next to Sari and barely spoke. My grandfather talked a lot about Vienna, while the two of them listened.

In my imagination Vienna was the dreaded, decadent city of high prison towers where the Habsburgs kept Hungarians in darkness till the end of their days. It was where ladies in crinolines ate petit fours while their silk-jacketed menfolk directed attacks on my country. It was where the Austrians had conspired with the Turks to give away Hungarian lands in exchange for peace in Vienna. It was where they had hanged Lajos Kossuth, hero of the 1848 War of Independence, in effigy. Luckily, it was the closest they ever got to hanging the real thing. Kossuth escaped their clutches. Vili told me Kossuth was one of our greatest heroes and the Austrians were hoping the hanged doll would bring him bad luck.

Back then Sari's daughter was called "little Sari" and she wasn't allowed to play with Kati and me because she had her own governess. Years later she would be called Carla and we would be reunited in, of all places, New Zealand.

When Sari, Kálmán and little Sari disappeared, everyone tried to pretend they were on holiday, but Kati and I knew they had gone to Vienna and, very likely, to a dark jail tower, where they would be fed only bread and water.

That was probably why my mother cried all that night and the next day after they left.

A few weeks later we moved to the Pest side of the river and no one mentioned them again until my father passed through our lives.

7

MY MOTHER WAS BORN in Budapest in 1924. She was baptized Maria Magdaléna Rácz, the only one of the Rácz girls to receive a New Testament name. It was an odd choice for a baby girl, Maria Magdalena having been a woman of exceedingly easy virtue, known for her voluptuous habits, for her luxuriant hair, and for being the only woman to accompany Jesus on his travels. There was a painting of her in the old Franciscan church where we went some Sundays before beer and pretzels. She was drying Jesus's feet with her hair. He seemed to be really enjoying it.

Nobody ever called my mother Maria Magdalena — she was too small for such a big name. Everybody called her "Puci" after the white schnauzer Vili gave Therese to celebrate the baptism. When Puci was born, her face was scrunched up just like the schnauzer's, and she made similar yappy noises when she was happy.

Leah and Sari tried to ignore her existence. She was too young to include in their games, too noisy to hide under the table when dinner guests came, too fragile to throw around. Sari thought she cried too easily. Leah thought she was spoiled by too much attention. Leah was four at the time, and Sari had just turned eight.

When she was old enough to listen to fairy stories, Puci recognized herself as Cinderella, the little girl always left on her own while her sisters were measured for the latest fashions. There was only one startling difference: Puci's sisters were the prettiest girls in the city. They charmed their tutors out of teaching; their lessons in arithmetic never progressed beyond simple multiplication; their language teacher was sacked for kissing twelve-year-old Sari behind the rose bushes while Leah stood guard hoping her turn would come. Puci had watched from her perch in the yew tree and told their parents.

Little Puci climbed trees and chopped her hair off herself so that it wouldn't hang in her face when she swung from high branches. She swam like a boy, practised lassoing the family dogs and hoped one day there would be a magical carriage and a fairy godmother to transform her into a golden girl with two glass slippers when she whirled in her prince's arms.

For my mother, there was never to be a prince — only a series of pretenders.

She sulked when her sisters went to dances and watched when they had male visitors.

When Sari put on her first white ball gown, Puci hid her sister's brand-new, elbow-length, form-fitting, matching gloves in her own panties, where she was sure no one would think of looking. She was only twelve when Leah went to her first ball, swishing down the parquet steps of the big house in Buda in her lilac dress. Leah didn't know till her beau brushed his hand over her perfectly slender back that Puci had pinned a piece of paper there with the word "pig" spelled out in capital letters.

Vili told me he decided to send Puci to boarding school because he was determined that at least one of his daughters should get a classical education. "She was the smartest," he said. "Already questioning everything, debating the reasons for all received wisdom, such as why only boys should play football, when it was obvious she could run faster and jump higher than any of them, and why girls should ride sidesaddle when it was so much easier to ride like the boys did. I caught her smoking one of my brother's Turkish cigarettes, and she just smiled at me: 'Does it say somewhere that girls can't smoke?'"

"They were all too busy for me," my mother said. "Father had his magazines, he had a great many friends, he had the theatre, he had bought the Lukács Baths, he had been a great athlete, he was famous and sought after, he was considering politics and he was pretending to keep aspiring starlets at bay. For each of them, just a mention in one of his magazines meant a new career. Leah and Sari were the belles of the balls. Young men stood in line hoping for a word with them. My mother was busy keeping the lid on everything. I think she was sorry they'd had another girl."

"Puci was Vili's favourite," Sari said. "She had all the advantages, don't you see?"

"He never thought I was worth an education," Leah said. "Only Puci."

Puci was ten years old when she arrived at the gates of Notre Dame de Sion School for girls on top of Sas-hegy (Eagle Hill). She put on the regulation long, blue, pleated skirt and top, the brown, scratchy stockings, the chunky, brown lace-up shoes, the rope belt to remind her of the saints. The whole thing was heavy and ugly, and she hated it so much she planned to escape the first chance she saw.

The gates were high and locked. The school was run by nuns who declined to speak Hungarian even in dire necessity. The only languages allowed were French and Latin. There were periods of silence for everyone, more frequent if you disobeyed the rules.

Puci snuck in nail polish and lipstick. She bobbed her hair. She rebelled against the silence and wouldn't keep her elbows flat against her body while she ate. She was locked in when everyone else went home for their first vacation, and she almost missed Christmas as well. Vili had to speak to the Mother Superior and promise Puci would change her ways when she returned.

"She was hoping they would expel her," my grandmother said. "But Grandpa was giving them too much money."

"She could do complex mathematical calculations, and she was fluent in French," Leah said. "I never had those advantages. That's why I drove trucks while she got a great job with the Road and Railway Company."

It was not until many years later, after Sari deposited me at a convent school in New Zealand, that I finally understood why my mother was prepared to do just about anything to escape — even marry the first man who proposed. No matter that he had been in love with one of her sisters, or both of her sisters, and maybe even with her mother; no matter that he was seventeen years older and set in his ways. He was her way out of the convent.

"It wasn't really like that," my mother said. "He was so handsome. He had big hazel eyes, and he was paying attention to me, not to my sisters. You don't know what it's like having older sisters whom the world comes to court and never knows you're there."

One day my mother and I were wandering around City Park. She suggested a boat ride, but it was early May and the boats wouldn't start till the next month. The willows were green already, and the tulips were blooming around Vajdahunyad Castle, a replica of the Hunyadi castle in Erdély. I threw stones into the pond, trying to make them skip, just the way Leah's latest bald-headed boyfriend had.

We walked toward the circus. We'd be on time for the two o'clock show, my mother told me, then she said she had met my father at the circus. She was sixteen, home for the summer holidays, and her parents had taken her along, though it was an evening meant for Sari and Leah. They were both between husbands, and there were men on leave from the front. It was 1940 and the war had barely been thought of. Count Teleki was running the country, and no one was much interested in Hitler.

"Has your grandfather told you about the war?" she asked.

"Which one?"

My mother sighed. "The Second World War."

"A little."

"He will," she said. "He will." We were standing in line for tickets. There was laughter inside. A man wearing a tall, black hat and baggy bloomers was leading an elephant up the animals' entrance.

"I want to talk about your father," she said.

There was no point in my telling her I didn't want to hear, so I looked up at her, thinking that if only she'd hurry up, we could get into the circus, where the laughter was getting louder.

"There used to be boxes — balconies where whole families sat," she continued, more slowly than I wanted. "István was in the next balcony. He had a few friends with him. All, except your father, were in uniform. He was very dashing, with his grey felt hat and kid gloves, his striped trousers and the way he came over and kissed Grandma's hand, then Sari's and Leah's, and last, mine. At sixteen, not many men kiss your hand. He bent right over mine and looked at me the way men used to look at my sisters, not the way anyone had ever looked at me before. Not counting the pimple-faced boy who brought out our skis at Innsbruck the winter before."

I thought she had forgotten I was there, but then she said, "I suppose there is plenty of time for you to find out what I mean."

I knew what my mother meant. It was the way her friend Benny looked at her when he thought I wasn't watching. As if she were a cream puff on his plate at the Gerbaud Café. It made me sick. I used to give him my evil stare, the one I thought would kill him if he ever touched her, but so far it hadn't worked. What must have saved him was that he never looked at me when I was casting the spell.

"I was just a child," she said. "When he whispered to me, and only to me, that he'd like to meet for coffee the next day,

I looked around at my sisters. Surely he must have meant one of them. But he hadn't. He was leaning toward me, only me.

"The coffeehouse the next day was the Emke, where I had never been. Cigar smoke. Flirtations. It was thought most unseemly for young girls to go there alone with gentlemen. My sisters went, but they were older. And I had been in that convent school for six years." She took a deep breath. "So I married him. I was so tired of being dragged back to the convent."

"You married him for that?"

"Why not?" she said defiantly. "He was polite and handsome. He was cultured, had travelled, knew art, read books, went to the theatre, talked politics, had manners. He had the right pedigree for your grandfather: a knight somewhere in his history. Old blood. My mother loved him. She flirted with him. He had a big sailboat at Lake Balaton, and he said he'd rename it for me. Soft-spoken. Debonair. A man of the world. He was thirty-two."

I told her it was hard to imagine. I had no idea what some of her words meant, but "debonair" sounded attractive. In the photograph Leah showed me, he had a round glass scrunched over one eye. He was balding.

"The monocle," Vili said, "was an affectation."

"That was taken the day Papa announced our engagement for the society pages of his "People" magazine. The monocle had belonged to István's grandfather. At the time, I thought it was very sophisticated," she said. "I don't think he liked being married once it was done. The challenge was gone. He went out alone to his old haunts, the coffeehouses, the nightclubs. He said I wouldn't enjoy it anyway — not a little convent girl. He went hunting in the Mátras and fishing on his estate in the South. His parents lived on the estate and didn't want me there. A big old house, built up again after the Turks left."

"What were they like?"

"His parents? I hardly remember. They didn't think he should have married me. I wasn't worldly enough. His mother bought her clothes in Vienna, her linen in Denmark. His father was an invalid. From the war before that war." She looked at me quizzically.

Yes, I knew about that war. It was the one Vili had fought in, the one that started with that silly Habsburg getting himself shot in Sarajevo.

"My father wasn't even there when I was born," I said.

"Men like that never are."

My aunt Leah said my father lost interest in my mother just weeks after they married. "After the first glow of love — you know the kind, young people, the scent of sex — he was tired of his young bride. He needed excitement, his own space. Puci couldn't give him the mystery a man needs to stay interested. She was a convent girl, no experience, what could you expect?" Leah had begun to pluck her eyebrows in the thirties and seemed to have lost them altogether by the fifties. She drew them thin and black with a pencil, somewhat higher than they might have been, giving herself a permanently surprised look.

"He was a sophisticate."

"He got the cigars out when he heard about your birth," Sari said years later. "It's not that he wasn't pleased, but those were terrible times. Not a good time for having a baby."

As if my mother had known enough to have a choice in the matter.

"The fact is," my mother told me later, when we were in jail, "he was too much of a gentleman to have been there when you were born. He wouldn't have wanted to embarrass me by having heard my screaming. Besides, he had expected a boy. He had the name picked out for you — Stephen. Had you obliged him by being a boy, he would have come and brought flowers. After the fact."

Leah slipped me another photograph of him, sitting in a white wicker armchair, dressed in creamy colours, his face and hands lightly tanned. He is wearing two-tone lace-up shoes. "I took this picture," she added proudly. "Sunday afternoon at the estate." She always referred to my grandfather's farm some sixty miles north of Budapest as "the estate." "Around 1940. I doubt he had met your mother then. He was one of the many young men who used to come and pay their respects in those years. There were so many, Sari and I could barely remember their names."

He had been attractive, as all the Rácz sisters' first husbands were. He liked pretty women, good wine, long books. He had the obligatory law degree, and he showered my grandmother with gifts of flowers.

"Some days, we would hide in the summer house by the lake, Sari and I. There were just too many suitors." Leah glanced down at her shapely ankles and pointed her toes as she crossed her legs. Even when she drove trucks, she found time to paint her toenails crimson. Her hair was still a deep blue-black, and she rouged her cheekbones slightly to give them a lift.

"But he wasn't your suitor," I suggested.

Leah laughed her high bell-like laugh. "Silly. Not mine? Sari's, then. Puci was still at school. She came home for the holidays, and even then she wore these dark, nunnish dresses that covered her legs all the way to here." She pointed at her calf. "She was just a kid. No man was going to notice her."

Still, Puci and István were married a couple of years after that picture was taken, and when I saw the wedding photos, I thought my mother looked anything but a child. They were hidden in one of her dresser drawers, under her silk panties, beige silk stockings and the woollen underwear she only used in the country. In the photograph, she has a long train, a white gauze veil, a dress with a high collar and maybe a hundred round, shiny buttons down the front. She holds a tiny bouquet of white flowers in lace-gloved hands. My father wears tails, white shirt front and bow tie and holds his top hat. She has a lot of blonde, billowing hair under the gauze. They both look very uncomfortable.

Vili said there were only fifty guests at the wedding. Wartime.

A year later I was born, and a few months after that István was gone.

I was reasonably convinced by the time I was five that one of the strangest things to have happened to my mother was her marriage to my father.

8

I WAS BORN DURING the German occupation of
Hungary. The British and the Americans were bombing
Budapest.

My grandfather had been trying to round up nurses to
attend to my mother in the emergency wing of the Frigyesi
Hospital. The nurses were too busy with the wounded and
the dying to pay attention to a young girl's first birth. My
mother was barely seventeen and no one had bothered to
tell her about childbirth. It had taken her quite a while to
figure out how people got pregnant, and that was shocking
enough without the pain that followed. Luckily, Vili had
the brilliant idea to knock her out with morphine and
extract me howling into the wartorn world.

He had chosen the Frigyesi Hospital because it was rela-
tively close to his magazine office. He still went by there
most days, in Kigyó Street (*kigyó* means "snake," and I
remember waiting for the snakes to appear when he later
showed me where the building had once stood), though he
had been forbidden to publish the magazines and the doors
had been padlocked by authority of the new State.

To make sure there was no mistake about it, the fascist
State had sent a troop to enforce its orders.

"What," Vili had asked the man with the skull-and-cross-
bones armband, "does theatre have to do with politics?" Vili's

most successful magazines were about the stage and movies.

"Nothing," was the little man's reply. He was a ranking member of the Arrow Cross Party — Hungary's own version of the Nazi Party — members of which Vili categorized as "little." "But we can't afford your kind of levity in the midst of changing the world. What we're engaged in, as you should know, Mister Publisher, *Sir*, is nothing short of a new world order. It's serious business." Then he ordered his men to lock the offices and affix the state's stamp to the lock.

"What he should have said was: Everything," Vili told me. "Had he been less ignorant and less vicious, he would have known that it's the stories we tell that make us think about who we are and who we might become. Stories are the natural enemies of all dictators. That's why the smart ones lock up the writers first." He was standing in front of the burnt-out building. I think it was 1949. There was a new stamp of authority on the one remaining wall where the office had once been. "All that's changed," he whispered, "is the name of the dictator. Now, we call them communists." In Vili's lexicon, communists were "little men" too, and they all, too, travelled in groups. "Safety in numbers. Not one of them could stand alone."

"Why did the Arrow Cross man call you 'Sir?'"

"Irony."

My mother doesn't agree. She says what made Vili different was his decency. Somehow, in the midst of chaos, he still commanded a bit of respect. That's why they called him "Sir."

"Nonsense," Vili assured me. "They handed me the most respectful title because they had no respect for me at all. Just as later a Communist Party emissary would call me 'Comrade,' though we both knew I was no comrade of his."

There is a photograph of Vili and me taken a few days after I was born. We are both bald. He holds me up to his face. We are both smiling, though my mother says that, in my case, it was most likely gas. I'm wrapped tightly in a white blanket. I'm about the size of his hand. By then we lived mostly in the basement of the old house on Lisznyai Street. The Americans and the British had been bombing since April. The Germans had been in charge for several months.

There was a large crowd of us in the basement, including several old friends of my grandfather's, Jews who were sought by the Hungarian Arrow Cross. Years later, I met one of them in London. He remembered the mewling baby and my mother looking frail and extraordinarily beautiful.

He remembered Vili going out for bread and water and returning with stray dogs whose owners had fled.

Vili left the basement and went upstairs when the Arrow Cross came to search the house for Jews. "He was a big man, exuded confidence. Invited them in and offered them *palinka* — he told them what with the war there wasn't anything else left, though we were sitting on crates of champagne in the basement.

"The furniture was covered with white sheets. He took the sheets off in honour of the guests. Lied and told them he lived alone now. It had been difficult to convince his wife, he said, to leave Budapest for the country, but he had had no choice. The war wreaked havoc with people's morals. He didn't want some red-blooded German recruit to mistake his wife for a woman of easy virtue.

"The Arrow Cross men guffawed at the thought. Two of them had girls to go home to. They drank and talked about the capture of Buda Castle. Your grandfather laughed along. When he returned to the basement, his palms were bleeding where he had dug his nails into his flesh to control his rage."

Years later, George Mikes, the Hungarian-born author of *How to Be an Alien* told me, "Vili was an old-fashioned man with old-fashioned standards of honour. It's an odd word in today's parlance, but the truth is your grandfather was a 'gentleman,' too civilized to do absolutely nothing while the Jews were deported. He belonged to another world."

In the beginning, my mother said, there were only two couples in the basement. One man was a journalist who had worked at one of Vili's magazines. The other had owned a small factory; he had been a Seventh Hussar with Vili during the First World War, and Vili said the man had saved his life once.

The two women had been society belles. Now they fought over who would get the corner bed, where a sliver of light fell in the mornings through a grate that opened onto the garden. They had brought their jewellery in identical mahogany boxes, and they argued over which of them had been the first to buy one and who had spotted it in the other's bedroom. One of them had brought her chihuahua. The men were quiet. The women talked too much. They were all frightened.

In late summer of 1944, Vili arrived home with another small group of people he had picked up as they were marched toward the Eastern Railroad Station. They were being collected for a work camp in the East or for Auschwitz. Somehow Vili had bluffed his way into the long, silent row of men, women and children the Arrow Cross was pushing along the boulevard and insisted he needed an immediate work detail for a bomb shelter for Arrow Cross families. "Little men," Vili told me, "used to taking orders are usually intimidated by loud, commanding voices of larger men. But you have to pick your targets carefully."

"The Arrow Cross were all short men?"

"Small, I told you already, has nothing to do with size."

"Mostly, he had bluffed his way through the war," Sari told me. "He knew everybody and knew things about them from 'peacetime,' from before the war. He reminded everyone he met of the way they had been. I think that might have been what saved us."

On a Sunday morning in October, when my mother went to look for milk to buy, she saw a few still figures standing on the Tabán, a hill playground in Buda. Around them stood a crowd of quiet spectators. When she approached, the others left quickly, as if to make sure they weren't caught in that place at that time.

There, on the grassy mound where children used to play on the swings, were five makeshift gallows. Five men had been hanged from the higher branches of the acacia trees; their arms had been tied behind their backs; their feet were only inches from the ground. The last time she had met one of the men, they had danced a risqué tango at the hussar ball, two springs ago, when the war had still seemed far away.

Two months later, in early December, my grandfather drove some of our basement guests to his farm. They travelled with our family's identity cards. If they were stopped, they would pretend they were Vili's daughters, sons-in-law and one of the children. Chances were that if Vili talked with the Arrow Cross men, they would only glance at the cards. "It was hard to make our guests look unafraid," Vili said. "Yet to show fear was suicide. The Arrow Cross men could smell it like sharks smell blood. When they stopped us, I joked with them about getting home for Christmas, and one of my Jewish friends offered to have them join us for songs Christmas Eve. A small family affair. His wife tried to look at the men as a woman might look at men at a party. She smiled. When we had passed the checkpoint she vomited."

My mother says, "I try to forget the Christmas of 1944. Your grandfather came home that night with a chicken for dinner and we brought up wine from the cellar. You had yellow fever and couldn't even drink water. We had some ten or more stray family dogs running around and a refugee turtle from the house next door. There were another sixteen people in the basement by now, and they were afraid to come up in case the Arrow Cross joined us for carols."

Three years later our family had a different set of visitors. It was 1947. The Russians had taken Budapest in 1945. The Hungarian Communist Party was now in power. Six men in black leather jackets came to our bombed-out house in Buda. Two waited outside, looking this way and that, their hands in their pockets, casual. They wore the brown trousers good party men wore after the war ended and the Russians remained.

It was already summer, but they didn't take off their jackets. The glass doors had been replaced, as had the patio and the steps, so you could walk out into the garden again. The big Titian had been rolled out and hung back on the wall. My grandparents' bedroom was still open to the sky. Their bed was in my grandfather's study. There was a tarpaulin over one corner of the livingroom where some of the plaster and bricks from upstairs had fallen. The smell of fresh paint mixed with the scent of lilies from the garden.

The two small dogs my grandfather had found on the embankment hid under the blue velvet chairs. One of them mounted a foolhardy attack on a pair of brown trousers and was kicked for his trouble. Not a big kick, just enough to send him scrambling and whimpering.

The four men strolled around the room, their hands in their pockets, looking at the pictures and at the small china animals my grandmother collected. They paused over Leah's green-hatted portrait, and one of them remarked that not everyone had enough money to commission portraits like that. They said no to the coffee my grandmother's maid offered.

They stood with their backs to the glass doors, blocking the light. Vili knew they had been told to do that. If you want to frighten somebody, make him look into the light, keep your own face in shadow. It's an old trick. The Germans used strobe lights for interrogations. The Turks held flaming tapers close to their victims' faces.

My grandmother's maid retreated to the kitchen. My mother carried me out into the garden. Vili told Therese to round up the family for afternoon coffee, but she wouldn't leave. She sat on the soft, padded arm of one of her brushed velvet chairs and smiled at the men as though they were invited guests, not agents of the government newly installed by the Soviet Army.

"The People's Committee overseeing publications has decided against your magazines," one of the men informed Vili.

"Why would they have done that?" Vili asked.

"We are building a new nation out of the ashes of the old one, Comrade. With the help of our glorious allies, we will determine which publications are useful and which are not." The man speaking was the shortest of the little men assembled in front of our garden.

"It has been judged that yours are not," added another who had the thick country accent of southern Hungary.

"One of them is about the theatre," Vili said.

"There will not be too much of that while we rebuild the nation."

"Who needs the stage when you can have such excellent theatre in the streets?" Vili asked rhetorically. "And the others are about literature."

"So you say, Comrade, so you say," the shortest man said, putting the emphasis on the "you."

"And what do you say?" Vili asked. He had been determined not to lose his temper because there was too much else to lose.

Instead of answering, the shortest man signalled to his comrades. Two of them fanned out on either side of the room and marched into the hall, where Leah and my little cousin Kati were waiting to see what would happen. They walked through the diningroom, out into the kitchen, through the second sittingroom, through my grandfather's study and back — more slowly this time — to position themselves by the door. They hadn't noticed Sari, my mother and me behind the rosebush in the garden. My mother says I was asleep.

"It doesn't matter what I may think, Comrade," the short man resumed. "It is the people's will. But since you insist on knowing my personal opinion, I think your house is too big for one family." With that he walked past Therese and toward the door, where his real comrades were waiting. On the way, he lifted a porcelain dalmatian from the mantel, looked at it for a moment, then dropped it on the iron legging of the fireplace. "Oh," he said, and he smiled at my grandmother.

Then they were gone.

Some weeks after the visit, the State formally shut down Vili's magazines again, and we were served with a document that informed us we were to move to more appropriate quarters for a family of our size. There were to be no more than three rooms. The house in Buda was being requisitioned by command of the armed forces.

That was what Vili would tell me.

9

THE DAY VILI LAUNCHED into our family history, he and I were walking along the embankment of the Danube — the Corso — on the Pest side, where the streetcars ran. There were droopy chestnut trees on the far side of the pavement; ice cream vendors pretending to belong to cooperatives lined the sidewalk. It was a sunny day. I was skipping from one paving stone to the next. Each time I landed, I threw a twig two stones ahead, marking where I was to land next. If I missed or didn't pick up the stick, I declared myself a loser. Quietly. I rarely interrupted my grandfather's stories.

His stories had many tellings, but the first version is the one I always remember the best.

This time he explained that, being who we were, we had a number of obligations he took seriously, and he expected me to do the same. "The old families," he said, "are responsible for keeping the memories. It's our shared memories that make us a country. The stories we tell and our language. Stuck between the Slavs and the Germans, and a thorn in both their sides, we have endured."

"Endured?"

"And still do."

I tripped over a dog that had darted ahead of me and picked up my stick. The dog offered it to me as I lay sprawled on the stones.

My grandfather slowed his pace but didn't stop to look back. "Stupid," I told the dog and ran to catch up with Vili.

"Did you know we are extra-special Hungarians? The Ráczes have always sent their sons to defend their country."

"Not their daughters?"

He shook his head. The status of gentry, he told me, had been granted to our family by János Hunyadi, governor of eastern Hungary, on July 21, 1456. To my grandfather that did not seem to be particularly distant. Merely fourteen generations, that's all. The man who earned it was another Vilmos. There had been other Vilmoses before him, too, but none like this one. My grandfather had been named after this illustrious Vilmos. That was why he had to be heroic and excel with the sword. All the Vilmoses had been great swordsmen.

In this Vilmos's day, the country was overrun by Turks. They were nasty, turbaned men with red sashes who burned villages, wrecked castles, slew everyone they met who wasn't Turkish and enjoyed carving little girls into many pieces to feed their dogs — dogs who were not at all like our dachshund, Jinny, but were bad-tempered, snub-nosed beasts grown fat on the flesh of Hungarians.

Vilmos was born on a smallish estate — no more than fifty acres — east of Arad in the Erdély highlands. The house and walled garden spread over a field of grass, part of a plateau surrounded by peaks so steep that sheep scrambled like goats when they climbed to the high patches of grass, their hoofs digging into the craggy earth. In the winter the snow piled up over the roof. The Rácz family had to chop paths in the ice from their door to the woodpile and to the barn where the animals slept.

In the summer the meadows were greener than any green you'll ever see, and balsam and spruce trees spread their branches so broad and thick you could always find shelter from the rain.

The house was spacious and airy, though the windows were small, to keep out the mountain storms. It had tall wooden towers and a courtyard so wide Vilmos's grandfather couldn't see from one side to the other. There were horses, and cows and sheep grazed in the fields.

No, Vilmos didn't have time for games, but he did fall in love once, deeply, with one of Hunyadi's relations. Her name was Klara. She was as blonde as he, as willowy as my aunt Leah, and she lived in the turret of her family's castle, not too far from ours, where she spent her time in contemplation and prayer — pretty much what was expected of young girls in those days.

("Was her hair so long it could touch the ground when she hung it out the window?"

"No. That's another story.")

Vilmos learned the art of swordplay on his family's fields. In Erdély, everyone knew how to handle a broadsword, a long curved knife, a lance, an axe and even the gentler blade of the épée. Once upon a time, the Tatars had overrun the land; now the Turks were marching in and out, looting, murdering, taking hostages, cattle and wives; you had to learn early how to take care of yourself.

As was the custom with eldest sons of the landowning gentry, his father sent Vilmos to court to learn the more refined ways of the gentleman's world. The court belonged to King Sigismund of Luxembourg, who had inherited the crown of Hungary with his wife's dowry. It was in Buda, where Sigismund had rebuilt the ancient palace of the Árpád kings on the bank of the Danube.

Because Vilmos was big and tough, the king picked him as one of his bodyguards. It was in the stone fort of the bodyguards that Vilmos met János Hunyadi, scion of Erdély's Hunyadis, as big and tough a young man as Vilmos and already a Knight of the Dragon, Sigismund's own élite order. János was as skilled in hand-to-hand combat as Vilmos, an excellent horseman, fearless and greatly respected in court, though he was only sixteen.

Sigismund was neither fearless nor greatly respected. Everyone had been surprised when the pope crowned him Holy Roman Emperor. He was a German and not in the least holy. He loved food and wine, courted the ladies, spent his inheritance with impunity and, unlike the real Hungarian kings before him, he was blond, ugly and a terrible loser both in games of chess and in one-to-one combat. In fact, had the general jockeying for more power and property not replaced the original tribal heritage by which the king was chosen as first among equals, Sigismund would never have been King of Hungary, let alone Holy Roman Emperor.

Even his wife despised Sigismund. It was rumoured that she had brazenly taken a lover and enjoyed embarrassing him in his own court. He was a lousy knight on the battle-field. He did have the smarts, though, to surround himself with men who knew how to fight.

Vilmos didn't much like court life. Far too much bowing and scraping, too much talk of fashion. Vili stopped to demonstrate how low a courtier had to bow before the king, how he had to hold his left arm behind him, the other lightly touching the ground, and how he would walk backwards when leaving the royal presence.

Vilmos didn't care at all for silk puffed pants, long hose or pointy boots. He made the most of his time at Sigismund's by learning languages. There were courtiers there from every country in the kingdom: Germans, Wallachs, Serbs, Croats, Czechs, Frenchmen, Hungarians, even Spaniards, and the only language they all spoke was Latin. Vili was particularly fond of Latin and hoped I would learn to speak it one day.

"A man is as many men as the languages he speaks," he said. "Each language gives him its secrets. In each, he can be a different person. Language, you see, is what makes us who we are. Each language declares its own history. János Hunyadi spoke sixteen."

One day, during a noisy jousting tournament in heavy armour, both Vilmos and János were spotted by George Brankovics, the great Serb despot, who was paying a rare peaceful visit to Sigismund's court.

("What's a despot?"

"A tough guy in charge of a country not your own. Had he been one of ours, he would have been a great king."

"Oh.")

He didn't come often because he was frequently at war with the Holy Roman Empire or the Turks. Being caught between the Turks and the Europeans, he told his biographer, was somewhat like slowly roasting on twin enemy fires. He had already given his daughter, Mara, to Sultan Murad's harem and supplied him with two thousand young men for the Turkish janissary forces. In 1439, though his forces had been brave and had lasted longer than most armies under attack by the Turks, he lost his lands, his two sons and even his stronghold in Novo Brdo. The Turks blinded his sons before they took them prisoner. Blinding powerful prisoners was thought to be merciful, because the alternative was death. Brankovics had been reduced to offering a tribute in gold to Sigismund and asking for his help because the sultan was still not satisfied.

After Vilmos and János were hoisted off their exhausted horses, Brankovics asked them to come to his court, where there was an urgent need for young men not afraid of the Turks. They readily agreed, János because he had vowed to beat the hell out of the Turks when he was still a tiny boy, Vilmos because he was seriously tired of Sigismund and his tournaments.

When János Hunyadi announced that he would raise a new army to beat hell out of the Turks, most of the despot's long-suffering men volunteered to fight on. As did our Vilmos. Carrying the Hunyadi banner, a black raven in a field of green, they rode across Serbia, their numbers swelling as they went, into the kingdom of Hungary.

Vili never watched to see if I had understood his story or its purpose. He strode along expecting me to follow. When he stopped, it was to gaze at the other side of the river, at the silvery waves or at a pretty young woman who went by. He would stop for a smile or to doff his hat for someone who called him by name. I followed so closely that I piled onto his feet, bumping my head on his hip. When I fell, he didn't pick me up. It was understood that I was to be brave on those long walks along the river. I was to be a young Vilmos. Fearless.

"There are," he told me, "great mounds of charred dead people to remind everyone that the Turks thought the world didn't need Hungarians at all. Between the Tisza and the Danube, south of Szeged, there is an island made of bones, and in the middle of the island, to this day (though I've never seen it), there is a bonecastle."

⊰ ⊱

In November 1997, at a Bácska-Hungarian get-together my mother and I attended in honour of my grandfather, a middle-aged man in a polyester suit tells me that the ghosts of one hundred thousand Hungarians haunt that castle even as we sit here drinking our too-sweet Badacsonyi wine. By 1450, he says, over one million had been slaughtered. Over our heads there are paintings of Hungarian heroes. Hunyadi wears a furry, black hat over his wavy, brown hair; he has a moustache like a racing bike's handlebars, a red jacket flung carelessly over his shoulder, tight, red pants, black boots; in one bejewelled hand he holds a green flag with a raven. The raven has a gold ring in its beak. In Hunyadi's other hand there is a gold-hilted broadsword.

⊰ ⊱

Wherever they went, Vilmos rode ahead of Hunyadi and stopped in village squares to announce that the great Defender of Christendom was coming this way and the people had better get ready to follow him into battle.

All he had to say to convince the reluctant was "The Turks are coming." No one wanted to be left behind for the Turks to find.

You can't think of it as a war. There were skirmishes and heroic resistance to save this village or that. There were battles lost and battles won, some men deserted and some remained, new armies were raised. A hundred men defended a wooden tower in the village of Latvár, for example, and were burned alive by the Turks before Hunyadi's army arrived. Some were slaughtered in their fields, their wives taken to the harems, their children killed in front of their eyes. In October 1448 Hunyadi lost a battle on the Field of Blackbirds in Kosovo, where the Serbs had lost their own Turkish war almost fifty years before.

Unlike the Hungarians and the Serbs, the Turks never seemed to tire of fighting.

In 1455 they were led by Pasha Mezid, a bloodthirsty type who had already burned and pillaged more than three hundred villages. He had become convinced that the way to defeat the Hungarians was to capture Hunyadi. "To kill the lion, his heart must be pierced," he told his men. Because Hunyadi wore a silver helmet and carried a shield emblazoned with a raven, he would be easy to spot. But the Hungarians came up with a plan. Vilmos and two others, the bravest of Hunyadi's men, would don Hunyadi shields and helmets and ride ahead of their men.

At first Hunyadi protested. He knew the three volunteers would draw the Turks' arrows and, if killed, would die of wounds meant for him. They stood arguing for almost an hour while the janissary army approached. You could hear the sharp thudding of horses' hoofs on the stones in the riverbed. It was late summer; the dry wind carried their shouts and the rattle of their armour.

Vilmos reminded Hunyadi that if he died, the Turks would rule the land he loved for over a hundred years. Finally Hunyadi relented. The three men wearing Hunyadi helmets and shields mounted their horses and, surrounded by troops, rode toward the enemy.

Vilmos was only eighteen at the time, a strapping, broad-chested lad with long, brown hair and flashing eyes. He rode a black charger named Lightning, *Villám* in Hungarian. He was so sure of his mastery of the sword, so convinced he could outrun any arrow and outmanoeuvre even a hundred men, that he didn't bother with the armour other fighting men wore.

The Turks never knew which of the three was Hunyadi, and all three seem to have survived. In their confusion, the Turks were defeated at Nagyszeben and, much to Brankovics's delight, Pasha Mezid's head was sent to Buda.

I cast furtive glances over at the Buda side of the river trying to figure out where I would stick a severed head. I decided on the top of the arch near the Chain Bridge.

The Turks were really annoyed about Mezid's head going to Budapest on a stick. They assembled a whole new army to wreak dreadful revenge and, once and for all, rid the world of Hungarians. This time they decided to attack in the southeast. Luckily, both Hunyadi and Vilmos were ready for them.

In 1456, at Nándorfehérvár, the Turks were led by Sultan Mohammed. His vast army seemed like the ocean, their turbans white waves, as they moved toward the city. They had five hundred cannons; some were twenty metres long. They had brought seven giant catapults, two hundred ships and enough armour to defeat an army ten times the size of that Hunyadi commanded. Their ships' guns blazing, they paraded up and down the Danube, terrifying the citizens who cowered inside their rough-hewn houses. There was no escape either by water, where the ships were, or by land, where the sea of turbans blocked out the grass.

Mohammed's flagship had a hundred-man band. They played Turkish military music, stopping only so that the Turks could shout insults at the Hungarians behind the barricades. At night thousands of bonfires lit up the Turkish camps and the men whooped and hollered in their time-honoured victory celebrations. Prematurely, as it turned out.

At first Hunyadi engaged the fleet, sending an advance guard of a hundred ships filled with nothing but sand. They travelled fast in the current and hammered the Turkish ships, sinking many, causing panic on the remaining vessels.

When the battle for the castle began, Mohammed's cannons bombarded the walls, his archers rained arrows on the defenders, his catapults tossed burning tallow into the midst of the villagers who had fled to the protection of the castle. For thirty days and nights, they held out.

On July 21, 1456, Vilmos and a contingent of knights rushed out of the gates.

"That foray into the midst of the enemy," Vili announced, "earned young Vilmos both a title and a crest."

"A crest?"

"More about that later."

Reinforcements arrived with John Kapistran (Giovanni da Capistrano, in Italian), the pope's own fighting priest, heading an army of a thousand men. The Hungarians beat back the Turks; Mohammed lay unconscious, bleeding from a head wound; his troops were demoralized, some fifty thousand dead, many more wounded. Mohammed was so discouraged he tried to kill himself. He failed. His sword slid off his breastbone, slicing into his chest — nothing serious, but embarrassing in front of his bedraggled men. Under the cover of darkness, they fled back to Turkey.

Sultan Mohammed outlived Hunyadi by some twenty

years, a bitter old man, not comforted by his harem, all experts in the art of love.

Hunyadi himself died later that year, on August 11, 1456 — almost five hundred years before I heard his story — of the plague. The pope bestowed on him the honorific, "Defender of the Faith" during a requiem held in St. Peter's in Rome. Giovanni da Capistrano was canonized.

Years later, I discovered that Nándorfehérvár had, somehow, become Belgrade and had taken the position that it was another country's capital city.

Vili promised to show me the family crest that evening.

In those years I slept in a narrow bed in my grandparents' bedroom, closest to my grandfather's side of the bed. That evening he only pretended to snore, waiting till my grandmother was asleep; he lit one of the candles he kept by his bed for the many electrical failures, and we crept out to the hall. He cast a huge shadow over the bookcases where I believed the family ghosts lived.

He pulled out the big art books he kept on the top shelf and took out a brown paper bag. Inside there was something wrapped in velvet and rolled up like a newspaper. He laid it out on the floor and we both got down on our hands and knees. He held the candle over our heads. The thing itself was thin and crinkly, yellowish, smooth to the touch. "It's dogskin," he explained in a hushed whisper.

"Dogskin?" I reared back. I was fond of Jinny. The little dachshund had been a comforting constant in my few years of life.

All family crests, it seemed, were burned into dogskin. It's just the way it was.

The centrepiece of the crest was a lion brandishing a sword. It stood on its hind legs, leaning forward, mouth open, teeth bared. "It's Vilmos," Vili told me. "He had fought like a lion defending Nándorfehérvár from the Turks."

In the centre court of the castle at Nándorfehérvár, there used to be a covered archway, where the governor's chair was installed under a velvet cover with gold tassels. The chair was elevated by three steps so that the governor could hold command over the whole courtyard.

"It was there on the blood-soaked flagstones that Hunyadi commanded Vilmos to kneel — on one knee only, as was the custom — and touched his bowed head with the flat of his sword, pronouncing him a Defender of Hungary and noble to the soles of his tattered boots. Incidentally, he gave him Klara in marriage. That's the only reason you're here listening to this story and I'm here telling it to you."

Vili rolled up the dogskin and hid it behind the books. It stayed there when my grandparents left for New Zealand. When I learned a little about what New Zealanders thought about such things, I decided he was right to have left it behind. People there would not have been interested in the crest and would have been utterly appalled by the skin of the dog.

Vili held my hand as we crossed the dark hallway toward our bedroom and, while the candle still burned, he lifted it to his lips so that I could see every word he mouthed: "No one must know our secret. Not even your best friends."

He tucked me into my bed.

"Would Klara have married Vilmos if he wasn't noble?" I asked when he bent to kiss me goodnight.

"I very much doubt it," he whispered, "but stranger things have happened."

10

MY AUNT LEAH LAUGHED when she heard the story of Vilmos and the Battle of Nándorfehérvár. Vilmos, she said, was in jail near Arad that whole year; he didn't see the light of day until after Hunyadi had died of cholera. It was being in jail that saved Vilmos's life. In those days nobody understood what caused cholera, and they left the bodies on the battlefield for the rats or wolves or whoever else fancied a meal of heroes.

In 1456, she told me, our Vilmos was not yet sixteen and was already a ladies' man. Our family's modest estate was up in the mountains on the banks of the river Mures, a rather forbidding place with fog year-round and sheep wandering down the paths toward better pastures. Even the goats found it inhospitable and kept straying onto other men's fields. Vilmos's one passion was accompanying the servant girls on their daily roundups of the sheep and the goats.

That's what took him into service at Sigismund's court, according to Leah. His mother thought it better that he learn the art of war than be trapped into marriage by someone below his status. You see what I mean? It wouldn't do to cheapen the line, would it? And by the way, being Holy Roman Emperor sounds grand, but there wasn't much of an empire, just a collection of nasty warring tribes, and the empire wasn't Roman, it was mostly German — Rome had been destroyed by our marauding ancestors, the Huns — and not even its greatest admirers think it was holy. Sigismund's court wasn't much of a thing.

Vilmos started as a page. Perhaps a little older than he should have been for his first assignment, but you wouldn't know about that, would you? In any event, he was a page. He wanted to be a knight. All the boys wanted to be knights, because it meant you didn't have to work for a living and ladies tossed you kerchiefs to carry into battle.

A page was expected to be virtuous, and no lady tossed you anything, least of all her kerchief. And that's where our l ong-ago ancestor got into trouble. While Hunyadi learned how to wield a broadsword as Sigismund's bodyguard, Vilmos made friends with Sigismund's only daughter, Elizabeth. This would have been an excellent match for Vilmos, but the decision was up to Mrs. Sigismund, who doubled as the Queen of Hungary and didn't think Vilmos had it in him to be Holy Roman Emperor. Both she and her husband were fairly determined to marry their daughters to Habsburgs — a great move for her, in hindsight — and they sent Vilmos home to Erdély.

The trip on horseback from Budapest to the shores of the Mures took many months. Vilmos, now sixteen, as handsome and tall as your grandfather once was, fell in with some Christian knights travelling toward the Holy Land. In the first village they came to, he proposed to a Wallachian girl by the water fountain, and he married her the next week, not even telling his parents, and certainly not revealing to anybody that he was Hungarian.

"Klara?"

"No. I don't know what her name was, but certainly not Klara. That's not a Wallachian name."

That's why Vilmos spent most of 1456 in a Wallachian jail.

"For marrying a Wallachian girl?"

"Certainly. Same thing could happen now. A Wallach man who marries a Hungarian might be stoned to death by his neighbours. Didn't Papa tell you about the Hungarians and the Wallachs?"

"And what happened to Klara, Hunyadi's niece?"

"She married Géza, Vilmos's brother. For a few years after the plague nobody cared much if you married under your station."

"The crest?"

"Came later. In seventeen-something-or-other. Another of Papa's favourite ancestors got it fighting the Habsburgs. He was in Rákóczi's army."

That was Leah's version.

II

I MET MY FATHER for the first time on Christmas Eve, 1948.

In our home, Christmas was always Christmas Eve, the twenty-fourth of December. At around dusk my cousin Kati and I would be ushered into my grandparents' big bed, where the duvet cover was of cool, blue satin and the pillows were stuffed with feathers. We were told to wait there till Baby Jesus and the angels delivered our gifts to the livingroom (which doubled as my mother's bedroom).

All that day my grandmother had cooked and baked, and we were exhausted from fetching what she needed, cleaning plates, carrying things, peeling, folding, slicing, listening to her instructions.

After my grandmother had lost her maid, her cook and her house, she had learned to cook, and she took pride in making complicated dishes whose cheap ingredients could never be exactly foretold, so Kati and I would be sent repeatedly to the grocer to buy more of this or that and be quick about it or the sauce would thicken, the soup would spoil, the cake would fall.

That's why, though we resolved to listen for whatever sounds Baby Jesus made when he arrived, we were asleep the day my father came. Leah trilled into the bedroom, all excited, her hands and hair flying, teetering on her special-occasion high heels (she worked a lot of overtime to have two pairs of shoes), giggling and shouting for us to wake up NOW or we might miss Christmas altogether.

Kati and I dressed quickly in our festive clothes. My dress was burgundy velvet, cut down from a long gown of my mother's, with white lace collar and sleeves. I was fussing with the matching burgundy ribbon for my hair when we heard the tiny silver bell that meant we were allowed in, that Jesus had been born and had left us his presents for Christmas. The bell, Vili assured me, was always rung by the smallest of angels, as Christmas was a special time for children. At other times the smallest angels were told to be seen but not heard, to keep out of the way of the big angels who were busy trying to fix the things people were breaking. They could never keep up with the demand, of course, which explains a lot even today.

In the end I left with the ribbon still in my hand. Leah led the way. It was dark and Kati and I were stumbling over well-known chairs in our excitement when Leah flung open the door. The tree, taller even than Vili, towered over us; candles flickered on every branch, white angel hair glimmered around the soft candlelight, silver and gold tassels and red candy wrappers hung from every branch. There was a huge gold star on the top.

Kati said "Oh" and, not finding her mother's hand, she grabbed for mine and held it as we approached, slowly.

There was a fresh wood scent in the air, sweeter than the candlewax, and the cherry *rétes*, sweeter even than the perfume my grandmother dabbed behind her ears before leaving the kitchen. Packages surrounded the foot of the tree, with the bigger ones at the back. I had been worried that I might be overlooked by Baby Jesus this year for disobeying my mother and spending too much time with the apartment superintendent, Mrs. Nemeth, but I knew as soon as I looked that there would have to be some things for me, and I heaved a sigh of relief.

I stole a triumphant glance at my mother to see if she had noticed that Baby Jesus hadn't minded so much about the super, after all.

My mother stood near the window, apart from the others. She wore a long, black dress that made her feet disappear, and she played with her fingers.

Our family used to sing a Hungarian Christmas song about angels and Bethlehem that had a great many verses and lasted so long I used to think it would never end and we'd never be able to open our presents. My mother had the best voice of the lot of us and the only one that could climb to the high notes the refrain required.

That evening she didn't sing.

She was gazing at the dancing lights. I thought that perhaps she hadn't seen me coming in and I started toward her, but Vili grabbed my shoulder and held me while everyone struggled through all the verses about all the angels and Mary and everything. The whole time my mother stood very still; only her hands moved as her fingers twined, untwined and twined again around one another.

Then the song was finished.

"Look what Baby Jesus brought you," my grandfather said, his voice playful and happy. He turned my shoulder toward the back of the room, where there was a figure I hadn't noticed before. It stood in the shadows.

The figure drifted closer. It wore a huge, greenish batwing of an overcoat and big boots that thumped on the floorboards as it approached. When the candles lit up his face, it was a dark, waxen, bearded statue-face, the image of the martyred Saint Francis in the Franciscan Church. His eyes were hollow and reddened, his lips parted, his forehead disappearing into a glistening peak, his arms reaching out slowly.

"Your daddy."

I shrieked louder than I'd ever shrieked before, louder even than the time when we found the cut-up dead horse behind the trees near our old house, and I ran through the legs of my relations and out into the darkness of the hall, through the chairs and around the oak table and under the writing desk in the corner, where I drew myself up into a tiny ball and tried to hold my breath but couldn't. It came in shuddering gasps no matter how hard I pressed my nails into my palms.

Someone turned on the light.

"Now, that's pretty much how I felt when I saw him early this morning," my mother said as she lowered herself onto the floor next to me. She sat on her haunches on the far side of the writing desk, her back straight against the wall. "It's the surprise, I think, seeing someone you don't expect to see, in a group of people you know so well you don't even look at them. She sighed. "And it's Christmas." She was still playing with her fingers, and I noticed she was rolling her ring around the finger it had always been on, as if she were trying to take it off. She wasn't, though, because I knew the ring was loose and she could have any time she wanted to.

From the next room I could hear Vili. He was protesting that I was an amazing little girl and not in the least spoiled. He said he had made sure of that.

"He used to be elegant, you know, and very well brought up," my mother was saying to me. "My parents liked him so well. He paid compliments to the ladies. He stayed up late playing cards with your grandmother. Gin rummy, I think. During the war, those things mattered very much." She reached in to take my hand. "Now they don't."

"Who is he?" I asked, still disbelieving.

"He really is your father." Her voice was almost steady. "Back from the war. Not that he was ever *in* the war, any more than the rest of us were. The war just went on around us and we tried to stay out of its way. Your grandfather told you he had gone out to get bread?"

I hiccoughed.

"He's been in Russia ever since. He worked in a uranium mine in a terribly cold place called Siberia. And he is very tired. Been travelling for a month. Not much water on the train and no food. That's why he looks like he does." She took a small parcel from behind her back. "For you," she said. "Why don't we open it together?" She peeled back the damp brown paper to reveal a tiny wooden horse. "There," she said. "Do be brave now." Then she took the velvet ribbon I had scrunched into a ball in my sweaty hand and tied it into my hair.

When we were back in the room with Christmas in it, Vili whispered in my ear that the tiny wooden horse was an exact replica of Vilmos's horse, Lightning, and he was sure that if I breathed on it during the night it would come alive in my dreams.

Always at Christmas Vili handed out the presents one by one. Everyone watched while a person opened a present, tried it on if it was clothes or showed it around if it was something else. Everyone clapped or oohed or said "How wonderful." But that Christmas everyone was distracted, and even my grandfather seemed to hurry through the presents, which he had never done before.

My mother was very quiet throughout and remained far away from the bearded man who stood nearest Leah and her third husband. Leah was very cheerful and kept pouring more red wine into the empty glasses. I think that was the first time I noticed that she had developed a habit of standing slightly pigeon-toed, her arms helplessly at her sides, her bottom sticking out, like a little girl.

I was too distracted to enjoy my presents. There was a small rocking chair with a pink ribbon on it; a doll with only eyes, no mouth; a book of stories with colour pictures; and a pair of blue, lace-up, ankle-high running shoes, exactly what I had wanted.

If my father hadn't been there in the back of the room, standing among the adults while Kati and I opened our presents, it would have been the best Christmas ever, because Baby Jesus had somehow remembered to bring me things I had really wanted. I was surprised he'd had time to do that with the world crumbling around us, as my grandmother said it was, since he would have known it was up to him and his angels to fix it.

Though I listened carefully, I didn't once hear the stranger's voice.

My mother tucked me into bed that night, on my cot by the window next to my grandparents' bed. "We've made up a bed for him in the hall," she told me. "Don't be frightened if you see him in the morning."

I didn't sleep much, worrying about the man in the hall and what it meant to suddenly have a father. Kati had had three of them already and she hadn't liked any of them. Her first father, the lawyer, had been very pretty and popular but not interested in small children. The second had a hole in his head. The third was there that night. She had said the best time with fathers was when they ignored you. She had been jealous of me for not having one.

My best friend, Alice, however, seemed happy with her father. Alice lived on the fourth floor; we lived on the third. I met her the day we moved in. She had been standing at the elevator, ready to push the button for our furniture. She was smaller than me, dark-haired, snub-nosed, wearing a fancy embroidered dress with brown stains, her white socks dirty, her knees bruised, and she had on a pair of large, red leather, high-heeled shoes that scraped along as she walked. I had liked her immediately.

Alice's father still worked all day in the grocery and didn't come home till after nine every night, and then everyone had to be quiet because he needed to rest. But sometimes he told her stories. She said she loved them the best, even though they were only about witches and dwarves and other things that never existed, not about real people like my grandfather's stories.

The biggest problem with not having a father, Alice had told me, was that you were expected to have one when you started school. The first question the principal had asked her mother when she went to enrol Alice was what her father did. I thought at the time that Alice had just said that because she wanted me to be jealous about her having a proper family. Proper families, she thought, included fathers.

Most of the night I listened to the murmur of voices as they ebbed and lulled, and to Leah's laughter and to the gramophone playing gypsy music. The new doll that had no mouth lay next to my old fuzzy bear, and the wooden horse was under the pillow. I had been blowing onto it, hoping it would change into Lightning during the night and gallop off with me. I thought it had just begun to breathe, when my grandmother came to her bed.

She turned on her tiny light and pinned her hair on top of her head for the night. When she was up and about, she parted her hair in the middle and pulled it down into a little roll that went around her head in a semicircle at chin level. She held it all in place with tiny hairpins that were almost invisible. I could never understand how she managed to do it so perfectly every day, especially at the back where she couldn't even see it.

My grandfather came a bit later, in his knee-length nightshirt and the small white cap he wore on his head to keep his bald pate from cooling. He said warm brains gave him a head start in the mornings.

When he saw I was awake, he came to sit on the edge of my bed. "Exciting day for you," he said.

I nodded, not very happily.

"You want to know about the horse Baby Jesus brought you?" he asked.

I said I already knew the story. Everybody knew the story. Lightning was Vilmos's huge black horse, the one he had ridden at Nándorfehérvár, where we had beaten the hell out of the Turks.

He smiled smugly. "Different horse," he said.

"But you said it's Lightning," I protested. "You said so your-self." I was about to cry again. One more bit of treachery to finish off this Christmas. There was no point blowing on just an ordinary horse; it would never come alive and, even if it did, it would be just a horse, like the poor wretches dragging the ice carts.

"His name is Lightning, too," Vili said quickly. He didn't like it when I cried. "He is the son of the Lightning who had served in the battle of Nándorfehérvár with the first Vilmos."

"Did they call all their horses Lightning?"

"Do you want the story or don't you?"

AFTER THE BATTLE of Nándorfehérvár, Vilmos took his bride, Klara, and his horse home to his family's house on the plateau in the Carpathian Mountains, where his mother taught Klara all the things young women needed to know. Vilmos encouraged Lightning to take a bride of his own, a pretty mare in a neighbouring village. She was as black as Lightning, but not as strong and powerful. When she had a foal, they called him Lightning, too.

When Klara and Vilmos had a son, they gave him Lightning's foal. Lightning was as strong as his father and as light on his feet as his mother. When he galloped through the hills, even the birds stopped to watch his sleek, shiny shape stretch over the green grass, his hoofs tearing up the soft earth, his mane and tail flying. He was even more beautiful than his parents. And smart. He was so smart, he saved our king's life.

"Sigismund's? Why would that be such a smart move?"

"Not Sigismund's. I'd hardly call that fool our king."

The life that the son of Lightning saved was a real king's life. He was Mátyás, son of János Hunyadi, and king of the Hungarians. He ruled his empire with kindness and respect for his people. Even as a boy-king, he was beloved by all, clever and fair in his judgements, unafraid of the argumentative nobles at court, a fierce warrior who led his army of Black Knights through the gates of Vienna when the Habsburgs continued to harass him. Here is how it all happened.

Sigismund's grandson, a weakling prince called Ladislas, inherited the Hungarian crown. He was only a child, but already richer than all the other kings in Europe. This Ladislas, the new Holy Roman Emperor, asked his nasty scheming uncle, Ulrich Cillei, to bring him up to be a worthy king. Instead, Count Ulrich taught the boy to be lazy in his studies, to hide behind his underlings in battle and, above all, to be suspicious of Hungarians. The new king barely learned Hungarian. Though he was king of the Hungarians, he was German at heart. So was Ulrich. Habsburgs. Never trust them.

Ulrich was keen to get his hands on the Hunyadi lands, and he told the boy-king to be particularly suspicious of the Hunyadis. Their father, János, the hero, had been granted lands on both sides of the Carpathian Mountains, castles in the south and rich farmlands in the west. Sigismund had been inordinately fond of him from the time he served in the Emperor's Knights of the Dragon.

The boy-king, hypnotized by his evil uncle, the bloated, greedy, show-off Ulrich, plotted against Hunyadi's sons. He agreed that Ulrich should have some of their lands in Erdély, even their magnificent castle, Hunyadvár (*Vajdahunyad vára*).

Vilmos heard that his friend's sons were in danger. He took his broadsword from its resting place above the mantel, his chain-mail vest, his cloak ("His pointy shoes? His stockings?" "Are you going to listen or heckle?" "Listen.") from the nail behind the door of Rácz manor ("On the Arges?" "Up the mountain near Tövis.") He led his horse, Lightning ("Which one? "The old one." "Oh."), from the stables, said goodbye to his family and set out for Hunyadvár.

The first night he was there, Count Ulrich sought admission at the gates. He had come with his men, no doubt to inspect the place, perhaps to decide how much redecoration it needed. A short stroll around the ramparts confirmed his worst suspicions: Hunyadvár may have been fine for the

Hunyadis, but it was too rough for the ladies of his own family. A great deal of work would be needed.

He remarked on this to his silent host, László Hunyadi, the eldest of Hunyadi's children. "My dear Laci" — he used the diminutive form of László — "this castle, quite frankly, is not up to standards. These modern times call for greater attention to the arts. You have no hangings, few statues, no frescoes, the stones have been left uncovered. It must be frigid in the winter." He talked like that and thought himself above the Hunyadis because his family's pedigree was longer than theirs. "The place needs attention to detail," he said.

The count himself wore all the fine trappings of his age: a red woollen long-coat with gold braid; long tight pantaloons; gold clips on his lacquered high-heeled shoes; his hair in braids. Greased and scented, face powdered, he was a dandy even by the standards of his dandified court. Entering the staterooms, he held his silk handkerchief to his nose. "We must install some carpets from Persia, and the kitchen will have to be moved."

When László told him he liked the place the way it was, Count Ulrich snickered. "Well, you would," he told him. "It's a Wallach stronghold. Given your heritage, how would you know any better?" He strolled with his hands clasped behind his wide back, his coat riding up over his rump to display his dagger and his leather-hilted sword. "Perhaps when Sigismund lent your father this land, he knew you'd be merely passing through. No need for creature comforts. A few years' stay. A hiding place from the Turks."

Everyone heard the word "lent," but no one was sure what happened next or how it happened. Some say that Count Ulrich, having failed to irritate László into battle, got tired of the game and drew his dagger, cutting Hunyadi's ring finger with the blade. And that the quick-tempered László lunged at his guest and killed him in one instant. Others say that László's men slew Count Ulrich.

But that night Vili filled in the details.

Vilmos had come a great distance, over treacherous passes where poor Wallachs and itinerant Saxon knights would kill you for a piece of bread — or just for the amusement you gave them, dying. He was tired and, as János's old friend and companion, much annoyed with Count Ulrich's antics. He was not amused by courtly pretensions, and what he remembered of the Habsburgs he didn't like. They had a habit of not turning up for battles when you needed reinforcements.

That night, when the portly count paused in front of a portrait of János Hunyadi and snorted with derision, Vilmos grabbed him by his golden braids and lifted him clear off the ground — just as his much later descendant used to lift men still seated in their chairs. He shook Count Ulrich by his fancy jacket and told him to get his hide back to Vienna where his kind belonged.

The count reached for his pearl-inlaid dagger, but, dangling as he was, he couldn't quite grab it. He commanded László Hunyadi to call off his dog. Once restored to the ground, his face red and steaming with anger, Ulrich lunged at László. Vilmos leaped in front of his friend's son and, in saving László's life, lost his own, thus greatly complicating our relationship with the Habsburgs (something Crankshaw fails to discuss in his history of the Habsburgs).

It's hardly surprising that Hunyadi's remaining pack of nobles slew Ulrich and his retinue on the spot.

King Ladislas was clearly miffed at his uncle's death, but he declared that he wanted peace with the Hunyadis and, to prove his good faith, he invited László and Mátyás, László's younger brother, to his castle in Budapest.

Their mother protested, but the two boys craved adventure and trusted the word of the king. Their enemies waited. When the Hunyadis were safely in their hands, they imprisoned them both. A brief trial found László guilty of conspiracy against the king and condemned him to immediate execution. Vili told me that the executioner's first blow missed Hunyadi's neck, the second faltered on his long, blond hair and the third cut but failed to kill him. Tradition called for the condemned to be released if three blows of the axe failed to finish him off. But when Hunyadi stood after the third blow, thinking he was free to go, the Habsburg king signalled his headsman to slash Hunyadi's throat.

His mother, Erzsébet, had the body brought home to Erdély and laid out with pomp and ceremony to allow the whole nation to mourn. There is a painting of the grieving mother and wife kneeling beside the body covered in a white sheet. Two tall candelabra fail to lighten the blackness around them.

King Ladislas died of a mysterious illness on November 23, 1457, exactly one year after he had given his word to Hunyadi's widow that he wouldn't harm her sons.

Less than a month later, in the middle of a cold December, Mátyás was proclaimed King of Hungary by the nobles of the land. They had come from all corners of the country, their armour shining, their swords swinging from their saddles. They met on the frozen Danube and carried the new king on their shoulders all the way to Buda Castle.

"What happened to young Lightning?"

"He was growing up. As was young Vilmos."

"I thought this was going to be young Lightning's story."

"I'm coming to that now."

By 1470 young Vilmos was only sixteen, but he was as big and strong as his father had been. He wanted to be a Black Knight, one of Mátyás's own army of soldiers. When he said goodbye to Klara, she asked him to take young Lightning as a gift for the king. Had he been a little younger, he might have refused. After all, it was his horse — he had reared it, cared for it, brushed its coat every day. They made the long journey from Erdély to Visegrad, at the bend of the Danube, on the highest peak of the mountain where the king had decided to build a new castle.

It was a bleak November day when young Vilmos arrived. He had a letter from Klara for King Mátyás. When the king saw the seal on the envelope, he recognized the Rácz crest immediately.

Mátyás welcomed him. He showed him around his magical hanging gardens, the wonder of all Europe. They feasted on wild boar and chestnuts and drank warm mead made by the monks of Esztergom. At first Mátyás was reluctant to accept the gift of Lightning, because he already had a very fine horse, but when Vilmos led him into the courtyard, Mátyás couldn't resist. Lightning's black hoofs danced on the marble flagstones, he shook his head and whinnied at so much pomp. The king thought this was the first horse he had ever seen laugh at the overdressed courtiers.

Wasn't it lucky for Mátyás, because a few days later, Lightning saved his life and led him to his one true love.

"A princess?"

"Alas, not a princess."

It was in the great walled city of Breslau, in Silesia. Mátyás had been invited by Mayor Krebs. When Mátyás entered the city, he was riding on his new horse, surrounded by his Black Knights, and the people tossed flowers under Lightning's hoofs. Except for this one rotten man who was paid a lot of money by fat King Podiebrad, king of the Czechs, to kill Mátyás. When Lightning saw the poisoned knife lunging to wound the king's leg, he bucked, tossing the regal rider onto the flower-strewn stones, right at the feet of the mayor's beautiful daughter. While the Black Knights grabbed the foiled killer, she bent down to help Mátyás to his feet. Their eyes met, and Mátyás forgot to be angry at Lightning for throwing him.

"Didn't he know that Lightning saved his life?"

"Maybe he did. Maybe he didn't. What he was quite certain about was that he was in love with Barbara. She was tall for a woman, almost as tall as he was, her hair the colour of honey, her face round and her eyes a soft green, like your mother's. When they danced together at the mayor's grand ball that night, they looked so perfect that artists took out their brushes and tried to capture their likeness, musicians' hands faltered and the music stopped, but Mátyás and Barbara kept dancing to the music in their hearts."

"What about Lightning?"

"Lightning?"

"What happened to him?" I wanted to know.

"He lived happily ever after, of course."

I slept well that night, all thoughts of my father banished by the magic of Vili's tale.

THE MORNING AFTER the Christmas my father ruined, everything seemed different from other mornings. Though it was light, my grandmother was still in her bed. She was lying high on her piled-up pillows, her hair tangled on top of her head. She was paler than usual, and she was always pale.

I couldn't smell coffee. I could hear my grandfather talking in the livingroom. No one had told me to get ready for church, though we usually went to church Christmas Day and afterwards to the Apostolok restaurant for beer and salty pretzels. I didn't care a whole lot about church, but I had been looking forward to the pretzels.

I opened the door to the livingroom. They were sitting at one end of the long table, my mother, Leah and my grandfather, leaning in toward one another, talking. My mother wore her silky pink dressing gown; my grandfather and my aunt were in their city clothes. Leah had a tiny hat on her head with a brown feather. None of them noticed me as I crept around the edge of the room.

There was a fold-out bed in the corner of the hallway. A big hump of overcoat in the middle stretched all the way from the head to the foot of the bed. A hand dangled from the end.

He was snoring.

I crept closer to see if he looked less frightful in the light of day. His face was turned toward the wall and hidden by the grey woollen blanket my mother must have pulled off her own bed to give him. The hair on the back of his head was a fringe around baldness.

When I was very close to him and he still hadn't moved, I decided to be truly brave and I sat next to him. I must have had delusions of being one of the Black Knights, because I waited for him to wake up. Close up like this, the greatcoat was just a coat, mended in several places, frayed at the sleeves and around the grease-stained collar. The sleeves had been patched over with some heavy, blue serge; there were no buttons. It felt rougher to the touch than my grandfather's chin in the mornings, and it smelled of horse manure and cigarettes.

His hand was square, yellow-white, the nails broken and bluish, the knuckles dark; there was hair on the top of his fingers. As I examined his hand, I noticed something shiny poking out from under the pillow where his arm was.

I got down on the floor and pushed my face into the opening, but I couldn't see what it was. Curious, I slipped my hand under the pillow and tugged at it, gently at first, then a little more forcefully. I was just beginning to pry it loose when he moved.

Suddenly he was sitting bolt upright in bed, breathing as hard as if he was still snoring, his coat fallen off, his chest bare, his eyes wide, his beard wild as the night before, and the thing I'd been tugging at fell clattering onto the floorboards and slid against the wall with a thud. I ran to get it, picked it up and offered it to him. It was shiny and black, oily to the touch, slippery.

"Put that damned thing down!" he shouted.

I backed away from him. His voice was hoarse, it croaked deep in his throat, but it was loud, and his beard opened to reveal yellow teeth.

"Now!" he shouted.

My grandfather was suddenly there, then my mother and Leah. He was still shouting. "Tell that damned kid to give me the gun."

"Quiet," my grandfather ordered. His voice was barely a whisper.

"A toy gun," my mother said too loudly. "How nice." She seemed to be talking to the bookcase.

Very gently my grandfather took the thing from my hand. He held it between his thumb and forefinger, glanced at it, then moved toward the centre of the room and laid it on the table. All the while he was looking at the man on the cot. My grandfather had dark brown eyes that turned to pinpoints when he was intent on something or annoyed, and I could see he was annoyed now.

We all stood there for a while and nobody said anything, then my mother took my hand and led me back to the bedroom.

"He is not himself," she said as I cowered into my bed.

"Who is he then?"

"We don't know yet. I doubt if he knows. He spent four years in Siberia, in the north of Russia. It was cold and damp there, much colder than you can imagine. Working sixteen hours a day. And not much to eat. Only raw potatoes. That can change a man." She spoke very softly. The string of pearls she had worn for Christmas was still around her neck.

He is definitely not my father, I told myself when my mother went back to where the adults were arguing. In fact, I thought, he is probably Turk.

14

THE DAY NEVER RECOVERED from its unpleasant start. Though I dressed in my absolute best Sunday clothes, squeezed my feet into the too-small black patent leather shoes from last Christmas, brushed my teeth with soap to make them shine and pulled on the pink skirt I already hated, no one came to tell me it was time to go to church.

I could still hear the voices from the diningroom, sometimes louder, then quiet again as someone shushed them. The doorbell rang and new voices joined the others. The sun was already high and the streetcars were rumbling and clanging along Rákóczi Street when my cousin Kati was ushered in to join me.

I was amazed that she was still in her flannel pyjamas, still holding her bedtime brown bear. She was three years older, and she was allowed to be up earlier and was urged to bed later than I was. She slept in the balcony room, on the far side of the livingroom that was also my mother's room. She shared it with her mother and her stepfather, Miklós. She had a white cot pushed up against the far wall near the balcony door, and she could go outside when her mother and Miklós were too noisy.

Their room had the Titian painting. Leah was really proud of having it there. It was a very dark picture, all browns and reds, blacks and tiny strips of light. One of the yellow lights fell on the man riding the donkey in the centre. My mother told me it was Christ entering Jerusalem. There were lots of people laying palm fronds under his donkey's feet. My favourite part of the picture was the two dachshunds in the bottom right-hand corner. One of them looked a lot like Jinny.

Leah and her husband often went away to the house he shared with his mother, and sometimes Leah took Kati with her.

I always knew when they were leaving because Kati had both her bedtime bear and her daytime smooth white bear with her. She liked to prepare them for the journey by reading them stories to calm them.

She stood just inside the door, glanced at our grandmother and whispered, "I think he'll be leaving soon. Your dad." She was allowed to have her hair hang to her shoulders already, but she still sucked her thumb. "You want to know how I know?" she asked between slurps.

I must have looked very keen to know, because she said she'd only tell if I let her have Lightning for a day. I wasn't too happy that Vili had also told her the story. I liked to think Vili's stories were just for me. The only good part of her knowing the same stories was that we could play story-games, starting at some point in one of our grandfather's stories and taking turns changing them a little, adding new details, even new people. The rules were that each of us had to carry the story to a crucial moment, then pass it over to the other to resolve and continue. If you lost the thread of the story, you lost.

I pulled Lightning out of my pocket. "OK."

"My mother was talking to a man last night who said he'd take your father to Vienna if she had the gold."

"What gold?" My grandmother sat up in bed, staring at Kati.

Kati shrugged and sucked on her thumb.

"Are you sure she said gold?" my grandmother asked.

"She had some stuff in her hands, it looked shiny, a bracelet, and maybe something red ..."

My grandmother leapt out of bed, got on her hands and knees then onto her stomach and laid the side of her head on the floor so she could see under the bed. Kati and I came closer and watched as she pulled out a cardboard box. The box rattled. She sat back on her haunches and started to pry it open, but her hands shook. She waved to Kati to come over, and the two of them pried the lid off the box. I was amazed that my grandmother would make such a fuss about anything. She was the least fussy person in our family. But then the last little while had certainly been quite unusual for everyone.

The box was full of earrings and bracelets, some strings of pink and white pearls, pendants with blue and green stones, and there was one long, shiny string with blue-green stones, some thin, glistening strands and a bunch of gold rings.

My grandmother said, "She wouldn't ...," stood up quickly and marched out of the bedroom without putting on her blue dressing gown. Her nightgown was pink and almost transparent. I was really glad she wore underpants.

Kati and I followed at a safe distance.

Everyone was in the livingroom. They were all smoking, even my grandfather, who didn't smoke. My mother was all dressed in her working clothes, skirt, blouse and jacket, her thick, blondish hair curling down her back past her shoulders. She held her cigarette lightly between her thumb and forefinger; the ash had fallen onto the carpet. Her face was closed, grey, expressionless, her eyes downcast.

My grandfather was next to her, his arm over her shoulder, and he was chewing his lower lip just like he often told me not to do when I was upset. Leah's husband was wearing his grey overcoat unbuttoned and stood with his back to the fireplace as if to warm himself, though I knew no one had set the fire yet. My mother had said he wasn't very bright.

To my great relief, my father wasn't there.

Leah was at the door. She wore her burgundy dress, her very high heels, the hat, her shiny black hair all frothy, her face powdered, her eyebrows outlined in perfect black arcs. She was telling my grandfather she would never again be told by him what to do. She seemed calm.

"It's my life, and I'll live it the way I want from now on," she said. "And where I want. And with whom I want. I'm not asking. I'm telling you, and I'm leaving." She strolled over to the corner table, her heels clicking; she twirled her long cigarette holder down into the ashtray, stubbing the burning cigarette, and flounced out of the room brandishing it between her first and middle fingers. Her shoes had no toes, though it had been snowing.

My grandmother stood watching Leah. It was odd how nobody seemed to have noticed that the three of us had burst in or that my grandmother was wearing only her thin pink nightgown. My mother never even turned to look our way.

Then my grandmother started for the door, and we could all hear her shout, "You took the ruby necklace, didn't you?" Pause. "And how much did you give him?" Her voice was rising. Longer pause. "*How much?*"

When Leah replied, it was hardly more than a whisper. Later I wondered if anyone else had heard. "Just the gold bracelet. No more than what you'd have given him yourself."

I joined my mother at the window, and the two of us watched Leah leave the building. "Silly," my mother said. "She never thinks about what she is doing." Leah made her way to the streetcar stop in front of the National Theatre, pulled on her gloves, swatted the snow off her shoes and climbed onto the streetcar. She didn't seem to mind that she had left behind her coat, her husband and my cousin Kati or that it was snowing still.

"Therese had been in love with your father," Leah told me once. She almost never called my grandmother Therese. "Not that she didn't love Papa. She always has, but with your father it was different. Her last chance to flirt, turning forty, wanting to have a man's full attention. With Papa, she never had his full attention. There were too many other things to interest him. And too many other women."

"Why?"

"It was his nature. Can't ever change the way a man is. Remember that."

"What about you? Did you also love him?"

"Me? I might have once, for a moment. Back then, in 1948, I thought I did. But he didn't love me any longer. Who cares? There were so many men, so many who loved me, one more or less."

"Did Sari love him too?"

"She liked that he loved her. Or she thought he loved her. In those days all we had to amuse ourselves were the men who came to court."

"And my mother? Did he love her?"

"You'll have to ask her that."

❧

"I don't think he loved me," my mother told me when we were in New Zealand. "He liked the idea of being in love with a Rácz girl, and I was the least threatening of the three."

"That Christmas then, why did he come home?"

"The Russians sent some of the prisoners back. Where else was he to go?"

❧

"There's not much sense his following Sari, now," my grandmother told my mother later that day.

"He isn't following her," my mother said.

"Nor, for that matter, will Leah be following him," my grandmother said.

"As you well know, he has his heart set on one woman, all you have to do is say the word," Vili said. "And you should forget about Kálmán, he is gone. And it's over."

My mother spent most of that day at the window looking out. My grandmother stayed on her bed, propped up on all the pillows, drinking her medicinal sherry. My grandfather went out for coffee and conversation. He didn't take me with him.

I do not remember what Leah's third husband did, but I'm pretty sure he left before nightfall. Nobody spoke to him.

15

FOR THE MOST PART, I grew up in that 1920s apartment building of grey concrete slabs, with a central courtyard, a rectangular patch of earth where our voluminous superintendent attempted to nurture a few vegetables. I liked to imagine that there were horses in the courtyard and that if I listened hard I could hear their hoofs clattering on the concrete, past the super's barred door, coming to a stop by her desolate vegetable patch.

For my grandmother, the move across the river to Pest had been a catastrophe. She had loved her pretty house in Buda, the house where Vili had promised her parents he would keep her in splendour. I think she was prepared to live in the rubble left by the war, to line up for food and be jeered at by the soldiers. But she had not foreseen that she would have to leave her house. Even during the bombardment of Budapest, when most of the city was destroyed, she refused to leave her own cellar until the last moment.

The State had taken the farm, the magazines, Vili's buildings near Váci Street, all his savings — the industrial shares were worthless — even his orchards north of Esztergom. Vili, ever irrepressible, would tell her how lucky we all were to be together and alive and that we had moved to a street still named after a great Hungarian hero, not like some people who were now living on Stalin Boulevard or Moscow Square or Liberation Avenue.

The apartment building was kitty-corner from the National Theatre. The yellow streetcars stopped just under our windows. We were on the third floor.

My mother had become the main breadwinner in the family. After the war she had studied at night school to be a surveyor for the State Road and Railway Company, an operation that took delight in sending her as far away from me as possible. She measured distances between villages for railway lines and roads. The work involved finding the most direct route between given points on the map. They used a viewfinder, long red and white poles, a metal tape measure, a big-headed hammer, wooden spikes and a grease pencil for the numbers. The greatest worry might have been that they would lose the markers in the deep, drifting snow, but what they really worried about was touching the metal tape measure without gloves and getting their fingers stuck. My mother promised that once her job was secure, she would take me with her, but for now I was to stay with my grandparents.

The superintendent, Mrs. Nemeth, was fat, red-cheeked and bowlegged, and she smelled of sweat and hot pepper sausage. She and her smallish, pale-faced husband had been transported to Budapest in 1947, courtesy of their local Communist Council in Pécs county. Their bulky son, Tibor, went to the police academy. The idea was that they were due for a break. They had been working the same small piece of land for generations. Luckily, it wasn't their own land; it belonged to a local landlord, now sagely behind bars for being a landlord (*kulak*). In exchange for cooking and caring for his family while cash was scarce, the landlord had wanted to give them a bit of land once Mrs. Nemeth's husband returned from the Russian front. Had the landlord not been such a stickler for formality, waiting for the man to return, she would have taken the land and been classified as a *kulak* herself, and she and Mr. Nemeth might now be behind bars with the landlord.

Not that she was delighted with their move. Neither she nor Mr. Nemeth had ever wanted to run an apartment building. They had never even been to Budapest. He had a talent for growing corn, and she had been a culinary artist. Her special-ty was chicken breasts with paprika sauce. It had never seemed to her that there was a war going on. Her husband, whom she always referred to as Mr. Nemeth, sent frequent cards from obscure Ukrainian places and never mentioned the army.

As far as she could tell, the war hadn't started till 1945, when the Russians came, requisitioned the corn and the chickens, raped the landlord's wife and daughter, carried off his paintings and silver, shot out his windows and took his horses. After the new government was set up in Budapest, they confiscated the land for the co-op and sent the Nemeths to Budapest to care for an apartment building.

Mr. Nemeth was so miserable in the city that he started drinking *palinka* before breakfast every day.

Though I had told her this story, my mother was convinced that Mrs. Nemeth did double duty as a watchdog for the Party and told me never to give any sign that I agreed with her when she complained about having to move to Budapest. In fact, my mother rebuked her once for her ingratitude to the Party. "Had you stayed back in Pécs county," she told the super, "Tibor might not have been able to train for the police force. Such a fine figure he cuts in his uniform."

Mrs. Nemeth harrumphed emphatically. I think she knew that Tibor didn't look great in his uniform; it was too small for him, or he was too big for it. She believed that he would have made a fine corn farmer. I heard her confide in my grandfather that my mother was becoming too much of a communist.

"How can you be too much of a good thing?" Vili asked with a wink.

Mrs. Nemeth kept an eye on the cavorting around the courtyard terraces where the apartment entrances were.

Most days Alice and I played Turks and Hungarians. We would race toward each other on a signal, and whoever got farther into the other's territory won. The loser would have to be the Turk for the day, and the winner got to successfully defend a castle, usually Eger, and pour very warm water on the other's head. It was tricky getting the water to warm because we had to get coal up from the basement first, set a fire in the bathroom water heater and wait. All that took a long time, and there was a good chance that my grandmother would see me sneaking into the bathroom and demand to know what we were up to, and when she found out "nothing," send me on errands or get me to walk Jinny.

Sometimes we had beheadings, but only when the Turks got too uppity.

16

IT WAS NOT ONLY my family that had an extraordinary preoccupation with the Turks; most Hungarian children knew enough about Turks to fear them. When I was four or five, my grandfather had read me *The Stars of Eger*, the classic tale of Turks in Hungary. It's by Géza Gárdonyi. It's a long book — it lasted many long evenings — but I loved every word of it, especially the way Vili read it to me.

He would hunker down in his wide-armed chair, the book balanced on his chest, waiting for me to settle next to him. He would sigh just before he began, a deep chestful of a sigh, and keep me waiting a moment longer, building suspense. During the exciting parts, he would lean forward, his moustache bristling, his eyes flashing, his voice taking on the voice of each person, louder or softer as the role required.

I would whoop with delight when I caught him using one person's voice for another, particularly if it was a child speaking like one of the adults. "Just checking to see if you're listening," he'd say.

The story is about the battle for Eger Castle. It's 1533, and the Turks, as usual, are invading.

Eger sits on top of the Mátra Mountains, where the air is clean and crisp and there are wild animals in the forest.

My hero was Gergely Bornemissza, about the same age as me when he is captured by a one-eyed janissary at the beginning of the book. Gergely is naked, swimming in the river, his pony tied to a nearby tree; his buddy, a little girl, is splashing about with him when the villainous Turk sees his horse. At first the Turk wants only the horse, but when he sees the children, he thinks, yes, they'll do as well. He grabs them, lays them over his saddle and takes them back to his unit. Even young slaves gave a man status in Turkey. Years later, Gergely escapes, as does the girl, and they find their way back to Hungary. They both end up in Eger with István Dobó, defending the castle. She is almost as great a swordsman as Gergely. It's the three of them, victorious, against the entire Turkish Army.

They hold out against an army of 150,000 well-armed Turks, confident of victory, having already destroyed resistance all the way from Transylvania to Budapest. What was left of the Hungarian armies had been destroyed on the battlefield at Mohács, after which King János had been forced to kiss the Sultan's hand, giving him dominion over the land. Naturally, said Vili, Ferdinand, the Habsburg, had sat out the battle.

In Eger, while the men fought like tigers, the women poured boiling water over enemy soldiers attempting to scale the walls. They beat back the Turks, the pope sang *Te Deum*s in Rome, everyone rejoiced.

The flags left behind by the retreating Turkish armies, Vili told me, were taken to Vienna, where they were displayed by the Habsburgs among their spoils of past victories. Perhaps they're still there.

Alice's father's grocery store was on the street side of the building. It was small and damp and smelled of dried rosemary, vinegar and pickles. He used to give me sugar cubes. My grandmother would send me down there for sour cream, bread, sugar and eggs, and he never asked for cash. Later, when the store was closed by authority of the Party, we owed him for about a week's groceries.

Across from our apartment on the far side of the courtyard, there was the Fothy family. He worked in the Ministry of the Interior, he told my grandfather, in a very unimportant job, as a paper-shuffler. He left each morning at seven sharp, dressed in a grey suit and tie. He kept his shoes shined. His wife cooked elaborate meals from old recipe books she guarded from prying eyes. Once my grandmother asked me to get her recipe for a rolled pastry cherry cake. Although I had seen it on their table at dinnertime, she denied that she had such a recipe and advised me to tell my grandmother to try something simpler, like a puff tart.

Alice and I used to watch her through the gap in their lace curtains.

She kept her hair in tight, tiny, pink rollers all day, combing it into tight little curls for her husband's evening return. He painted her toenails pink. Whenever she left her apartment, she pulled on a girdle that must have been made for someone a great deal thinner than she was. In any event, she took a long time pulling and tugging and stuffing her flesh into it. Sometimes he helped.

When Kati was with us, we never spied on the Fothys, since Kati was friendly with their daughter, Moci. They were at school together.

Years later, when I discovered that Mr. Fothy worked for the Hungarian secret police, filing pieces of information about people, and that Moci followed in her father's footsteps, I no longer felt guilty about the day I stole Mrs. Fothy's rolled pastry cherry cake recipe for my grandmother and her blue feather boa for Alice and me, or for not owning up to either crime when I heard Mrs. Fothy accuse the tearful Moci.

In the apartment below us, there was a piano tuner and his daughter. A doctor lived upstairs with his wife and two older sons. We played ring-the-bell-and-hide on both families until the piano tuner talked to my grandfather and Alice's father about it. Alice's father told her the worst thing you could do was to draw attention to yourselves. It wouldn't be the kids who were reported to the authorities, it would be the parents.

Vili told me he could see why we enjoyed the game, but the piano tuner's daughter and the doctor's wife fed pigeons on their windowsills, just like my grandmother did. If I persisted in making them mad, they'd attract all my grandmother's pigeons over to their windows and Therese would be too distraught to make our dinners.

Next door to Alice's apartment, there was a woman who lived alone with her son. He was very sick. Once when we rang her bell, she came to the door with the boy in her arms. He was almost as tall as we were, but so thin she could carry him with one arm. His skin was yellow and the bones stood out in his face. Alice's mother told her he had tuberculosis and wouldn't live till the end of the year.

The woman had made such a point of not being noticed that she never called the doctor. Mrs. Nemeth thought she might have been a big *kulak*'s wife or widow, still living off what they had saved, since she didn't have to go and find work like everybody else.

We used to leave gifts for the boy — shiny buttons, a comb we had found, a coloured pencil, a papier-mâché doll we had made — but I doubt his mother ever gave them to him. She asked Alice's mother to tell us to leave them alone.

He died anyway. His mother cried so loud and for so long that Mrs. Nemeth had to call the police. She said she hadn't liked to do it, but the noise had to stop.

Perhaps Mrs. Nemeth's supposition had been right. The woman was never seen again after the police came and the state undertakers carried off her son's body.

My grandfather said it was best never to ask about people who disappeared. We lived in times, he said, when disappearances were common.

Mrs. Nemeth rented the place to another woman who had no children. She wore black lace underwear and went out most nights. One morning, early, when Alice and I were lurking outside her apartment, peeping in through her velvety curtains, she opened her door and let out a man. I thought he looked like Leah's third husband. She saw us at the window and winked.

The Christmas my father came and went was the last one before I was to start school about six blocks from the apartment building. My mother took me there to show me what it looked like. I didn't find it frightening; in fact, I was quite looking forward to September. My only worry was my father.

Both Vili and my mother had already coached me to say that my father had disappeared during the war, that I had no idea what had happened to him and that he was probably dead. Now he had spoiled that whole plan by reappearing, and chances were that the principal would want to know where he had gone again. Worse, rather than maybe feeling sorry for my being fatherless, he was bound to ask what my father had been doing before the war.

I already knew that to be a trick question. Never, under any circumstances, was I to tell anyone that my father had lands and especially not that he had owned factories. Not even Alice. If there was one thing worse than a *kulak*, it was a capitalist. Capitalists were "class enemies."

That's why I didn't tell Alice right away that my father had been there on Christmas Eve. I thought that perhaps I could pretend it had never happened.

My mother didn't mention him for a while, and whenever my grandmother started to talk about him, Vili would cough or say "Nicht vor dem Kind."

Some days after my father left, Vili had taken me out to the bench in front of the National Theatre and told me we must never talk about my father in the house. It was a cold day, wet snow freezing in the gutters, and an old man was scattering bread on the sidewalk for the sparrows, who fluffed up their feathers to keep themselves warm.

"The walls," Vili said, "have ears. And some people think it's a crime to leave this country. They might even put us all in jail if they find out we helped your father leave."

"You mean with grandmother's gold and ruby things that Leah gave him?"

"Exactly. And they wouldn't just blame Leah. They'd blame all of us."

"Even me?" I asked.

"Possibly. Anyway, with us all gone, who'd be there to look after you?"

I shrugged.

"That's why we can't talk about him in the apartment. Someone might be listening."

For years afterward I imagined that the walls had tiny ears, and sometimes, when I was lonely, I whispered to them.

"Your father had to leave Hungary," Vili explained. "He was in danger while he was here and everyone he met was in danger because of him. Think of it like the chicken pox. Or whooping cough. Contagious. Soon as you touch another person, she gets it too." I nodded. I knew about the whooping cough. "Why," I asked, "was he in danger?" "Because he was anti-communist, and he said so. Now he is in Vienna. That means he didn't like it here. Not liking it here is enough to send a person to jail. Just knowing someone who doesn't like it here can send you to jail. That's the way it works. Do you understand?"

I didn't quite. Still, I was surprised he had asked. He always assumed I understood. "Why Vienna?" I asked. "Hungarians don't go to Vienna unless they're in chains. And he didn't have to, did he? Did he go to be with Sari?"

"No."

"Will Leah go too?"

"No."

"Anyway, they'll all be in jail in Vienna, the Habsburgs get them all," I said quite cheerfully.

"They won't stay there," he reassured me. He thought for a while, then he said, "A lot of things changed between us and the Habsburgs over the years. They lost their throne, you know." He looked very pleased about that. "And another thing. Did I tell you about the time King Mátyás took Vienna hostage? He almost became Holy Roman Emperor. If it hadn't been for the treacherous king of Bohemia, he would have done it ..."

"Podiebrad?"

"... then no one would have cared if that silly Archduke Franz Ferdinand was assassinated. He wouldn't have even been an archduke, a member of a forgotten family of lesser nobles, and who would have bothered to do him in? Nobody. Then there wouldn't have been a First World War, nor a Second, and we wouldn't be in this mess now, would we?" He held my hand as we crossed the street to the entrance of our building. We stopped to say hello to Alice's father and pick up a few dill pickles for dinner.

"The villain, no doubt, is Podiebrad," he said as he bit into one of the pickles and offered me another.

17

VILI AND I WERE SAILING paper boats off the balcony of our apartment on Rákóczi Street.

Out of the blue Vili mentioned that there was a good reason why my father hadn't been at the hospital for my birth. I had no idea why Vili was broaching the subject now. I hadn't been thinking about my father at all.

Vili made elaborate ships of flimsy newspaper pages, I coloured them basic red, yellow or blue, then we shoved them into the prevailing wind, their prows high, their sails shaking in anticipation, over the rails and beyond the balcony above our heads. We watched them cross Rákóczi Street and disappear behind the garish lights of the Corvin department store, then Vili sighed, "They are on their way to Erdély," or sometimes, "to New York."

That day, he flew them straight up in the air, trying to see if they would jump over the roof and go east. "The way your father had gone in '45," he said, much too nonchalantly, as if he were talking about the colour I'd put on the sails. "Back behind the house, and as far as you can imagine going, there are the Great Hungarian Plains, and beyond them, the Great Russian Plains, and beyond them still, that's where your father went. The Great Russian Taiga." He cleared his throat, as he sometimes did when he began a new story, but the rest of it came in a burst, not in his usual tale-telling voice. "The

Russians took him to a cold place where the sun shines for only the smallest part of the year. In 1945." Vili stopped looking up into the sunlight. "The rest of the family was huddled in the basement of our old house. Your grandmother and aunts. Your cousins. Your grandmother's maid, the cook and her helper, and some of the people who had been hiding there since '43 and '44."

"He didn't care much about me, did he?"

"The point is," Vili added, sensing the wind's changing direction, "that he didn't have a chance. He was nabbed by a group of Russian soldiers while he was lining up for cabbages near the Franciscan Church."

"Not bread?"

"Cabbages."

"But now he's gone to Vienna and we don't have to think about him anymore," I said.

"The story isn't over yet."

And it wasn't.

My mother was the next person to bring up the topic. That spring she was home for one of her infrequent reassignments. We had a day to ourselves, and she said we could go to Heroes' Square after breakfast, and Városliget, if I liked.

I wanted us to take Alice, but she wouldn't let me. No Alice and no Benny — it was a deal. Benny was one of her friends. A bulky man who wore a lot of grey and had brown, thick hair, button eyes, lumpy hands and a grating niceness I thought he wouldn't be able to keep up for long, but he did. He had tried very hard to like me, and I doubt if it was his fault that he failed at the task.

My mother knew I loved Heroes' Square; she had loved it herself when she was a child. The square dwarfs everything else in the city. Its sheer size is breathtaking. The ancient bronze heroes stand, each on his own massive pedestal, around the huge Millennial Column, itself almost forty metres tall. When you stood under it and looked up at the top, you got dizzy.

Once Vili had played a game with me of who could look longer at the top of the column and stay standing. He made such a fuss about the contest that a small crowd gathered to watch. He lost spectacularly by flipping over and stopping himself with his hands in a push-up position just before he fell. Everyone clapped.

The heroes, Chief Árpád and the six tribal chiefs, are much bigger than real people. They have pointy headgear with bronze feathers, swords hanging by wide belts from their waists, huge capes hanging from their huge shoulders, and they sit in the saddle like men who have ridden far. Their horses are decorated with bronze bangles and beads, their saddles and their leads with bronze bloodstones from the lands of the Avars. Vili said their stirrups were fashioned from bone. Each chief carried a gold-inlaid bugle, whose sound reached into the far corners of the plains between the mountains and Buda where the tribes settled and where Árpád ruled.

Behind the chiefs there are the fourteen heroes of later history, including King Mátyás. He has the face of a fighter, lips pressed together, chin jutting out, thick, curly hair, an array of heavy armour and a sword you'd have to be a giant to wield. Yet he is the only one of the heroes with a tiny smile around his lips, as if he thought standing here in such ceremonial surroundings was not what he'd had in mind for the afterlife, but it amused him anyway.

My mother said Mátyás was a lot better looking than the statue. His hair was auburn, almost dark red, his cheekbones high, his shoulders broad, his carriage straight. His laughter was raucous; he loved funny stories and rewarded those who told them well. "Your grandfather would have been a wealthy man."

Princesses and countesses from all over the world vied for his hand in marriage, she said. At festivities, they were all trying to catch his eye. They wore glittering gowns of silk and brocade, just like Sari and Leah had in "peacetime," and more jewellery than a king's ransom; but no one pleased Mátyás. When he finally fell in love, it was with a commoner, the daughter of the mayor of Breslau.

"Barbara."

"Oh yes, Vili loves the story of Barbara. Of course, they couldn't marry, though he continued to love her all his life."

"Why couldn't they marry?" I asked again.

"Because a king could only marry someone who was of noble blood, someone who could bring an inheritance of wealth, possessions, rank, respectability, connections with other nations." My mother sounded as if she disapproved but there was not a lot she could do about it.

"But he was the king, he could do whatever he wanted," I protested.

"Being king didn't make a difference; you still had to do what was expected of you. Perhaps being king made it some-what worse."

It was a warm, hazy day, with pigeons strolling and court-ing all around us and the scent of cherry blossoms from the Városliget.

"I need to talk to you about your father and me," she announced.

"About my father? Why?"

"The war," my mother said, "has changed everything. For all of us. He had to work in a uranium mine. And on an underground tunnel near Kazakhstan. His fingernails were gone. One of his ears froze and broke off. He's had dysentery for more than a year. His father was killed by a drunken Russian soldier. His lands are gone. His mother died last month. And I have grown up." She took a deep breath. "I think we should give it another try." She paused and looked at me. "We are going to join him in Vienna."

"We're *what*?" I yelled. "Are you crazy?"

She put her forefinger to her lips. "Shssh ... No one must know."

She wouldn't answer my whispered questions on the streetcar home, because there were other people around, and when I said, "You don't even like him," she scowled.

"When you're older ...," she said, but I didn't let her finish. I moved to the far end of the car.

We got off, and there was Benny waiting at the corner near the Astoria Restaurant. He must have had a bath and shave not much earlier, because his hair was all plastered down and wet around his shining face. He had a little box for my mother and a stuffed pink rabbit for me.

I told him to keep it and gave him my evil look.

"We could all go and have ice cream," he said, his eyes all over my mother.

"I'm not coming," I yelled at my mother and started to sprint home. I didn't look back once, but I knew she knew I hadn't meant the Astoria for ice cream; I was talking about going to Vienna.

She didn't call after me.

VILI SAID A WIFE had a duty to be with her husband. That was one of the problems with being a wife. He added the admonition, "Never get married." He was serious. "Marriage," he said, "is not for the fainthearted. It's messy and complicated and emotionally draining. And it's particularly tough for women."

I was in the kitchen helping my grandmother roll plum balls. She had cooked the plums in sugar water and made the dough overnight in a white Herendi ceramic bowl she had been given by an aunt as a wedding present. My job was to drop the oozing plums onto the centre of the flattened dough pieces, fold up the sides to hide them, then roll more or less round balls.

Vili, who hated to spend time in the kitchen, stood in the doorway. I could tell from the hunching of his shoulders that we weren't to talk about Vienna and my father now. At least, we weren't to talk about it here. The kitchen was one of the rooms that had ears. The grown-ups often talked in riddles.

My grandfather thought the livingroom (my mother's bedroom) was the only safe room, since it was surrounded on three sides by other rooms, and on the street side the noise from the streetcars and buses would have made it difficult to overhear what was being said. That's where he would sit, late in the evening, his ear to the radio, listening to Radio Free Europe or "thevoiceofamerica." The rest of us had to keep up some friendly chatter to confuse anyone listening from above.

Vili had shown me how to use a glass against a wall or door to hear what people were saying on the other side. It didn't work through the floorboards. That also gave Vili confidence in the livingroom.

My grandmother glanced at him. She was stirring soup. "She is only five," she told him.

"Not too soon to learn the truth about the world, is it?" Vili said. "Perhaps she'll not make the same mistakes others have."

Therese made a lot of noise stirring. Then she wiped her hands on her white apron and turned around. "You mean like me, don't you? Don't you mean the mistake I made? How was I to know you needed more than one ..." Vili moved so fast I didn't even see how he got from the doorway to the gas stove, but there he was with his huge arms around her waist, his neck bending down to her face, and I knew he was going to lift her before she did. He spun her around and kissed her on top of her head where the part in her hair was. My grandmother squealed and hit him over the shoulders, her tiny hands flying like Mrs. Fothy's white canaries. "Oh Vili, stop that," she said as loudly as she could with all the air pushed out of her.

They were both laughing when he deposited her by the stove again.

"Come," he said to me, and the two of us took Jinny for her evening walk.

⚹ ⚹

"Of the two women, who would you rather be? Beatrix or Barbara?" he asked when we were outside. "Both were beautiful; the king married one, but loved the other. One had been arranged, the other chosen. Back then a woman had no choice.

Her father made her decisions. Beatrix's father, one of the Italian kings, decided she would marry Mátyás. She would much sooner have married an Aragon painter at her father's court or the son of another Italian king, but there was no choice. The best she could do once she arrived in Buda was to try to recreate her own home in what had been a rather grim fighting man's castle."

She brought in Roman musicians, Parisian goldsmiths, Venetian master weavers, builders from Florence and painters from Aragon. She spent all her days following her husband in ceremonies and directing the household work.

Meanwhile Barbara could come and go as she pleased. Nobody's wife, she could make her own decisions.

"What about her father? Mayor Krebs. Didn't he want her to marry someone rich and polite?"

"He must have thought being with a great king was enough for her," Vili said impatiently. "For a few years she enjoyed the king's company in Buda, where he had bought her a very nice house. One day she decided to leave. It was rumoured that she rode a magnificent black stallion on her way from Budapest and that she was accompanied by a Black Knight."

"Who was the Black Knight?"

"Nobody knows. Her son János was Mátyás' favourite for the throne. Poor Beatrix remained childless."

"Did she love Mátyás as well?"

"Beatrix?" Vili thought. "Might have, in the beginning. But she didn't later. Still, you see, she had to stay and be his wife. Wives go where their men go."

"That's why we have to go to Vienna?" I asked. "Because he and my mother are married?"

"It's the way things are," Vili said. "When your turn comes, just remember never to get married."

Later we were walking along the Danube Corso. The thin white trunks of the new birch trees were peeling from the late

March frost. There were young green shoots on some of the branches and there were blackbirds whistling. The ice had melted and the Danube was noisy, rushing, high on its banks.

Vili started into another of his Turkish stories.

For two hundred years after Mátyás, Turks wandered about the countryside as if they owned it and were part of the landscape. You might leave for your fields one morning and never return. A man's cows would be driven off, his children taken prisoner.

Those children never heard their own language again. They were trained to be soldiers, to obey commands in Turkish. They were rewarded for showing no emotion, for being merciless when faced with a challenge. Then one day they would find themselves facing their childhood friends across enemy lines. They'd have forgotten who they were. That's how the Turks built their famous janissary armies: out of boys they'd scooped up in other countries. On the Field of Blackbirds, the Serbs lost their king and their kingdom to a janissary army. Many of the men who fought them had been Serbs.

And there were Hungarian janissaries at the terrible Hungarian defeat at Mohács.

In the days of Mátyás, our family lost many of its children to the Turks. Some day, Vili said, I might be wandering about a street in Istanbul, a tourist checking out the carpets in the souk, and I would suddenly come face to face with a girl just like me, only Turkish. She'd be a long-lost Rácz.

"It's really vital," Vili said, "to remember always that you are Hungarian, not to forget your language, so if the time is right, you can return to your own land."

"Won't I become an Austrian in Vienna?" I asked. "Isn't that what happened to the young people whose parents sent them to the Habsburgs' court? Didn't they speak only German? Didn't they forget who they were?"

"The good ones never do."

⊰ ⊱

Vili said we should go to the National Gallery again. I couldn't remember much about our last visit, a lot of paintings of battles and men in chains.

There is an oil painting of Ferenc Rákóczi. He wears a black velvet riding suit, a red cape with white fur trim, a high fur hat with feathers and red leather boots, and he holds a big silver mace. He has a jowly, unsmiling face, a twirly brown moustache, wavy brown hair. The fez-like fur hat looks Turkish, as does his shiny red belt with tassels. Vili stood in front of the painting, his feet apart, his hands clasped behind his back.

"There," he said, "is the true Hungarian hero. A prince who loved his people more than he loved himself. A man who valued liberty over money. A man who never forgot who he was. No matter how far away you go, you must remember him."

I had heard the Rákóczi story before, but only through the eye of another Vilmos, five or six generations on from the one who gave Mátyás his horse, Lightning. This Vilmos had lost his whole family and one eye to the Turks, his lands in Erdély to the Habsburgs. The Austrians had become worried about the Turks on their doorstep, and they considered Hungary to be their doorstep. Stationed all over Hungary, the Imperial Army took food wherever it found it. Taxes to keep the Austrians in finery had become so onerous that many of the lesser nobility had to abandon their lands and flee. Poor Vilmos spent years in the woods eating what he could find or kill. Luckily, he had been a great warrior, and he became a fair hunter.

He volunteered to serve Ferenc Rákóczi's mother, Ilona Zrinyi, at Munkács Castle, and he fought the encircling Habsburg Imperial troops for three years. He lost his eye in the final days of bombardment. He escaped through an underground tunnel.

That last day before my mother and I set out for the Austrian border, Vili wanted to tell me about the young Rákóczi. He was only twelve years old when his mother's castle was taken by the Imperial troops under the dreadful General Caraffa. It was the end of March 1688.

There is a painting of Ilona Zrinyi — "Remember that name" — with her children after the surrender. Young Ferenc Rákóczi stands close to his mother, her arm over his shoulder, each protective of the other. She is white-faced with grief and exhaustion; he is wild-eyed, angry. Caraffa has the sharp, long-nosed features of a Habsburg. He is greatly overdressed for the occasion.

Ferenc was separated from his mother and placed in a Jesuit school in Bavaria where he would never again hear a Hungarian word spoken. He was not allowed to receive letters from his mother or his sister, nor was he to see them again. "The lion cub," as King Leopold called him, had to be tamed and taught the civil ways of Vienna. Hungarian, Leopold said, was not a civilized language.

Ferenc was attired in German finery, married off to a German princess; he graduated in Latin and German from the university of Prague and spent endless hours gambling at cards and the horses in Vienna, just like the other courtiers. Some said he flourished in the presence of his godfather the Emperor.

Yet when Ferenc returned to his estates in Hungary, the layers of German schooling peeled off him, and what he found underneath was his Hungarian skin. He had not forgotten his language, and he now found that he had not forgotten his people.

It was only a few weeks, Vili thought, before our Vilmos convinced Ferenc that the Habsburgs were bleeding his country dry. Ferenc, ever willing to think the best of everyone, travelled to Vienna to reason with the Emperor. The Emperor put him in jail, a deep underground cell in Neustadt.

Vili thought that perhaps he didn't know then that it was the same cell where his grandfather, Péter Zrinyi, had spent his last night before being executed for opposing Austrian rule in Hungary.

His grandson escaped from jail and armed over a hundred thousand men to fight Austria. And there was our Vilmos, barefoot and ill-fed, but ready to fight again.

Rákóczi declared Hungary's independence from Austria.

He rewarded our Vilmos with new lands in Erdély near Tövis. Though it was not where his old home had been, the lands were beautiful, with fields for grazing cattle, a forest that stretched over seven hilltops, four small villages and the remnants of a fifty-five-room manor house. Vilmos married a young Czech girl with blonde pigtails and had a bunch of children. And that's why we're all still here.

"And what happened to Rákóczi?"

"He lost the war. At the end of 1711, while he was searching for help in the other European kingdoms, his army surrendered to the Imperial forces, thus ending the longest period of Hungarian independence in over one hundred and fifty years. It had lasted around three years."

That's the story Vili wanted to tell me that day in the National Gallery.

19

LEAH SOLD HER ROOM to a married couple from Csepel and moved in with her third husband and his mother. When she came to collect Kati, who desperately didn't want to leave, our grandmother and I were the only people in the apartment. My grandmother said she thought Leah had timed her visit perfectly. She knew my mother would be at work and Vili in the coffeehouses talking politics. There had been a lot of anger about the couple from Csepel, though less than there would have been had my mother not decided she was going "West" herself.

Leah stuffed all her clothes into two large suitcases. She took the old clock from the hall and her green-hatted portrait from the livingroom. She told my grandmother she'd send Miklós for the rest of her things. Then she stood with her hands on her hips, defiant, as if either of us had argued. "The only reason Puci is going," she told my grandmother, who had not been watching her pack, "is because she doesn't want me to have him. She doesn't understand the meaning of love."

"I don't want to go with her," Kati said.

"And I suppose you do," my grandmother told Leah.

"At least I've damned well tried, haven't I? I tried. What's Puci done to qualify? Nothing. You should've left her with Kálmán. They deserve each other."

"If you hadn't been in such a hurry to get István gone, they could have had a chance ... Puci might have been able to go with him. She would have had time to think about it. But not you. You helped him buy his way out ..."

"I really don't want to go," Kati whined. "I'm going to school here. I've made some friends."

Neither of them heard.

20

MY MOTHER AND I left on the 7 a.m. train from the Keleti Railway Station. My grandfather was on the platform, saying very loudly that he'd see us both next week and wishing us a great vacation. "There is a poem," he told me, "by Endre Ady — and you have to remember that name because he was one of the greatest poets ever — that goes like this." And he recited a couple of verses for me. It's a poem about a stone thrown up into the air and landing, always, back on earth, no matter how hard or how high it flies. The stone is like the poet who, no matter how far he wanders, always returns to his own small country.

Despite the poem, Vili was pleased that I didn't let on that I knew he was saying goodbye, in case somebody was watching.

I sulked for most of the journey.

My mother and I sat on opposite ends of a wooden bench in one of the passenger carriages. She slept for a while, but the train kept jerking her awake, stopping and starting as people got on and off. There was a man carrying baskets of potatoes, and he gave me a handful; another man with two chickens under his arms; a family with a dog and a goat; a woman with a big apron and a crying infant. My mother bought a strawberry drink from a passing cart. We didn't talk to each other.

All the time I held onto my suitcase. It was brown with patched corners, small enough to fit on my knees. It had metal snaps that made a lot of noise when you opened or shut them. After my mother had packed it for me, I had removed several items at random to make room for Lightning and my fuzzy bear. The bear had never been anywhere, but I'd had it ever since I could remember, and even though he wasn't very heroic, I thought he would miss me awfully. Lightning came along because he was new and brave.

I couldn't imagine what it would be like not to go back home again. I sat, looking out the window, thinking that we would most certainly go back soon, that Vili would be waiting and so would Alice, and I could tell her all about this adventure. I didn't want to be like the young Rákóczi, trying to hold on to my memories while speaking only German. I remember worrying about starting school at the end of the summer. I slept a while.

My mother took my hand and said, "We get off here," and I woke with a start.

We got off on a long platform. There was a squat building with a small, dark room where my mother told me to wait with our cases while she went to find the person who was to meet us. I climbed up on one of the benches and looked outside at the fields of poppies and the chickens pecking in the yard. There were crows bigger than Jinny.

My mother returned with a man in a brown suit, sandy hair falling over his wide, angular face. His arms were too long for his suit jacket. He carried a canvas sack with grease marks. "She is too young," he told my mother, talking about me as if I wasn't there. "A little kid."

"I'm not," I said.

"You didn't tell me there would be a kid," he said. His voice was high-pitched, like a girl's.

"It makes no difference." My mother gave him some bills

from her pocket. She grabbed her suitcase and mine. "Let's go," she told him.

We set out across the platform and over the railway tracks, the man in front, my mother next, then me. She glanced back frequently to see if I was keeping up. We were moving fast, but she knew I would hustle to show him I wasn't a little kid.

At first we went along a kind of road, though not one I could imagine a taxi would choose.

There were chickens clucking at us when we got too close, as if to say they didn't like strangers. There were women bending over in the fields. My mother said they were picking the first harvest of peas or beans, but the man in brown said they were looking for live ammunition. The Germans had retreated this way. Then the Russians came and grabbed everything the Germans hadn't already taken.

He told us the women had hidden in the cold cellars or in the woods, though not much woods remained once both armies had gone. Any woman or girl caught in the open was fair game. "Some were not much older than that one," he told my mother, pointing to me.

She said she knew all about that — it hadn't been any better in Budapest.

The brown man shrugged as if he didn't believe her.

The women wore full skirts and black rubber boots, kerchiefs on their heads. They nodded at us when we passed, then went back to work. It was warm for this time of year, one woman said, as the man tipped his hat to her. He had taken off his jacket and slung it over his shoulder.

There were big yellow flowers with dark centres. My mother told me to watch them following the sun as it started to go down. "Too early," she said, "for sunflowers." Blackbirds circled overhead and landed in the plowed fields like dark clouds, their cries louder than the streetcars slowing down on Rákóczi Street. There were a few cows with young calves pushing at their teats. Some of them came up to look at us. They're curious, haven't seen city folks, my mother said. My new running shoes got stuck in cow dung, and my feet slipped out of them. Wet cow dung squished between my toes.

I still wasn't talking to my mother.

We picked small, pink cherries from a tree by the roadside where we'd stopped to rest. My mother unwrapped salami sandwiches, one for each of us. The man had a chunk of dark bread and a piece of lard with red pepper. Though it was late, the sun was still hot. He told my mother we would be cutting across the fields and heading for the woods. He unfolded a hand-drawn map, laid it flat over the reddish earth, and they studied it.

That night we slept in a haystack in the middle of a field filled with similar haystacks. We hollowed out the lower part of the stack and crawled into a warm cavern of hay. It smelled beautiful, but the stalks were prickly. We spread out the thin blanket my mother took from her case and put our coats over it. There were rustling noises and movement in the hay.

"They're mouse noises," my mother said. "We are sharing some tiny fieldmice's homes. They're annoyed at our lying all over their places, and they're complaining to their friends."

Brown suit said he'd find somewhere else to sleep.

"I don't like him," I told my mother.

"Neither do I," she said, and we both giggled and laughed until I had forgotten that I was really mad at her about this whole trip.

THE NEXT DAY STARTED with the man's voice in the dark.

There were still stars when we crawled out of our warm space in the haystack. A strong wind blew across the field carrying bits of grass and the scent of flowers. "Wheat flowers," my mother said. She buttoned up my coat and brushed me down, which annoyed the brown man, who said we should hurry before first light. With luck, no one would see us, and who cared what the kid looked like; better that she should blend in with everyone else, since any cityfolk in these parts were assumed to be up to no good. He called her "my lady," with an edge in his voice.

We marched single file like soldiers. To keep me going, my mother recited long poems she had learned at her convent school and others Vili had read her when she was a child. I remember the one about Erzsébet Hunyadi's letter to her son, László, in Prague at King Ladislas's court. She pleads with him to come home to Hunyadvár, because she thinks his life's in danger. She sends her letter with a raven, but the bird arrives too late. László is already dead.

The sky lit up slowly, but then it started to rain, softly at first, then in gusts, with the wind beating our faces, soaking through our clothes, turning the earth into mud and pools of blackish water. Short stalk stubbles scratched our ankles. The sunflowers stood dejected, unable to find the sun. We cut across dense fields of alfalfa and young corn, the leaves snapping at my face as I followed my mother. The brown man pulled his hat down over his forehead, and told her she should have been prepared for rain. Overnight he had acquired a black slicker that kept him dry. Only his shoes and the bottoms of his pants were soaked.

"You should've left her at home," he repeated, not even mentioning my name, though he knew it by then.

"Soldiers march like this," my mother said. "They go on even if it rains or snows and when their feet are cut." Her own feet were bleeding. She had worn her best flat shoes. They were, she said, older than I was. She taught me the tune of the Rákóczi March, and she called me her little soldier.

The brown man had us stop under an oak tree and told us to wait for him there.

My mother wrapped her feet in her white cotton handkerchiefs. Blood seeped from the cuts on her toes, through the handkerchiefs and over the tops of her shoes. Her ankles were sliced in many places, as if by a paring knife; her heels had blistered and her shoes had stretched and split so her feet slid out of them sideways. She said she should have known better than to wear them for the journey.

We sat on a patch of wet grass under the oak tree, attempting to make the handkerchiefs thin enough to fit into the shoes yet thick enough to absorb the blood. My shoes were ruined, but they had kept my feet safe from the sharp stalks.

"We should have waited till you were old enough to carry me," she said, standing up and walking around. She was worried that her feet would swell so much she might not be able to walk.

"I could carry you now," I told her, thinking myself to be as tall as all the Vilmoses and as strong as the best of them.

"You may have to," she said.

"Do you think *he'll* buy you new shoes?"

"He'd better." Then, when she saw I was unconvinced, she added, "Doesn't matter if he won't though, does it? I'll get new shoes for both of us. In Vienna everybody has lots of shoes. And it's not because they've saved up their old ones from before the war. They can afford to buy different coloured shoes to match their many dresses."

"And when we come back, we'll bring new shoes for Grandfather and Kati and Alice?" My grandmother had saved more shoes from before the war than anyone else.

"When we come back," my mother said.

I wasn't reassured. "We won't be back in time for school," I said. I was sad I wouldn't be starting with Alice. "And I won't go to school in Vienna. Not with all the Habsburgs. Speaking German."

She walked around the tree slowly, trying to place her feet as lightly as she could, humming the Rákóczi March, her hands held to either side and slightly away from her body for balance. She had put a small, square, black scarf over her head; its two corners barely reached under her chin. Her hair was clinging to her neck, wet and curly, a thin strand over her forehead. She had turned up her collar and buttoned her coat.

Except for a few heavy drops that splattered off the broad leaves, it was dry under the tree. There were mounds of dead leaves left over from the previous autumn. I sat on one of the mounds and leaned against the tree trunk, my knees pulled up to my chin. If I put my head back against the bark, I could feel the tree breathing.

I took the fuzzy bear out of my bag and held it tight against my chest under my coat. He had been shivering. I told him very quietly that everything would be all right and he had nothing to fear.

I wasn't sure he believed me.

The brown man came back so quietly we didn't know he was there until he stood under the tree. I saw him before my mother did. She was still walking around the trunk, humming. He waited for her to come to where he stood.

"It is time, my lady," he told her when they were face to face. I hated the sound of his thin voice calling her "my lady." "Wake her up," he jabbed a thumb in my direction.

I wasn't sleeping.

My mother took my hand when we stepped out into the rain again. It had become even darker. The fields were a flat, smoky green, the sky inky. The rain was soft and steady. There was no wind now.

"There is the border," he said, pointing past the fields, past a white wooden fence lying on its face to our right, toward a copse of trees so dark they looked like shadows. "Five minutes and you're in Austria."

My mother seemed confused. She looked all around us and asked, "Where are the guards?"

"There are none here now, and you'd better get going before they show up. Wouldn't do to wait for the rain to stop. You cross that road," — he pointed to a flat piece of earth stretching alongside the woods, but in our direction — "down the other side, and into the trees. No one will see you there. Halfway, there is a wire fence. Low. You can climb over it and lift the kid. Keep going about half a kilometre. There should be a farm house. Austrian."

My mother peered towards the trees, still uncertain. "You're not coming all the way?" she asked.

"This is as far as I go," the man said. "Brought you to the border, my lady. What you should do is hurry while you can see a little, or you'll be spending another night out. And maybe on this side, not where you want to be."

My mother opened her case and removed a bag from the side pocket. It was flat, black and oily-looking. The man took it without a word, turned and started back to where we had come from. We watched him pick up speed, taking big steps, his black rubber boots sinking into the earth.

"Let's go," my mother said, and we walked, then ran, toward the flat bit of earth he'd said was a road, climbed onto it, our hands snatching at bushes, and slid down into a low trench on the other side, where the water came up to my knees. My mother's mangled shoes were sucked off her feet by the mud. I grabbed one as she reached for my hand, and we started toward the trees.

"Stop," A man's voice shouted from somewhere beyond us. She didn't.

"Stop!" — louder, and a yellow light swept the field between us and the woods, perhaps five metres away.

She hauled me in front of her and tried to run faster, but I was too big and she couldn't carry me running.

"Stop or I'll shoot!"

We stopped then.

She turned, shoving me behind her now. There was a large truck on the bit of road we had crossed; its lights were turned on us. As we watched, a tall figure came into the light, walked a few steps, then stood with the light spread out behind him, a flashlight aimed at my mother and me.

The voice was calmer now. "Put your hands up over your heads and come slowly."

We did.

22

OUR CELL HAD NO BEDS. Two bunks, one over the other with narrow metal planks, no mattresses, no windows, a tin bucket in the corner, the smell of urine and cigarette butts. We could hear men talking and laughing, but we couldn't see them. Faint yellow light came from the passageway between the cells. The cells were like cages, with widely spaced bars. I thought I might slip through the spaces, but my bum was too wide.

A man in khaki uniform had taken our suitcases, including mine with Lightning in it. He had grabbed the bear, felt along its sides, held it at arm's length, looked at it, frowning as if he thought the bear might bite him. When it didn't, he returned it to me.

Years later my mother told me she had planned to tell them we were heading for the woods to pick raspberries, but, what with the suitcases and a few days' worth of clothes, it would have been a tough story to sell. So she told them the truth. They didn't believe her. She thought they imagined that she was a currency smuggler and had taken me along for cover.

She sat on the lower bunk, her knees drawn up under her chin, her arms around her knees, her back against the wall. I examined everything in the cell and asked questions she didn't know the answers to, like why did we have a bucket, and would they really expect us to poop in it even though there was no door to close and no paper, and why didn't they have mattresses on the bed frames, was it because they had a room for us somewhere and this was just a place to keep us for an hour until they knew for sure what to do with us, and what were they going to do with us, and how long did we have to stay here? She tried to sound reassuring, so I kept on with the questions until I hit one she did have a good answer for: Did she think my father would be really sad we weren't there yet, and did she think we were going to be able to go on tomorrow and meet him anyway?

"No," she said. "We're not going to your father anymore."

"Next week?"

"No."

"Maybe never?"

I took her long silence as confirmation of never and heaved a huge sigh of relief. "That's great," I told her. I could hardly wait to get back to Budapest. "I'll be able to go to school then with Alice."

I put the bear on the ground and lay down with my head on it. I remember smiling, looking into the yellow light and imagining what my grandfather would think if he knew we were in a cell just like a whole bunch of his great Hungarian heroes — and it wasn't even all that bad. I must have slept a while, because I didn't hear the cell door open, but I did hear it clang shut and heard my mother say she'd be back in a bit, I wasn't to worry.

There were three men with her, two behind her, one in front. It was too dark to see their faces, but I figured they were soldiers. All three wore peaked caps. They towered over my mother, who was not much taller than five feet.

"Where are you going?" I asked, suddenly frightened of the dark.

"I might bring you back some supper." she said, "These nice men will get us some food for sure, right?" She had turned to one of the men behind her for reassurance.

When it didn't come, I started howling.

The man in front stopped. "How old did you say that kid is?" he yelled over my howling.

I heard my mother say I was five. It was not strictly speaking true because I was about to turn six, but I was howling too hard to correct her, and the man in front shouted that he was going to get some bread and cheese and even a glass of milk if only I'd shut up. "You heard, she'll be back in a bit."

She wasn't, but he was. He said he had the food and my mother outside, and he took my hand to take me with him, down the long, narrow passageway with cells just like ours on both sides, six of them, but only a couple with people in them. They had come up to the bars to see me. A man with grey hair in the next cell whispered not to worry, not even these bastards hurt kids. The guard told him he'd be quiet if he knew what was good for him. His voice crackled when he said that, like firecrackers on New Year's Eve. We walked to a table at the end of the passageway, where it opened out into a bigger area. That's where the yellow light bulb was. His hand was sweaty, but I didn't try to slip my hand out of it. I had begun to shiver and I liked the feel of his warm palm.

"You talk funny," I told him. I was still hiccoughing a little. I always hiccoughed after I had been crying, even if it was just howling and not the real thing at all.

"I do?" he asked.

"Not so much now. Back then. Now you sound like Mrs. Nemeth, our super, who doesn't like Budapest very much and wants her son who is in the army to be a corn farmer near Pécs where she almost got some land, but didn't because the guy who was going to give it to her went to jail for being a *kulak*. You know what a *kulak* is?"

"You always talk so much?" he asked.

I shook my head. "Not always. Only because I don't know where my mommy is."

A man with grey hair and a moustache came through one of

the doors at the far end. All the guards stopped laughing when they saw him.

We went into the room he had come from. A bunch of chairs, a table, a jug, glasses, yellow cups with black coffee, a half-eaten apple, a metal ashtray, clumps of papers, pens, white-painted walls, a couple of windows, blinds pulled down, a standing lamp, a frayed rope rug in front of the other door. A large, black and white, framed picture of Stalin between the windows. I held on to the guard's sweaty hand as hard as I could, though it finally slithered away.

"A little kid," grey hair said, obviously not pleased.

One of the young guards lifted me onto a high stool facing the grey-haired man. I banged my heels into the wooden legs of the chair. A lamp's bright light shone into my eyes.

"Where were you heading?" the grey-haired man asked.

I shrugged.

"Didn't your mother tell you?"

"We were going to visit my father."

"She was taking a gift for him," he said.

"Why? Was he hoping for a gift?" I was surprised he'd think that.

"Usually when you go visit someone you take them a gift, don't you? Something shiny like gold? Now, that's a nice gift, isn't it?"

"Gold?" I shook my head. "She doesn't have any gold. Unless it's the ring she wears."

"Do you know what happens to people who lie?"

I shook my head again. "Do you line them up and shoot them?" I asked.

"No. That's not it," he said. "We stick them into a dark cellar with huge, hungry rats."

"I like rats," I told him. "There are lots of rats in the basement of the house we live in on Rákóczi Street, some bigger than Jinny — that's our dog — and they are fine, they never bother Jinny, I think maybe they think she's a rat like they are. She's got the long nose and that tail, looks like a rat. I give them old bread and things ..."

He didn't know that I knew all about the old "light in the eyes" tactic. The Turks had done it to young kids they caught to find out where their parents were hiding. The Germans and the Russians used it to get the answers they wanted. The thing to remember was that there was only "a little man" behind the light. He thought he was stronger than you because he could shine the light in your eyes. Never let on that you're afraid.

Still, I thought about panicking when he reached for my bear, but I didn't want him to know it.

"There was a letter," I said quickly. "Came from my father in Vienna. He was hiding there, waiting for us to come and help him get away from the Habsburgs. It's tough being in Vienna."

"Why?" The grey-haired man seemed really surprised.

"Because of all the Austrians, of course. They've been trying to do nasty things to Hungarians all the time. Even when the Turks were here for a hundred and fifty years, killing everybody and stealing all the cattle, they didn't stop."

The grey-haired man laughed, and all the others laughed with him.

"Who told you that?" he asked.

"Everybody knows that," I said. "About the Turks. And the Habsburgs."

The grey-haired man laughed again and said yes, that was true, and asked if I'd like an apple and some bread and drippings. He turned the light down toward the table and told the man whose hand I had been holding before that it was alright, he could take me back.

My mother was already in the cell. She grabbed me as soon as the door opened and hugged me closer than she ever had, then held me at arm's length, feeling along my chin and eyes. I kept telling her I was fine.

"Damned barbarians!" she shouted down the empty corridor toward the guards' table.

23

IN THE MORNING we were trucked to a much bigger jail, a low, concrete building with a concrete yard, two guard towers and barbed wire all around. No trees or plants, just asphalt.

Inside there were only women. They all wore slippers or thick socks. Some of them had rubber bands holding back their hair, others had cropped their hair to a stubble. There was a big room with tall barred windows. I could just squeeze my arm and one shoulder between the bars.

We all slept on the floor on white, straw-filled sacks. You had to pummel the straw when you lay down. Sometimes the stalks stuck into your skin. Everybody ate together at long wooden tables. There was black bread in the mornings, tea, soup and more bread at lunch, and bread and pork fat in the late afternoons. All the water you wanted. The guards were women during the day and men at night. They all wore the same green uniforms, carried black-handled pistols in leather pouches and rubber sticks they sometimes swished against their thighs.

I never saw them hit anybody. But one of the women told my mother never to question anything they said, because when they whipped you, you knew it. And if they got really angry, they hauled you into a tiny cell, the size of half a sack of straw, and kept you there, in the dark. "A person could go mad there by herself."

You also had to be careful to stay where they could see you. A woman with a ragged red kerchief around her neck told me that the whole point of being locked up was that you were never allowed to be alone. Not even in the toilet. There were six toilets side by side, with no partitions between them, no wooden seats. A guard would always stand close by when someone went to the toilet. She looked out the barred window and told people to hurry up.

You had to ask to use the toilet and you were never allowed to go at night when the male guards were there. If you had to go really badly at night, they told you to use the buckets in the corner of the room where you slept.

Some of the time you weren't allowed to speak.

At daybreak a few of the women went out to dig ditches or pick fruit, but most of them just stayed there, sewing sacks and taking the fluff off chicken feathers. Then they would stuff the feathers into the sacks. At the end of the day the male guards took all the finished bags away. The next day there would be another load of feathers and flat sheets of sacking.

I was allowed to help with the feathers but not with the sewing. I thought of my grandmother's aversion to dealing with chickens. She hated the idea of killing them herself. She didn't even like to pluck them, but we did it when we had to, standing side by side at the sink, a pot of boiling water to one side. She held the chicken by its stiff, yellow legs and dipped it, head first, into the water to loosen its feathers. She used plyers to remove the hard-to-get ones. Without its feathers, the chicken had gooseflesh, just like I had when I got out of the bath water.

We sat in a room with fluorescent light and no windows, a red tile floor, the walls covered with stick drawings and writing. The women sang when they worked — mostly sad love songs, but there was one with a lot of verses that told the story of a couple who decide to leave the country. They pay a specialist to take them across the border, but they are caught while the specialist escapes. Taken in for questioning, they insist that they were just picking berries to go with their wine. The border guards don't believe them. The couple is charged with attempting to escape the workers' paradise, and they are sentenced to six months in jail.

I still remember that song. The word for border crossing was "*bokorugras*," which translates into "jumping over the bush."

At first the other prisoners didn't much like my mother. A woman named Magda, who made stuffed animals in the late evenings, told me it was because my mother thought her shit smelled better than anyone else's. That was the funniest thing anyone had ever said about my mother, so Magda and I became friends. She let me help her stuff the animals with sawdust and rags. She told me they were for her little girls and she couldn't wait to get home to them and see their faces when she gave them all the animals she'd made. There were rabbits and bears, a tiger, an owl, a frog. My favourite was a kangaroo mother with a baby kangaroo that fit perfectly into her tiny pocket. The mother kangaroo even had a little polka-dotted kerchief on her head. I introduced them to my fuzzy bear, and I could tell right away they would be friends. I made a little carrying sack from a piece of white cloth for my bear. Then he could take turns with the mother kangaroo carrying around the baby.

Magda had long, brown hair and blue eyes, a round face and wrinkles on her neck. She said that was because she had once been a big woman, but she had shrunk in jail. She didn't like the food. All that was left of her former self were her strong arms — her biceps bulged just like Vili's when she flexed them to show me.

Most days the guard who had held my hand would come and take me out for a walk. Sometimes he gave me a sugar cube or an apple. He said he had a little girl my age at home in Győr and he only got to see her once a month, when he got time off. He let me sneak an apple back to my mother. He returned my bag with Lightning in it, and though someone had cut into his belly with a thin knife, I could tell he hadn't complained once. He was the toughest horse I had ever met.

I made him rest under our straw mattress during the day but let him roam around when it was dark. I imagined he went on a trip home once he felt better. I had to wipe the sweat off his flanks in the morning. He told me my grandfather missed me.

At night my mother told me long stories to help me go to sleep. There were some about magic dragons that could swoop in through the tiniest of openings and rescue maidens from captivity and one about a miraculous tree whose leaves made such fabulous music that everyone came to see it from all over the world, though it was only in Hungary, where not so many people ever came unless they were in an army and marching over it. The dragons had been rather quiet and withdrawn for the past several years, she said. It was thought by those who knew much about dragons that they were busy in China. The miraculous tree was still growing in a faraway forest on a slope of the great Carpathian Mountains, but people had forgotten where it was. Maybe one day we'd go and see it. While its music played, you could climb up its huge branches and visit the fairy folk who lived on its giant leaves. Maybe the pink dragon's castle was still there at the top, where Lucky Jancsi had found the white talking horse and fed him the live coals it craved.

Because we all slept in the same big room, the other women could hear my mother's stories, at least those women who were near our straw mattress. I could see them listening. One night she told the story of a young boy called Attila who set out to bring back the king's golden crown that had been stolen by the leathery Witch of Erdély, and one of the women told my mother to speak up, she was sick of straining on her elbows to hear.

By the time Leah and her red-haired boyfriend came to pick me up, everybody liked my mother. Some nights they would ask her to tell a story she had told before. She had learned all the words to their songs, and sometimes they would ask her to sing something of her own because her voice was so nice.

When we said goodbye, she said she'd be home really soon, but I knew that was a lie; the guard told me she got six months, just like the couple in the song, for trying to cross the border, and I was lucky to be only five. I could go home after only three weeks. I cried a whole lot and so did my mother.

The young guard looked sad when I said I would miss him, too, and I meant it. Magda gave me the baby kangaroo to take home. She said she could make her children another one, she had time. She gave me such a strong hug, the guard had to separate us. "You have to be careful with that one," he told me.

I cried a little for Magda.

The guard told me that pretty much everyone there was serving time for trying to emigrate. Magda was different. She was in jail for murdering her husband and their two children.

24

I WAS WEDGED BETWEEN Leah and her red-haired boyfriend in the space between the two seats of an old motor-cycle that was passed by every truck heading toward Budapest. His name was Laci. The bike farted foul-smelling, blue-green gas that he was proud of having mixed himself for this special occasion.

Leah had stuffed her blue cardigan under me, because the body of the bike heated up after it travelled a few kilometres. I kept my face pressed into the back of the boyfriend's black leather jacket and my ankles out wide, away from the hot parts of the bike, my heels wedged into his woollen knee socks. This last bit was to keep my feet steady. When I let them float in the air, the bike wriggled and Leah yelled that we were going to crash.

Leah complained that she'd had to report in sick; she could hardly have taken the day off to retrieve her sister's kid from the jail that everyone knew was for failed emigrants. Trucking jobs weren't easy to come by.

"How long do you suppose it will take them to find out my sister tried to defect? A few more days and I'll be called up to answer for it. The amount of grief this will cause the whole family ... She should at least have succeeded while she was at it." She was talking into the wind and mainly to herself, rather than to me or to Laci, who couldn't hear anyway because of the engine's noise. "I'll have to join the bloody Party just to keep the job now, and you know what that means. Attending the re-education classes and getting ready for all those damned celebrations and marching on my days off. With Puci in jail, there will be talk. Class enemies. And how's Papa going to get a job with this on his slate, tell me that. With Puci in there for six months, there's only my bit of pay. He'll have to find something for himself. Why couldn't she stay in Vienna the last time? She was already in Vienna. The little fool. Right?" Leah kept complaining and grumbling the whole time. "We could have sent you on by post."

I wanted to ask her about "the last time," but she wouldn't have heard.

I kept my face shoved into the boyfriend's jacket.

It turned out that she had left her rig at her husband's place at Székesfehérvár, and that's where we were headed.

"You heard, this one's name is Laci — László — but you're not to talk about him when we get to my husband's house," she told me as we came off the main road.

"Same as Mátyás's older brother who had his head cut off by the king," I said cheerfully.

Leah laughed her high bell-like laugh for the first time since she had come to pick me up. "Let's just hope he can keep his head," she said. "He's a man I work with. And he was kind enough to take us home. At any rate, that's what we tell them. Alright?"

I shrugged.

"Unless you want to stay in my husband's house till your mother comes for you."

When I met her mother-in-law, I knew why Leah was worried. She was short and square with bluish hair pulled back so tightly that each strand was dragging skin, puckering bits of her temples and cheeks. She had small, grey eyes and a pursed mouth with lines pointing to it all the way up her chin. Though it was a warm day, she wore thick, black clothes down to her ankles. She had made the house dark by closing the wooden slats outside the windows, and the windows themselves. The house smelled of cooked cabbage and rosewater.

Laci stayed outside with his motorbike while Leah ushered me in.

"You call her Grandma," Leah said after the introduction. "And you do everything she says."

"You're not my grandma," I told her.

She stood with her hands behind her back, her eyes squinting at me from her black-framed glasses, looking down without lowering her chin. There were grey hairs in her nostrils.

"And I don't want to stay here," I added. "I want to go home now."

I tried to run after Leah, who was flying out the door. She grabbed me hard by the shoulders and propelled me back into the house toward the stairs. "Remember what I told you," she warned.

"You're putting your bag into Kati's room, top floor," the old woman said. She had a gravelly voice like a man's. "And you're to stay quiet and be grateful we're letting you stay." She tossed my suitcase after me. It bounced off the bottom step so that I had to go back to get it while she stood over me, the smell of rosewater wafting from her. She gave me a push as I slowed a little; my knees grazed the wood. "And you're to stay there till I tell you it's time for dinner. Understand?"

I mumbled and climbed the rest of the way wishing I was back in jail, where people were nicer. The stairs between the second and third floors were just like a ladder going almost straight up, so I had to take two trips, holding the banister with one hand, my fuzzy bear with the other, on the first trip, then go back for my suitcase.

The room at the top was shaped like a tent, tall in the middle and very low on the sides, and there was just the one squat window near the floor. Kati's bed was in the middle. She had her stuff in boxes along the sides. Both her bears were on her pillow; the daytime white bear had its paws around the brown bear. I thought they looked a little scared.

I crawled around to see if Kati had any new clothes in her boxes or new books or toys and found last Christmas's gifts packed in the one nearest the window. I played a bit with her giraffe and showed him to Lightning and my bear. They were just starting to thaw out after the ride and I would have put them with Kati's bears to play, except they didn't look happy and there was no sense in depressing them soon after we had arrived in a new place. The giraffe said Kati would be along in a bit and we could all play together, but it turned out he was wrong.

A long time later the dreadful woman with the tight bun called for me to wash up for dinner and to make sure I was properly dressed before I came downstairs. Although it was dark, I managed to put on my clean pair of pants (the ones I hadn't been wearing on the bike) and a sweater of my mother's that she had said I might as well take home for her. It was soft angora wool, a deep bluish-green colour. It came in at the waist on my mother, so she looked really beautiful whenever she wore it, but on me it went down to the knees and I had to roll up the sleeves. Still, it felt good just to be wearing something of my mother's when I went downstairs.

There was a murmur of voices coming from the ground floor. The diningroom was closest to the door where I had first entered and, I hoped, would soon be leaving. There was a dark wooden, shiny sideboard with printed porcelain dishes, big plates propped on their sides to face the door, cups hanging by their handles, four brownish paintings in gold frames on the wall, each with a different face. All the faces had long noses and big chins, and I thought they looked like the Habsburgs in my grandfather's books. One even had a tall, yellowing wig, its sides curled in toward his face. The only woman among them had her hair done up just like the old witch did hers. I hoped it hurt like hell to pull it back so hard.

Miklós sat at one end of the shiny brown table, his mother at the other end. He looked much the same as when I had last seen him the morning after Christmas — brown button eyes, thin hair, no lips, pale. At first, I think, he was a little confused about who I was, at least until his mother said, "It's Puci's daughter; she'll be here a while." Then half his mouth turned up into a smile and the other half remained still, as if he couldn't decide whether to be pleased to see me or not.

I remembered my mother saying that it might have been the shell that exploded in his trench during the war that made him so stupid.

Kati sat in the middle. She had become taller and thinner, her face all beige, dark around her eyes. Her hair, parted in the middle, had been clipped to an even length just under her ears. She grinned at me, but she didn't shout hello or run to me like she usually did when we hadn't seen each other for a long time. She didn't even speak until the witch said, "You can say hello to your cousin."

There was only one chair with no one on it, so I sat down, grabbed the white napkin, tucked it into my mother's angora collar and glanced around for dinner.

There was a long silence while both Leah's husband and Kati stared at their plates. Then the witch said, "We don't do things in this house the way you may have learned in the Rácz household." She wagged her thin finger for emphasis. "Here, we act like the gentlefolk we are, and that means never — and I mean never — sitting at table until you have been invited to sit. You go back to the door now. Now." She waited until I complied. "And you start again."

I waited.

"Would you like to join us for dinner?" she asked, as if I'd just arrived.

"Yes," I said and proceeded to sit down again.

"Now that wasn't so difficult, was it?" she rasped.

I thought of Vilmos swishing off the heads of his enemies with one stroke of his mighty sword. "No," I said.

She sliced pieces of pork hock from a deep dish in front of her, giving her son a huge portion, me a bit of skin, brown bread, a dollop of sauerkraut, potatoes and onion gruel, another huge chunk of pork for herself, and nothing for Kati. When I looked at Kati's plate and thought of risking a question, I noticed that there was a big mound of green mush in the middle of it, a few stray peas on the side, all sitting on a thin film of congealed fat.

"Kati is not very hungry," the witch said. "She's been getting ready to eat her spinach since lunchtime, haven't you, dear? And she's not yet ready for her supper. She won't be ready until she's eaten her lunch." She continued speaking to her son, as if Kati and I had vanished altogether. "I don't know how they rear their young, the Ráczes, dear. All that pomp and all those parties in peacetime, and now when we all have to learn to survive, they throw out food like the world hadn't changed. And Leah out on the road, supporting the whole damned lot of them, how would she feel knowing good food she's worked for was being thrown into the garbage? Too much devil may care, dear, must come from the soil in Bácska, certainly not from around here. Oh no. We have to learn to make do with less."

I was hungry and ate everything on my plate. Kati ate nothing. I thought I had eaten much worse food during the past few weeks. I slipped the bread under my mother's sweater for Kati.

When she had finished eating, the witch told Kati and me we were excused, and while I waited for an explanation, Kati slid off her chair, came around to my side of the table, grabbed my hand and pulled me along behind her to the door. "Say thank you," she whispered in my ear, "and goodnight."

After that we both ran up the stairs to her room.

"I hate her. I hate her. I hate her," Kati kept repeating as she lay between her bears. "I hate her so much I could die. I only don't want to die because I know she'd be really pleased if I did die and I don't want her to be happy. Ever. I hope she dies and I can go and do hopscotch on her grave and piss on it. I hope she dies a horrible horrible death. What's the most horrible death you can think of?"

"Getting impaled," I whispered.

"That's it. She should be impaled through the bum and left to die." After that, Kati felt a little better. She even ate the bread I had kept for her.

We talked most of the night. Kati was hoping her mother would settle on a fourth husband soon, one who had no mother. Laci, for example, was an orphan; his parents were killed when the Russians bombarded Budapest. On her days off the two of them could travel places on his bike and let Kati stay with us at Rákóczi Street. Then she could return to the same school she had been in with Moci.

Though I was still worried about Lightning's stomach wound, I let her hold him for good luck.

The next day we were awakened by Leah's husband. He had only a pair of white shorts on and was giggling and bouncing up and down on our bed. "Mommy has gone shopping, you want to play?" he kept asking in a high voice.

Kati said it was best to go along with it, or he'd make up some ghastly story about us and tell his mommy when she returned. "He doesn't get to do much," she told me as we followed him to the top of the stairs and played who-can-slide-down-the-bannister-fastest-and-jump-farthest-when-we-hit-the-bottom.

Naturally, he won.

25

WHEN LEAH CAME FOR ME in her two-ton rig on Sunday, she was radiant. She wore a red silk blouse and fitted trousers, and she had a bunch of lilacs on the seat next to her. I think she regretted the fuss she had made on the way to her mother-in-law's place.

She took me for a spin around the garden of ruins in the centre of Székesfehérvár, the site of the White Palace, where most of Hungary's early kings had sat on their thrones, and the remains of the cathedral where they used to be crowned.

Of course, the Turks had destroyed the city when they took it in the mid-sixteenth century, and the rebuilt parts were completely annihilated during the bombings of the Second World War; barely a hundred people survived them. "Nobody knows why both sides decided this was such a good place to dump ammunition," said Leah. "No one bombed Vienna, you know."

I didn't know that.

On the way to Budapest, Leah had told me she was definitely leaving Miklós, though she hadn't quite decided to marry Laci. She thought she'd move into his apartment in Pest, see how it went and decide later. Meanwhile, Kati would come to Rákóczi Street.

I figured Lightning had done his job.

26

ALICE'S FATHER HAD BEEN WILLING to close the store earlier. But unlike Mrs. Nemeth, he was an ambitious man; if the State wanted his store so much, he had hoped it would offer some small compensation that he could use to start something else. He told Alice and her mother that there would have to be a price offered for the space when the State nationalized it.

"Nationalize," my grandfather told me, was communist for "steal."

Governments, he said, developed their own special language. For example, when the wartime government officials said they loved to listen to Wagner, they meant they were Nazis and held special positions in addition to their official roles. When the Arrow Cross held clean-up operations, they were really hunting for Jews and dissidents. When the communists talked of cooperative farming, they meant they were taking the land from the peasants and giving it to people they thought they could trust more. The same with nationalizing grocers. The government saw them as small pockets of possible resistance. No man should be independent of the State.

When the State served Alice's father his notice, they gave him only one day to clear out his stuff. A week later the store was the State's, and it never opened its doors again.

Alice's father and mother carried as much food from the store as they could into their fourth-floor apartment, filling every room. At first, everyone in the building went to shop there as if he were still the grocer, but when things started to smell bad, he had to drastically reduce prices. Then he went to work in a box factory south of the city and came home each night after dark. Now Alice's mother would have to find a job as well, or they'd have to move to a one-room apartment. Alice was utterly miserable.

My grandfather tried to get work in the same box factory, but they told Alice's father they had no room for aristocrats. Alice's father just slipped by as a former grocer, and even so he had to attend lectures on communist history and the meaning of Marxism.

Eventually, Vili landed a job in a button factory.

When he applied, the factory boss asked him what his occupation had been before the war. Vili replied, proudly, "Publisher."

"And what, Comrade Publisher," the man asked, "are your qualifications for this job?" As Vili told it, the factory boss wouldn't look him in the eye. His voice made it clear he knew Vili was not a comrade. He was practising communist humour.

Vili simply lifted the oak desk behind which the "little" man sat, held it aloft for a moment and replaced it exactly where it had been. "My qualifications are this," he told the interviewer. "I have strength and know how to use it. That's what your posted requirements are. Nothing more." Not one sheet of paper on the table had slipped out of place, and the man's cigarette was still burning in the orange ashtray.

Vili started the next day.

My mother sent me a card wishing me a great first day at school and telling me she would think of me all day. On the front of the card she had drawn a picture of a little girl dressed in blue with white socks and blue and white running shoes. The girl had a wide-mouthed grin on her round face.

One of her socks was hiked up to her knee, and the other had bunched around her ankle. I wondered how she knew the rubber band holding up one of my socks would break before I was even at school.

Vili couldn't take me the first day because he was carting around heavy button boxes. He said he was not yet ready to miss a day of work. While I had some sympathy for my grandfather's position, I was annoyed with my mother. I still thought she should not have tried to escape and meet my father.

Kati led both Alice and me up the steps to the principal's office and signed us up for first year. She filled out the forms about when we were born and where we lived. For occupations, she put Alice's father down as a box maker and mine as dead. She said that would get us by for the first while, and if my mother wanted to revive my father, she could do so when she was out of jail.

Kati wrote in the space for my mother's occupation that she was a land surveyor, which she surely was, even though she was working with chicken feathers just then. Kati was almost ten and she knew all about what not to say. To make sure, Vili had sat us both down the night before and rehearsed the answers. If they asked me anything about before the war, I should shake my head. At six, a person didn't have to know all the answers.

Alice pretended her father had always been a box maker. She reasoned that if the government liked grocers, they would not have taken away his store. Why start off in school with a black mark against you?

The best thing about that first day was when I noticed that I was one of the tallest in the class and thought that if I squared my shoulders and pulled in my tummy, I would seem fierce. Vili had told me that seeming fierce was the best policy, since people tended to pick on the defenseless.

Alice was the smallest of the new girls. The boys called her "Chipmunk." She asked to sit next to me.

At the end of the day, as Kati had warned, we were given a sheaf of papers for our parents to fill out and return within two weeks.

When my grandfather came home from the button factory, he took me down to the Emke Café on the Boulevard. I loved the Emke for its fusty smells, its plastic palms, its silver mirrors, its paper flowers in silver vases. I loved the way the waiter bowed to Vili and called him Doctor Rácz and swished ahead of us to one of the window tables. Everyone looked at Vili as he strutted in, his moustache twitching hello this way and that. He waited for me to climb onto my seat before he plonked down on his.

He ordered an espresso for himself and a Viennese *dobos* torte for me, and we studied the questionnaire. He had taught me to read a little, but my knowledge was restricted to simple words. "This questionnaire," he said, "was especially designed to confuse the reader. We have to be extra careful of trick questions." Those were questions that appeared to mean one thing but meant another.

For example, "What are the names of the child's grandparents? Give full names and occupations." "What part of Hungary does the family come from and what was it doing before it settled here?" "What wars did members of the family take part in and in what capacity?" All these, he said, were intended to reveal that we were not true proletariat, not ready to embrace communism and possibly class enemies. "Those are people who are neither peasants nor proletariat," Vili said. I had to appear to love communism if I was going to do reasonably well at school. No true communist had a dogskin with a rampant lion, had ever owned anything, was a captain in a war or had been educated beyond high school.

No one was going to expect him, Vili said, to be a communist anyway, so it hardly mattered what *he* said, but I had a chance, why not take it? It's how the country had survived for more than half its history: playing along.

I shared the *dobos* torte with Vili because I knew we had little food at home. With my mother in jail, we didn't have enough money for dinners.

27

IN MY GRANDFATHER'S HUNGARIAN history, there hadn't been a legitimate Hungarian state since the brief season of euphoria that began on March 15, 1848. His last heroes were all of that era. They included Count Stephen Széchenyi, Lajos Kossuth, Sándor Petöfi, Mór Jókai and a range of generals who died in the last defence of independence from the marauding Austrians in 1849.

Petöfi was young and passionate, a university student, a poet. He led the student revolutionaries who demanded that their "Twelve Points" be met by Parliament. These demands included freedom of speech, a free press and freedom for the serfs who had been working on the lands for their owners."

"Serfs?" I asked.

"People who were owned by someone else."

"Owned. Like Jinny?"

"Like Jinny, but more useful. They tended the vineyards and planted and tilled and harvested."

"You had them in Erdély?"

"Yes, about a hundred, but your great-great-grandfather was a good owner. He made sure they were all fed and clothed ..."

"Like children?"

"Don't you want to know about Kossuth?"

I'd already heard about Kossuth. He had a big black beard, and he led the *Honvéd* (Home Defense) Army against the Austrians. He was a strong-willed patriot, Vili said, a good speaker, a writer, a revolutionary. Revolutionaries are people who decide how the world should be and go about changing things. They usually have a lot of opposition.

When Kossuth was imprisoned for his writings, he read all Shakespeare's works with the help of an old English grammar and emerged three years later with an education that he had never before had time for. Like the Ráczes, the Kossuths were members of the lesser nobility, having to think about making a living for themselves. Like Vili, Kossuth became a newspaper editor. And his paper was shut down by the government like Vili's papers were.

Széchenyi, who also had a big black beard, had studied democracy in England, fought in the Imperial Army against Napoleon, owned 70,000 acres of land and founded the first Hungarian Academy of Science. He was the richest of them all, yet when he entered Parliament, he advocated equality for all.

"Even the serfs?"

"Especially the serfs."

These may not seem like fighting words now, but they were most upsetting to the Habsburgs and their princelings in Hungary. The great Hungarian aristocracy had gone along with whatever the Emperor of Austria demanded, so long as their own serfs and privileges stayed. Those pretty pink and yellow façades on Castle Hill hid successive families of grand nobility, born to wealth, paying no taxes, bearing no obligations except to uphold Habsburg rule.

Széchenyi thought they would listen and learn, that Kossuth was wrong to get into a fight with them. For a while it seemed Széchenyi was right. For instance, the Imperial Council in Vienna agreed for the first time in three hundred years that Hungarians had the right to use Hungarian as the official language in their own country.

The Emperor-King, Ferdinand the Fifth — long face, big nose, white muttonchops — managed to open the Hungarian Parliament in Hungarian, much to the general merriment of all. Hungarians laughed at Ferdinand's unfortunate use of the language, while the Viennese took his effort as a sign that the king was an aging imbecile.

On December 2, 1848, the Austrians deposed Ferdinand and substituted his nephew, eighteen-year-old Franz Joseph, who was delighted with the thought of a good fight. There is a gold-framed, round painting of the new emperor in Schönbrunn. The artist positioned his subject's face at a quarter-turn from the viewer, somewhat disguising his prominent chin and nose. He has a light growth of blondish fur on his upper lip, and his brown hair is carefully parted on the right, smoothed down over his forehead but unruly on the sides. His full lips tend toward a girlish smile. It's impossible to imagine this child-king leading an assault on Hungary. Well, he didn't have to. He could stay home and play croquet while Prince Windischgrätz led the Imperial forces.

A few days after Franz Joseph nabbed the throne, the Austrian Army, with the help of some border minorities, attacked the last legitimate government of Hungary.

"Border who?"

"People who had moved in and settled on lands made empty by the Turks and the Austrians. Some of them had lived there for a couple of hundred years, but they hadn't become Hungarian."

"Why?"

"Old habits don't die easily. They were mostly Slavs. The Hungarians aren't. They're a strange Asiatic people, stubborn as hell."

There were battles and sieges, but none the Hungarians couldn't handle. In 1849 Franz Joseph called on the Russian czar, his distant cousin, and told him the Hungarians were driving him crazy. They wanted to rule their own country and free all those serfs. It's the kind of idea the Russian czar would hate, because he and his princelings had more serfs than anybody else, and they had all quite forgotten how to do even the simplest little things for themselves, like slicing bread or washing their own hair.

The czar, who ruled all of Russia, called up an army, and they, too, attacked the Hungarians.

Kossuth had been hoping that some other countries would come and help the Hungarians, but, as Vili saw it, though a great thinker and statesman, Kossuth couldn't have been a student of history. The other Europeans hadn't come when the Hungarians held out against the Tatar invasion in the thirteenth century or when Pope Calixtus begged them to relieve the Hungarians fighting alone against the Turks; they didn't show up when the Turks settled in for one hundred and fifty years, and there was no sign of them when Ilona Zrinyi defended Munkács from the Austrians or when Rákóczi gathered an army to defend the country from the marauding Imperial forces in 1848, so why would they come now? Besides, in 1848 the other Europeans were battling their own civil wars.

Great Britain's prime minister, Lord Palmerston, announced that his country had no knowledge of the existence of a Hungarian state, except as part of the Austrian Empire. There is not a word of this in Palmerston's biography.

On August 13, 1849, on the field of Világos, Arthur Görgey, commander of the Hungarian forces, capitulated before the vast Russian Army. He knew that the Austrians were a few miles away.

Görgey was not one of Vili's heroes. He died a lonely man. To this day there are feverish debates about the reasons for his unconditional surrender and its inevitable results. The reign of terror under General Haynau, the "Austrian hyena," lasted nine months. Soldiers, young and old, and government officials of all stripes were shot or hanged as the hyena satisfied his masters' bloodlust.

On October 6, at five o'clock in the morning, when the roosters were still asleep in Arad, general Haynau of the Imperial Army had the thirteen top officers of the Hungarian Army executed on a field near the town, which had stayed loyal to Kossuth till the end. The first three generals were shot by firing squad; the next nine were hanged. One had died of a heart attack the night before. He was hanged anyway.

On Haynau's orders, Count Lajos Battyány, the last lawful prime minister of Hungary, was shot by firing squad in Budapest.

On October 20, in Tövis, Vili's great-grandfather, who had been a judge during Kossuth's brief stay in Parliament, was killed by a single bullet through his forehead while he was dining with his young wife, Petronella Hlatky. He was forty-nine years old, a big man — a Rácz — broad shoulders, thick, bristly neck, thinning hair, a ginger beard tending to grey. He was near six foot three and weighed two hundred and fifty pounds the year that he died. Petronella was eighteen years old, a slender waif of a girl, round-eyed, small-mouthed, with a look of surprise about her arched eyebrows.

The Austrians now brought more Serbs and Wallachs into the east and south, and settled them on Hungarians' lands. They encouraged Slovak settlement in the north and hoped to contain the Hungarians in a ring of enemy fire should they ever get above themselves again. The war had consumed over sixty thousand Hungarians, not including those the Austrians later forced off their lands, hanged, shot or burned. There would be, Haynau said, plenty of room for newcomers.

It gave me some small satisfaction to find out that when Haynau visited London a year after the war, he was attacked and severely beaten by workers at Barclay Brewery. Palmerston, perhaps somewhat penitent about his lack of help for Kossuth's cause, resigned rather than, as the queen demanded, apologize to Haynau.

In Hungary, October 6th is a national day of mourning.

28

I TOLD THE TEACHER I had lost the questionnaire. Unfortunately, she had a fresh supply in her drawer, since quite a few of us had done the same thing.

I acquired a spiffy blue scarf to indicate that I was a member of the very young Communists. I had a white dress shirt for special occasions. I volunteered to make class posters with pictures of our various leaders cut out of newspapers. The teacher gave me a signed, glossy, black and white photograph of Prime Minister Rákosi to paste above the door to the classroom. It was a gift from the prime minister himself. Our teacher was proud of having stood in line at the Leader's office to obtain the photo.

I hung Comrade Stalin's picture over the blackboard, at the head of the classroom, and made a small Russian flag for one side and a Hungarian flag for the other, the two intersecting over his forehead to form a kind of arch. The teacher said that was very pretty.

The seventh of November was going to be our great debut as new kids. We would be allowed to join the rest of the school in a vast spontaneous celebration of the Soviet Revolution, certainly the most important moment in human history, the day the Russian people threw off their feudal shackles and declared the new Republic. "Spontaneous," Vili said, "means they will organize every detail, all you have to do is watch and listen and you can't go wrong." Vili was right — there were hours of rehearsal to get it right.

In preparation for the great day, the teacher took us to a movie showing how heroic the Russians were and what a bunch of bloodthirsty nasties they had to deal with back in 1917 when they decided to take matters into their own hands. There was a terrific scene with thousands of happy Russians storming the Winter Palace where the rotten old czar lived, and at the end someone held up a smiling child around our age.

Everybody in the movie spoke Russian, and our class couldn't read the subtitles, but we figured out what was happening anyway.

The seventh started earlier than usual schooldays. I marched along Rákóczi Street with my classmates, singing the *Internationale*, a few happy Russian marching songs and some Hungarian songs about gathering wheat.

We strode up the Boulevard all the way to Heroes' Square, where King Mátyás and Lajos Kossuth still sat proudly on their iron horses, and the leaders of the seven tribes who first arrived on the plains of Hungary must have wept to hear our leaders shouting slogans of gratitude for all the good fortune the Russians had brought us. Just a few years earlier, the Russians had bombed the hell out of Budapest, destroying most of the buildings around Heroes' Square. Over to the right of our proud entry at Andrássy Avenue, they had destroyed a church and installed a towering metal statue of Stalin. It was in front of the statue that our own leaders stood waiting for the crowds to pass with their spontaneous expression of joy.

They stood on a raised dais, Comrade Rákosi, the prime minister, in front; Comrade Gerö, the Party secretary, next to him but slightly behind; a bunch of other men in brown suits. Rákosi was round and completely bald, his face a pink disc in the morning sun. Alice said Comrade Rákosi must be getting pretty tired standing up there all day, and I thought it would be very odd for him to be in that place, under the Russian flag with Kossuth only fifty meters away, waving at us while huge photographs of his own face went by.

Of course, there were more pictures of Stalin and Lenin than of Comrade Rákosi, but Lenin and Stalin weren't there to wave.

I carried our class banner, a pretty red flag with a building in the middle. The building didn't much resemble our school, because I drew it to look more like a castle, adding turrets and even a small gargoyle. Alice had to carry the Comrade Stalin banner. She managed to leave it by the water fountain after we left Heroes' Square, but the teacher told us we would have to go back for it.

It had been a sunny day, but now it started to rain. Neither of us had raincoats and it was cold for November, so we collected the banner and ran with it down between us, each of us holding one end. When we rounded the corner of the Corvin department store just a block from the school, a man's voice told us to stop. "What's that you got there?" he asked, friendly, a man with reddish hair, getting wet like we were. He bent to have a better look at the banner, then righted it so Stalin was facing him. "Hello, there," he said to Stalin, then he hoisted the banner and smashed it against the pavement. He put his boot through Stalin's face. "Bastard," he whispered. Then he ran.

We told the teacher the banner must have been stolen from the fountain by someone who desperately wanted to take Comrade Stalin home with him. We were afraid to admit that we had let the man wreck it.

As it was, Alice had to stay an extra hour at school because she had been careless with Comrade Stalin.

Vili thought we had done well not to tell the teacher what happened. "Sometimes you get blamed for stuff just because you're in the wrong place at the wrong time," he said. "Take, for example, Sissky the butcher at the foot of Castle Hill, who lived through the Arrow Cross campaigns and the coming of Hitler. Sissky kept his shop open when the British bombs fell, cut up horse carcasses while it rained Katusha rocket balls, kept his head down serving his remaining clientele. He never imagined he'd be taken to Siberia when the Russians came. But it seemed to the Russian commander that any man who was willing to serve meat on Castle Hill had to be part of a conspiracy. And he has never come home again."

That wasn't the first time I had heard about the butcher, but Alice must have looked puzzled, because Vili added, "The lies you tell at school are not really lies. They are self-preservation. Only the lies you tell at home count."

My mother returned before the end of November, after nearly eight months in jail (she didn't know why they sentenced her to the extra two months), just in time to personally hand in my spotlessly filled out school questionnaire at the first parent-teacher meeting. She was thinner than before; her long, fluffy hair had been cropped short and it, too, had thinned. Her skin had turned somewhat yellow. But she seemed really happy to be home.

She said she'd had a lot of practice answering questions during her national re-education classes in jail. She knew exactly what kind of answers would keep me out of trouble.

As Kati predicted, when the new questionnaire came, she left my father dead.

29

THE WINTER OF 1951 was one of the coldest ever. There was frost on the windows in early December. One of my grandmother's favourite pigeons died on the windowsill. The first snow froze into sheets of ice; we could slide most of the way to school. The touring exhibition "Stalin's Wartime Life" arrived in Budapest, and our class was taken to see it. We were allowed to go home afterwards to read the small illustrated booklet about Stalin that the teacher gave us. The teacher said there would be a test the next day.

My mother spent most of her days trying to find work, but every interviewer asked eventually about where she'd been for the past few months and why wasn't she at the Road and Railway Company any longer. Then she had to admit to our foiled attempt to reach Vienna, and that was the end of it.

After lifting and carting boxes at the button factory, Vili now volunteered for extra hours at the cement works. It still wasn't enough to pay for all the coal we needed.

There was not enough coal to heat both the apartment and the water heater in the bathroom. My grandmother would often choose the water heater so that Vili could wash in hot water when he came home. We all wore extra socks and pullovers, and we visited friends and relatives in the evenings.

Benny came with a big package of coal for my mother as an early Christmas gift. Peter, another of her friends, brought wood and mittens. She went out to dinner in the evenings to save food for the rest of us.

In February she acquired a new boyfriend. His name was Jenö. He was a high-placed engineer at the State Road and Railway Company. He was a worker's son. He had gone to university, supporting himself as a barman in an all-night club on the Corso. He had joined the Party during the war. He hated most forms of religion. "Opiate of the masses," he told me before I knew what the words meant. He brought us sacks of coal. He brought wine and salami and played chess with my mother.

In June, the State Road and Railway Company rehired her.

Vili was very quiet when Jenö was there. He stayed in the bedroom, read from his papers or his books and never listened to "thevoiceofamerica."

Then Benny disappeared and my mother applied for one of the tough winter assignments on the prairie. There was to be a new railway line from Kecskemét through Debrecen and into the Ukraine. It was to be wide-gauge and it had to have a new bridge over the Tisza.

"If anyone should ask you about Benny," my mother said, "act stupid. A seven-year-old isn't expected to remember everything. Say that I have several boyfriends, you don't know all their names."

She did have several boyfriends. "Is Jenö going to disappear next?" I asked her hopefully.

"No. Jenö will stay."

With my mother working, we could heat the apartment again. Kati had begun to relax about her school year, since Leah made no effort to come for her. Leah had left Miklós but took a bit of a detour from her devotion to Laci and moved in with an old man we called "the Raven." He dressed in black; his winter coat had a black pelt collar and belt that he said were panther fur. He had a shiny wooden cane, its handle a black carved bone that he said was the charred head of the panther; its eyes were made of amethysts. He had gold rings on his baby fingers and on his middle fingers. Leah said he worked for the government and his job was so special he couldn't discuss it.

He hissed when he talked.

He bought Leah an orange at a Party store that he said no ordinary person could enter. Kati and I were allowed to watch while he peeled it for her. He cut circles into the skin, then pulled it off in one long strip. He explained that oranges grew in countries where the sun was always hot; that's what made them orange. He wouldn't let Leah share even the smallest sliver with us.

Vili said the handle of his cane was made of ordinary black African wood and was hollow. Inside it, he probably carried a microphone and recorded anything he thought sounded interesting. He worked for the State Security. If the State Security didn't like what you said, it could make you disappear just like Benny and the woman who had lived on the third floor with her son had. Vili was even more quiet when Leah's new boyfriend visited than when Jenö was there. Now not even the livingroom was safe.

"Luckily," Kati said, "this one hates children."

30

IT WAS RIGHT AFTER the Raven's second visit to the apartment that we found the man in our coal cellar.

The door to the basement stairs was usually left open, because the basement light didn't work. There were low, wide, fenced-in, glassless windows that allowed in barely enough light in winter to find where each apartment's own cellar was. The cellars were separated by cement partitions that Mrs. Nemeth said were the foundations of the building. "If anything happened to those partitions, the whole sorry old heap would collapse," she said. "Then Mr. Nemeth and I could go back to Pécs. Wouldn't that be a shame?" Her whole body shook and wobbled as she laughed.

The partitions didn't reach all the way across to the other side of the wall, so you would pass through other people's cellars on the way to your own. People kept the strangest stuff down there close to their wood and coal heaps. There were brass canary cages taller than I was, huge vases with fake flowers, rolled up bear rugs, stone cherubs and glass Madonnas, a corner closet with priest's garments, bookcases stuffed with mouldy, leather-bound books, an empty coffin with ivory handles and puffed purple velvet padding, a complete butcher's stand, black mirrors, silver bedstands, stuffed deer heads, mounted antlers, and much more besides.

In our own area, my family had put away all the things they

had salvaged from the old house and couldn't fit into the apartment. My favourite was the blue plush livingroom set, the sofa longer than Alice and me toe to toe, armchairs wide enough to sleep in, the low oak table that had taken the shrapnel shots in its centre but hadn't caught fire. The gold drapes were now rolled up over the sofa, and there was a stand-up closet full of ball gowns.

Alice and I were playing "Turkish wars" when we found the man. It was after six, and the light was so dim we thought, at first, he was a new piece of furniture, but he moved when Alice shouted "Surrender or die," challenging me from the sofa. He had been crouched down behind our coal pile, one of the old drapes wrapped around him. He tried to stand and say something, but he was unsteady on his feet and fell headlong over the coals. He continued his murmuring.

Alice leapt off the sofa and stood beside me, our hips touching, hers at the lower part of mine.

"Who? What?" Alice squawked, her voice high from fright.

The man murmured some more and tried to raise his shoulders.

I had one of Vili's old fencing épées, the practice one with the button at the pointy end, but if you didn't know it, it looked fierce enough. We took a few steps toward the man and I prodded the coal pile with the point. "What are you doing here?" I asked.

He lurched over onto his side and turned his face toward us. It was too dark to see him and he was too black, but we could smell him now. It was a nasty stench, like the dead horse that had once lain behind the house. I kept thinking about that horse with its hoofs in the air and its belly all cut to pieces.

He whispered, "I need some water," his voice as dry and soft as autumn leaves. "Please." He breathed in deeply. "I don't get water, I'm going to die. Please." His breath was like rotten eggs.

Alice was the first out of the cellar, bounding toward the Nemeths' door, but she stopped abruptly and veered off in the direction of the back stairs. "I'm not sure about the Nemeths," she whispered, as we took the stairs two at a time, bouncing past Kati and Moci trying to smoke on the landing at the third floor and up to Alice's door on the fourth. Alice carried her own key now that her mother had gone to work for the Ministry of Agriculture. Her grandmother was sleeping in their kitchen.

Alice's grandma was very old and, unlike mine, she never asked questions.

Alice climbed on a stool and grabbed one of her father's old vinegar jars, washed it, filled it with water and hid it inside her father's brown derby, and we took the front stairs down, slowly, chatting like a couple of ladies. We enjoyed pretending that there was nothing out of the ordinary going on. Of course, if anyone had been watching, they would have known that we absolutely never walked down those steps — we always ran and we always jumped the last five or six steps on each turn of the landings. And we never chatted like a couple of ladies — we always either shouted or whispered.

When we got back to the cellar, the man took the jar in both his hands and drank all the water. I thought the whole building could hear his swallowing, it was so loud. Then he vomited. "Thank you," he told us, though we could both see that the water hadn't done him much good. "I shouldn't have drunk it so fast," he explained. His breathing was softer now. "I'm sorry."

He wiped his face and hands on the curtains wrapped around him. He was shaking, his voice barely there at all. "My mother always told me not to drink too fast, it'll make you sick." He hiccoughed. "My mother ..."

It was too dark to see, but I thought he was making crying noises.

Alice and I went for more water, and she snatched an

apple from her kitchen. Her grandmother was awake now, but she was peeling potatoes, her back to us.

"Mommy left it for me, but I don't need it," Alice said. Apples were special in the winter; she wanted me to know she was making a sacrifice.

After that, I knew which one of us would have to venture into the dark again. She said she had to stay at the top of the basement stairs to make sure the lightbulb by the main entrance was on so I could find my way back.

I went down alone with the water and the apple. You hardly ever saw the rats in the daytime, but they were out in force in the evening. Still, they never did anything but watch.

I knew the way, knew where everything was. The Nemeths' coal pile and the tulip bulbs Mrs. Nemeth had scrounged from the Kerepesi Cemetery, the doctors' lounge set. The chandelier with the broken crystals, their woodpile, the Fothys' locked hardwood boxes and Mrs. Fothy's beauty salon set, the piano tuner's ancient accordion, the furniture restorer's newspaper-wrapped paintings.

When my eyes adjusted to the darkness, I found the man. I was careful that our hands wouldn't touch when I gave him the water and the apple.

He thanked me.

This time he drank the water slowly, his throat again making that awful glugging sound, stopping, starting, stopping. "Is it an apple?" he asked, looking into his fist.

"Yes. We thought you might be hungry."

He was crying now in earnest.

"I have to go," I told him. "I'm sorry; it's dark."

"I'm used to the dark," he whispered.

Alice and I swore on our best and longest friendship that neither of us would tell. He would be our secret. It didn't occur to either of us to call the police. Throughout our childhoods, "police" meant late-night knocks on the neighbour's door and walls with ears to listen. Even the Nemeths' fat son was terrifying in his tight uniform. The only people more frightening than the police were the government. They made people disappear. Alice and I never discussed these things; we just acted by the rules.

I barely made it into our kitchen in time to help my grandmother. She expected me to take part in her cooking, and if I wasn't there when she started, she would leave me the salad to fix. That night it was cucumbers.

My grandfather liked them sliced very thin, transparent. I had to use the thin side of the grater. She had already made her sugary vinegar dressing. I cut my knuckles as I scraped the cucumbers up and down on the grater, my blood dropping into Vili's favourite salad. Then we set the table, got his warm washbasin ready and waited.

I could almost hear myself telling Vili about the man in the basement and see him taking charge of what to do next, but I didn't tell him. I watched him tuck his napkin into his shirt collar and eat the cucumber salad with great gusto.

It was one of the few nights my mother came home, but she didn't stay for dinner. A new man called Tibor was waiting to take her to the Mátyás Pince. He was taller than Benny, thinner than Peter, younger than Jenö. He had sandy hair and high cheekbones. He kept his grey suit buttoned up. He said good evening to my grandparents, but declined their invitation to sit at the table. He waited near the door, shuffling his big brown shoes.

He had brought her a tiny bunch of violets. He spared us both the effort of trying to make friends.

The next day my mother was gone by the time I woke up. She was still assigned to a possible road construction site on the prairie, some three or four hours' travel from Budapest.

Jinny was getting older and fatter and could hardly wait till six for her first walk of the day. She would try to climb into my bed to nuzzle me awake, and when she could no longer jump, she would whine near my head. She could create an entire operatic production if she judged me too slow to react.

I grabbed the coal bucket in one hand, the dachshund under the other arm, and ran down to the basement.

The man took shape in the thin shaft of morning light. I could make out his features more clearly than the day before. His face was long, his nose slightly twisted to one side, a dark blue bruise over the bridge. His lips were puffed. He had large, watery eyes fringed with black lashes, and there was the deep well of a cut over his forehead, splitting one eyebrow into two distinct halves. His hair was dark, matted, sticking up from his head in tufts.

During the night he had taken one of my aunts' pink velvet ball gowns and wrapped it around his chest. He had pulled a cushion from the old blue plush sofa and propped it against the wall where he sat on the ground, behind the tall closet. If you didn't know to look for him, you wouldn't have seen him.

When I arrived Alice was already there. She was perched on the back of the sofa, her feet dangling on either side. She was banging one of her heels against the backboard.

"I brought him bread," she said. "You?"

"He can have half my sandwich," I said, hoping he wouldn't want it. Alice's bread was still on the arm of the sofa.

Unable to wait any longer, Jinny pissed in her lady-like manner on the Fothys' old rolled-up carpet across the way, then she went in search of a perfect place for a shit.

"Your dog?" the man asked.

I said yes.

"I used to have a dachshund," he said. "Black with brown patches around his snout and on his chest. Little brown booties. Loved to take him for his walks. Is yours a boy?" His voice was throaty, as if he had a very bad cold.

"Jinny? She's a girl. You live around here?"

"Not too far," he whispered. "You tell someone I'm down here?"

"No," we both said at once. It felt great saying it at once, as if Alice and I were the same person — not just best friends, but living in each other's skins. I knew how much I had wanted to tell Vili and figured she'd wanted to tell her dad, but we hadn't.

"You don't live in this building," Alice said. It wasn't a question. We all knew he didn't live here. When the man didn't reply, she went on. "Why did you come here then?"

We both waited for the answer. Alice beat her heel harder on the wooden frame of the sofa.

"We're going to have to go to school soon," I said.

"I didn't know where to go." His voice was soft and scratchy, like dog's paws on the carpet, "I was afraid to go home. Afraid they'd come after me again ... I thought the doctors would help ..."

"Doctor Apatheky?" I asked.

"He was my doctor in peacetime, I thought he might ... Then I got here and I thought he would be afraid to do anything for me. And he might call them."

"Who?" Alice asked, all conspiratorial. "The police?"

He took a deep breath, his chest wheezing. "Yes."

We waited for a bit, saying nothing.

"You're going to live down here, then?" Alice asked.

"Don't be stupid," I told her. "Nobody lives down here. Only the rats. Besides, he'll be found. Everyone comes down for coal."

"I don't know what I'm going to do," the man said. "I'm afraid to go home. It's not just them, it's everyone else. It's my friends ... even my wife ... When she finds out ... And the others ..." He was crying again. "Maybe it's too late for the others ... They'll be picked up now. Down to Andrássy Avenue. They'll know it was me. That I told them. I wasn't going to tell them anything, but the pain ... I'm not brave, you know ... I am a coward ... And none of it's true ... none of it. All lies. They made me tell them things they wanted to hear ... lies. About my friends, and other ... people I hardly know ... You can't imagine what it's like." His voice had gone from the hoarse whisper to a shrieky whine, like a rat crying when it's caught in a trap.

He shrank into the drapes, his face buried in the soft gown, his hands scratching at his split eyebrow. I noticed that the ends of his fingers were dark, caked with blood, swollen; he didn't seem to have fingernails.

"That must have hurt," I said, trying hard to think of something helpful to say because his shoulders were shaking.

"They won't understand ...," he cried. "They won't understand ... And then there'll be the trial. And the lies ... all the lies ..."

"We'll come back after school and bring you some more water and food," Alice said in an attempt to be reassuring. "You'll be alright till then?"

He didn't reply.

I took Jinny and the coal bucket up to the third floor. Vili had already left for the factory.

We ran to school, our bags banging against our legs, the cold January air tugging at our lungs; we slipped on patches of ice and muddy snow. But it felt so much warmer than down in the cellar, and the air was clean and sharp after the dampness and the strange man's crying.

All that day, I half-thought we had imagined him. We played so many games imagining people who seemed real enough to frighten us, when we were shot by Turkish arrows or killed by a single cannonball, and we were generals and brave men-in-arms. As the day progressed, the man in the cellar seemed to shrink into one of our long story-games, a secret only we shared. Alice would look at me across the classroom, and I'd know she was thinking the same thing.

Between arithmetic and spelling she whispered to me: "Do you think he'll still be there when we get back?" And I said yes, I was sure he would be, though I really thought he would have disappeared.

But he was still there. He had come out of his corner, shrunk into the shadows near the Fothys' closet. He wore one of Mr. Fothy's old black suits and a sagging coat with a turned-up collar. His hands were wrapped in bits of Leah's gown. He was smoking a cigarette. I could see right away that Alice's apple was still on the arm of the sofa. My pork fat and paprika sandwich was gone.

"I'll wait till it's dark," he told us. "Then I'll go. Can you please get me some more water?"

Alice went.

"Don't tell anyone you saw me, will you?" he asked me. "You never know, they could misunderstand. It's better not to have seen me. Better for you. And your parents. You have parents, don't you?"

I was about to tell him about my mother and Vili, but he put his velvet-wrapped fingers in front of his mouth and shushed me. "Never. Don't tell me your name. I might remember it. It's not safe to tell me anything ..." He hid behind the woodpile when Mrs. Fothy came down for her evening coal. And Alice hid the glass of water behind her back. Then Mr. Nemeth came down with his buckets and took a bottle of *palinka* from the woodpile.

"What are you two doing down here all the time?" he asked, glugging from his bottle. "No good, I'd bet on it. No damned good at all, the pair of you little vixens. Don't you tell Mrs. Nemeth, and I won't tell on you. Fair's fair."

When we were alone, our stranger thanked us for the water and told me to take care of Jinny, he missed his old dachshund a whole lot. They were the best kind of dog. Smart. Then he told us to please go, in case someone saw us together or suspected.

I said it was alright, I'd already been to jail, and it wasn't all that bad.

He laughed, I think, though it was hard to tell — there was a sound like a door creaking and he shook some. "Please go," he told us. "Please. You're good kids."

"What's the big deal about Andrássy Avenue?" I asked my grandfather.

At the time, he didn't answer.

But he took my hand early one Sunday morning, earlier than we would get up for church, boarded the streetcar on Rákóczi Street and the bus to the beginning of Andrássy Avenue, renamed Stalin Boulevard, though everyone still called it Andrássy Avenue. It's wide and there were old expensive houses, a boulevard for strolling on a warm summer afternoon, in "peacetime."

He said we would walk slowly, but not so slowly as to attract attention, and I shouldn't say anything till we were past the far corner and onto Teréz Road.

It was a long street, a few desolate winter trees embedded in round holes in the pavement here and there, four- and five-storey yellowing buildings with peeling paint, a couple of them still missing roofs. A wide sidewalk. It was quiet, no music through the windows, no people, no dogs barking.

There was just one noisy building. It looked very much like the others, yellowing white, fake pillars by the front door. But there were bars on all the windows. Some cars were parked in front, the drivers in olive-green uniforms, shiny boots, leaning back on the hoods of the cars, laughing and smoking. There were more young men, wearing leather jackets, on the balconies, one blond man with his hands on his hips who looked like he was telling a joke, grinning at the other men. When he saw me looking at him, he waved, a flick of the wrist, full of vigour and self-confidence, acknowledging my gaze. Then he stopped talking, and the men all guffawed with open mouths, slapping one another on the shoulder.

Vili took my hand and put it under his arm. "We are going to walk past that building, slowly; don't talk, and don't stare; we'll be a strolling old man and his granddaughter taking a bit of air on a Sunday morning." As we went by, I felt the big muscle on his arm tighten. One of the young men shouted hello. We kept walking.

"That's number 60," Vili said when we were well past the corner. "Nothing to see from the outside. Like all the other buildings along here, a boulevard, spacious, turn of the century, but number 60 has doors that once entered, few people ever leave. Less than ten years ago, when you were born, the Arrow Cross was quartered there. They wore somewhat different uniforms and badges on their lapels, smart armbands, shiny boots. They picked up innocent people on the street and in their homes for being Jews or socialists or for just not cooperating with the terror of the day, and number 60 is where they beat them, that pretty house with the balustrade and the balconies, until they were no longer human. And just a couple of years later, by sheer coincidence, you'd imagine, the State Security Police settled on that same haunted building for their own macabre playground. This is where they bring people they think are enemies of the state, or people they simply don't like, and they torture them and murder them."

"They kill them all?" I asked.

"Most, not all. A few survive. Some turn on their friends, and then they let them go."

It was the time of the long show trials in Hungary. At first, Vili would read the daily newspaper and crack his knuckles in rage as the accused were convicted and executed one by one, but as the long winter continued, he began to laugh as the communists turned on one another and Rákosi began to execute his former colleagues. "The insanity continues ... the lies ... Did I tell you before that Hungarians don't make good conspirators? We make dashing soldiers, brave fighters, spectacular victims, but we are lousy conspirators."

Every day *Szabad Nép* ("The Free People"), the one daily paper allowed to publish, ran headlines about the new trials, photos of the accused with their heads bowed, their lengthy confessions featured in bold type.

One Communist Party faction, men who had been to Russia during the worst of the war, decided to purge all its rivals and any future opponents, however remote the possibility of opposition. The charges varied. Some were accused of spying, some of selling secrets to the United States or Britain. Some were just enemies of the people or enemies of the workers. A few were found to have conspired with the Yugoslavs against the Soviet Union or were about to defect to Yugoslavia. Some conspired with the conspirators or might have done so.

Most of them admitted to everything.

All the trials were held behind closed doors.

Szabad Nép demanded the maximum penalty, death by hanging. Afterwards, it applauded the brave men who had the courage to execute the enemies of the people.

In the 1990s I met the two sons of the man who had written those "death by hanging" headlines.

The older brother now ran a privately funded computer software venture on the outskirts of Pest. He talked proudly of raising money in the West. Investors could see that Hungary was on the way to becoming a new capitalist state, one where their money was safe, and his venture was just the firm to offer them an opportunity. He strutted around his office in his English suit, his tassled Gucci shoes, his hair fashionably long, his tie askew with the excitement of his story. He spoke English well, German passably. He had been educated in the fundamentals of Samuelson's *Economics* and the theology of the free market. I never asked him about his father.

But I did ask the younger brother the night I met him in London. It was at an East-West "exchange of ideas" gathering. There were few there from the West, and the Easterners drew into groups by nationality, the Czechs close to the Hungarians, the Slovaks near the Baltic states, the Romanians off by themselves near the exit. All seemed more interested in the free food and wine than the free exchange of ideas. By then the Easterners had seen quite a lot of the West's ideas at home.

He was sitting at one of the Hungarian tables. Taller than his brother, thinner, with a long, pale face, dark, curly hair greying near his temples; he was wearing a dung-coloured, off-the-rack suit like those favoured by Russian diplomats in the heyday of the Soviet empire. He said he was an editor in a publishing house, reading history and biography, and found comparing old versions of history to newer versions fascinating.

His father had been Rákosi's closest friend.

His family had lived in a spacious apartment on the Buda Hills overlooking the Danube. In the evenings his father would come home from the trials where men were condemned to hang and he would eat his meals with the family. Most evenings he returned to his office to write his editorials and the headlines demanding the death penalty. But at home he never talked about his business. A gentle, kindly man, he had never raised his voice to his children or to his wife. Even when Comrade Rákosi came to dinner, they never talked about politics or the events of the day.

Comrade Rákosi was a frequent visitor. The man I had seen waving to us from the podium in Heroes' Square, the man who had eliminated all his rivals, who presided over the laws that sent my mother and my grandfather to jail, ordered sudden arrests, sanctioned disappearances, torture, and murder, used to like his chicken *paprikás* extra spicy.

"And now, looking back, how does your father feel about all that?" I asked.

"He still thinks he did the right thing back then. Some people had to be sacrificed. He was willing to make that sacrifice." The old man was very ill now and rarely ventured outside their apartment. A few years earlier he had gone blind. His son couldn't remember when, but he thought it was even before the old communism ended and the new post-Berlin Wall era began.

He said his father would act the same way now, should history repeat itself.

What was strange about post-Wall Hungary, he said, is that Hungarians were so eager to bury the past and rush into the future. There had been no trials of former leaders, and groups of former prisoners brought no charges against their guards. There appeared to be no sense of guilt. The children of the murdered and the disappeared went to work for the corporations that the children of their parents' killers founded. The educational advantages had gone to the latter group because they had studied economics and banking and spoke English. They were the ones best equipped to start the new ventures the West wanted to see.

When he was growing up, his mother had a cook and the children had a tutor. Their school taught only the children of the Communist élite, and no one mentioned the show trials or his father's part in the pre-agreed verdicts.

At home his father would put on his slippers, read his paper and indulge in an occasional glass of wine. They talked about the children's adventures at school and the latest movies they would be allowed to see. He remembered that one of his father's favourite actors was Gérard Philippe. He had taken the boys to see the movie *The Count of Monte Cristo* four times.

EARLY IN 1952 our history teacher, Comrade Sipnovich, replaced the modest ten-by-ten-inch smiling photograph of Comrade Rákosi with a more serious photograph roughly twice the size.

There were a few minutes of mild terror while he tried to decide what to do with the cheerful picture. We all knew that throwing it out would have been unthinkable, and tossing it in a drawer was dangerous. There was no room for it anywhere else on our walls, what with Comrades Stalin and Lenin continuing to occupy equally large areas, and Marx and Engels, even in their smaller incarnations, had to have some air to breathe. Of course, the map of the Glorious Soviet Union in all its redness had to stay exactly where it was, and the map of Hungary could hardly be removed just when we were launching into a study of the two world wars.

Klara Toth, who had once said that she was the daughter of a landowner aristocrat and a countess, offered to take the photo home. It was a transparently desperate gesture. She couldn't take back the bit about aristocrats. She argued that their Rákosi photograph was not nearly as nice as this one, and she said her mother would be so very pleased. Nobody believed her. The teacher ignored her suggestion.

In the end, another tall girl and I reverently carried the picture out to the hall and stuck it above the second-floor noticeboard, where each day's events were announced.

A good part of our schooling consisted of acquiring and upholding good communist values. Most days there would be singing, sometimes with dancing in the gym, or there would be marching practice in the quadrangle or in front of the school. There were frequent special days to prepare for, such as Comrade Stalin's birthday, Comrade Rákosi's birthday, the commemoration of Comrade Lenin's death, the entry of the Glorious Soviet troops into Hungary, and later, the whole miserable country, and the start of the Glorious Bolshevik Revolution and its success on the seventh of November, to name just a few.

On Stalin's birthday and on days that had anything what-soever to do with the Glorious Revolution or the Great Soviet Army, we wore our white shirts and blue neck-scarves (the older children had red scarves) and blue skirts or pants and marched, four abreast, to Stalin's statue in City Park. Stalin wore boots, baggy pants and a loose jacket. Vili had told me that the biggest joke in Budapest was the inscription on Stalin's pedestal. It read, "To the great Stalin, from a grateful Hungarian people."

There was usually some form of music, and drums to keep our feet moving in unison. When we got there, we would find crowds of other kids, all waving banners, marching, singing and generally having a good time.

Twice a week there were meetings of the Young Communists League.

At first Comrade Sipnovich, who supervised the group, was reluctant to admit me, but once he realized that I was eager to paint and hang weekly signs, he relented. Though there was no question that my background was bourgeois, my father, fortunately, was dead and my mother was making every effort to contribute to the common good by laying down new highways on the Great Hungarian Prairie (Alföld). At the time I worried that Mr. Sipnovich hadn't brought up the

subject of Vili. I imagined he was holding that bit of poten-
tially treacherous heritage in store for some later occasion.

For now he was glad to encourage my volunteering. Mr.
Sipnovich had a mild case of vertigo, and the weekly signs
had to be positioned high above the blackboard, on either
side of Comrade Rákosi's bald, unsmiling head.

The signs were somewhat simplified Marx or Engels, dis-
tilled into easily digestible sayings, such as "It is necessary to
continue the armed struggle against the oppressors" and
"Class struggle is inevitable in a society based on class." My
favourites, because they were the shortest, were "Work enno-
bles" and "Long live the proletariat." These and a few similarly profound phrases by Lenin, Stalin, and our very own
Comrade Rákosi ("The Revolution never slumbers," "The
people's sports build a strong, healthy, brave workforce")
were painted on long, white sheets of paper and nailed up on
the wall. I favoured reds and blues and a simple brushstroke,
with occasional flourishes that included a beige wheatsheaf
and a yellow hammer-and-sickle decorative motif that I knew
would please the Russian language teacher.

Comrade Sipnovich tackled head-on Hungary's role in the
two world wars. Unlike my grandfather, he had a simple
explanation for everything. The *kulaks* (rich landowners
unwilling to share with the more deserving poor), the gentry
(even bigger landowners, even less willing to share) and the
capitalists and industrialists (bloodsuckers on the bellies of
the working poor) marched gaily into battle following their
traditional partners, the Austrians, who were even wealthier
than their Hungarian equivalents and whose king had been
festering on the Hungarian throne for centuries.

Naturally, our textbooks took a dim view of all monarchs,
who were inherently lazy, bloodthirsty drones, long overdue
for elimination by whatever means, including, if necessary,
another war. It was obvious, for example, that British workers
were going to rise up against their wasteful monarch quite

soon, and we'd be there to help them when they called on us.

It was not only Hungarian *kulaks* and gentry who went to war on the backs of peasants and the proletariat, mean-spirited aristocrats had done the same throughout the Eastern Bloc. But we were all friends now, because we were all ruled by the proletariat and peasants, none of whom ever willingly fought one another.

Even before the First World War broke out, Hungarian workers had demonstrated their distaste for their masters. In 1912 there was a hundred-thousand-man mass demonstration in Budapest. One hundred thousand people on strike, opposing the government's bid to increase arms production. That's why we observed a special day of singing on May 23, to commemorate the heroes who died that day. For years before the beginning of the First World War, the proletariat of Europe had been hoping to prevent it. But the two Imperialist alliances were determined to wage war to gain more for their already bulging coffers. The shooting of Archduke Franz Ferdinand, heir to the throne of Austria-Hungary, was just the pretext. These capitalist-imperialists were determined to run amok no matter what.

Didn't the Soviet Union quit the whole sorry mess the very day it rid itself of the czar? Their proletariat desired peace.

Comrade Sipnovich had assembled a range of heartwarming pictures of brave Russian peasants and workers taking part in the storming of the czar's palaces, breaking bread in sorry-looking hovels, dancing in the Moscow streets and, finally, gathering wheat all over the Ukraine.

He proudly displayed *Szabad Nép*'s front-page stories about *kulaks* hoarding sugar and flour in lofts and cellars. They would all be hauled off their land and punished while the rest of the villagers shared the booty. There were funny cartoons of fat *kulaks*, their arms full of bulging sacks, their bellies overflowing their belts, their necks bubbling over their white collars — they always wore black suits and had white shirts — being kicked in their ample butts by thin, check-shirted, barefoot peasants.

As a special treat we went to a film about the Glorious Bolshevik Revolution. It starred a young man called Chapayev who seemed to kill, single-handedly, over a thousand bloodthirsty supporters of the czar and still had time to fall in love with a pretty blonde girl.

At the sight of the new freedom for workers in Russia, Hungary's workers started to shake off the yoke of centuries and declared themselves to be opposed to the imperialist war machine. The soldiers, forced to fight on the front, now rebelled and deserted by the thousands. Councils of workers, peasants and soldiers took matters into their own hands as the monarchy disintegrated toward the end of the war.

Barely a year after our proletarian allies in Russia swept out the old and swept in the new, Hungarians elected the first Communist Government. On December 7, 1918, the Red Newspaper declared, finally, the "class war." This was the war we were still fighting, because, alas, the class struggle is never over. The first attempt to wrench power from the bourgeois didn't work. They came back in force, defeated the communists, enslaved the people and launched us into yet another war in 1940.

Luckily, in 1945 the Glorious Soviet Union's victorious soldiers liberated us. But there was no time to relax. The imperialist Westerners wanted to take away everything we had gained during our friendship years and give it all back to the gentry, the *kulaks* and the bourgeois elements among us.

That's why we had to remain vigilant. The enemy was clever and could resemble, physically, any of us. Comrade Sipnovich asked that we keep a watchful eye for the "enemy within." Our country was threatened by enemies so wily they could infiltrate even classrooms like his.

32

MY GRANDFATHER'S VERSION of that same period of history was a whole lot more complicated than Comrade Sipnovich's and took many tellings, whispered confidences in old coffeehouses, walks along the Castle streets or just sitting in the Sunday afternoon sun on a bench in front of the National Theatre watching the actors come and go. Most of them tipped their hats to him or smiled and waved as they hurried by.

He told me about the wars. Both wars. "I am still trying to think how we might have avoided being caught in the middle. Whether there ever was a choice. Another road we could have travelled. Could we have avoided the First World War?"

Vili believed that it was the Compromise of 1867 that had sealed our fate. After the devastating 1848 War of Independence, the theft of our lands and the disinheritance of our peoples, the Austrians offered a kind of peace. This was the Compromise of 1867. The court in Austria would let Hungary have its own parliament in a dual monarchy. Some of the swaggering nobles on Buda Hill thought this was a lovely idea and promptly crowned Franz Joseph king of Austria-Hungary.

Austria-Hungary. It had a certain ring to it. The problem was that the Hungarians agreed to fight alongside Austria should Austria want their help.

Kossuth, still in exile, warned that a clash between the Great Powers was unavoidable and that no matter what the outcome, it would mean the collapse of Austria. He was sure that the Compromise would "assign us the role of the stake on which the Austrian eagle will be burned." The world, he warned with extraordinary clear-sightedness, would "regard Hungary as Austria's accomplice." It would ignore our history of resistance to Austria's oppression.

The aristocrats argued that Austria was a safer friend than Russia. They signed to stay west of Russia's influence.

"The danger," Vili told me, "is in not seeing the connections. While history is never as tidy as cause and effect, there are connections between the things that happen."

There had been a hundred and fifty years of Turks, one lifetime's respite, then two hundred years of Austrians, followed by a few shining moments and more hangings, slaughter, executions, rapes and burnings, stifling all attempts at independence. Always there was the pressure to forget your language, to blend into the Empire. With their survival at stake, is it any wonder that the Hungarians compromised?

"What is a compromise?"

"It's when you want something badly enough that you're willing to give up other things you cherish so you can have it. It's like hanging pictures of Rákosi and Stalin on the walls at your school so you might get to go to university one day. That's a compromise. We do it every day when we don't say what we think of the people running this country." Vili sighed. "Trouble is, it uses so much energy." In 1867 the Hungarian nobility's desire for peace and prosperity was so great, they gave up independence.

In my grandfather's version, about the last thing the Hungarians wanted in the summer of 1914 was war over the fate of Archduke Franz Ferdinand, known in Budapest coffeehouses as Ferdi Habsburg, a weak-chinned, straw-haired nephew of Franz Joseph and next in line to ascend to the throne. He was stubborn and stupid, and he passionately disliked Hungarians. He once remarked that it had been "an act

Vili in his Budapest University Athletic Club outfit, around 1910, two years before he took part in the Stockholm Olympics.

A formal portrait of Vili in his 7th Hussar uniform, home from the Russian front, 1916.

Vili and his bobsled team, 1911.

An early photo of Vili and Therese, possibly just after their wedding.

Vili and Therese, in "peacetime."

The young Therese, in the twenties.

Vili and Therese in the back garden of their house in Buda.

Therese and the girls:
Sari, the oldest on the left,
Leah on the right,
Puci, a little annoyed about
the photograph, in front.

Leah in one of her
many ballgowns.

Puci, age 15,
in her first grown-up dress.

Puci and Sari in the late thirties. This photograph appeared in one of Vili's society magazines.

Leah in the mid-fifties.

My parents' wedding.

Therese and Vili with some members of
the family during the Second World War.
Kati is sandwiched between our grandparents' knees. Both of her parents are
missing from this photo.

The three Rácz girls
(Sari, Leah, Puci)
and their three
daughters.

The Apostolok
Restaurant, where
we used to go for
beer and pretzels.

Vili and I at the beginning
of our friendship.

My mother on my father's yacht,
somewhere on Lake Balaton.

That's me, age 3, or thereabouts.

Later.

Vili in New Zealand.

With Vili in Hastings, shortly before we said goodbye.

Vili, resplendent in his bowling outfit, Christchurch, New Zealand, 1962.

of bad taste on the part of these gentlemen ever to have come to Europe."

In the end it wasn't his hatred of Hungarians that got him killed. It was his stubbornness and stupidity.

There had been bloodlettings in the Balkans, wars between Albanians and Greeks, Bulgarians and Turks, Serbs and everybody else. Yet on a pleasant sunny day in late June, when he could have been skeet-shooting in the Imperial Gardens, Ferdi decided to take a trip to the Balkans. He picked Sarajevo, the capital of Bosnia. Bosnia, then as now, was next to Serbia, and the Serbs had no great love for the Austrians. Very few people in the Balkans liked the Austrians. The Serbs even warned the Archduke that Bosnia was not a nice place to visit.

Not only did Ferdi ignore their advice, he chose a special day for his visit: June 28, the anniversary of the Battle of Kosovo. The Field of Blackbirds.

"Where the Serbs lost to the Turks?"

"And their king was killed."

"Why do they call it the Field of Blackbirds?"

"It used to be a vast, green field where blackbirds gathered in the spring. Perhaps they still do."

June 28 is a day of national mourning for the Serbs.

When his chauffeur found a bomb under his car in Sarajevo, Ferdi could have called off his plan to tour the city, but being stubborn, he didn't. Thus it was that he and his unfortunate bride, Sophie, got themselves killed. They were shot dead by an asthmatic Serb student who was waiting on the wrong side of the street.

The only reason they were on that street at all was that their driver took the wrong turn. The patriotic student was almost as stupid as the Archduke. But he got lucky, and the rest of the world got unlucky, because that was the shot that began the First World War.

The Austrians were outraged. The Compromise of 1867 said that the Hungarians had to be outraged as well.

Russia was already fully armed and prepared for war. Czar Nicholas II made no secret of his intentions. Long before the "shot heard round the world" had sounded, he had recalled Russian troops from Asia and found a willing ally in Serbia. The Serbs, having grown more confident with their victories in two Balkan wars, saw a chance to add southern Hungary to Greater Serbia. Southern Hungary is where the Habsburgs had settled Serbs after the Wars of Independence.

Austria-Hungary declared war.

The Russian Army began its march toward Budapest.

When it was over, more than half a million Hungarians had died. The Habsburg monarchy was no more. The head of a new National Council, Mihály Károlyi, ordered the soldiers to lay down their arms and went to Belgrade to ask for a separate peace for his countrymen. The French General d'Esperay consulted his Romanian and Serbian liaison officers and treated Károlyi with utter contempt.

Meanwhile, Romanian troops poured over the eastern borders. Budapest was in ruins. Mobs of angry men fought one another, some demanding peace, some justice, most wanting a new government. The Romanians entered the undefended capital, looted what little they found, blew up a couple of Catholic churches and murdered a few people.

The recently formed Communist Party grabbed the government and executed two or three thousand more Hungarians. That was the first "red terror." The man who led them was Béla Kun.

What followed the war was the terrible Treaty of Trianon and the tiny new State of Hungary under Admiral Horthy.

"Admiral?"

"He liked to think of himself as an admiral, though we had no navy and barely an army left." The few soldiers still to be found had been assembled by Admiral Miklós Horthy and led, triumphantly, to the capital. Most people were glad to see him, then.

Béla Kun escaped to Russia. In 1937, during one of Stalin's periodic roundups of fellow communists, he was arrested, and in August the following year, he was hanged.

When I asked Comrade Sipnovich about him, he said there was no such person as Béla Kun, and where had I heard that name?

33

MY GRANDFATHER'S STORIES about the Second World War never came as a package. He talked about people, mostly, and about how the war had crept up on Budapest. In the fifties it was still too recent. There were too many painful memories.

Vili told one story about his friend, the humourist called Zoli. He had been living in our basement in Buda for over six months. He was the funniest man Vili had ever worked with. He never forgot a joke. During the long, dark days he used humour to keep the other basement guests laughing. The day he ran out of jokes, he said, he would have to leave. Who'd want to share a cellar with a funny man who was no longer funny? One morning he told his last joke. It was the one about the Jews the czar orders out of their village. When nobody laughed at the punchline, Zoli fled. He was shot crossing the Chain Bridge to Pest.

"Why was he shot?"

"Because he was a Jew. The Arrow Cross were hunting humans all over the city."

"What was the punchline?"

"Something about the village deciding not to leave. It was not very funny."

Vili had had another friend who was a cartoonist. He died of hunger north of the city, waiting for the Russians to come.

He had filled the abandoned villa where he was hiding with his drawings. When he had used up all the paper, he had continued to draw on the walls. But that was in 1943.

In 1936, though the Italians and Germans supported Franco in the Spanish Civil War, Hungarians fought with the international brigades against Franco. "Franco was a fascist," Vili told me. "The Germans wanted to see how their troops handled battles out of the trenches. An uncivil civil war against civilians, where babies were thrown against the walls and women were bayoneted alongside their weeping children."

In Budapest it had been hard to tell when the war began or when it was too late to turn back.

Hungarian intellectual life had been full of prominent Jewish writers, philosophers, politicians, artists, lawyers, doctors. In 1937 the Hungarian government excluded fascists from public life. When a few right-wing politicians began to talk about too many Jews in the professions, it seemed like the ravings of a fascist minority. There were some grumblings about new Jewish immigrants from the East, but much of the grumbling came from Hungarian Jews. They thought the newcomers were not sufficiently civilized.

On March 12, 1938, when the German Army jackbooted down the Kaertnerstrasse in Vienna, there was only a ripple of regret in Budapest coffeehouses. Some felt relief — perhaps Hitler would be satisfied with Austria. Hungary remained neutral.

There were Hitler jokes told in public places. Little boys imitated the goose step. Comedians put on fake black moustaches and gave Hitler's ranting speeches in fake German laced with German-sounding Hungarian words.

Then the government passed the first Jewish Law. "The first act of cowardice," Vili said. "The Germans were insisting that Hungary do something about the Jews, and that was, they thought, a way of appeasing the Reich." The first law allowed that no more than twenty percent of certain professions — the press, the law, medicine, engineering, banking — could be Jews. No one took much notice of the percentages. On Sunday evenings, the group of intellectuals who had been gathering for talk, food and cigars in the Hungaria Restaurant still gathered there and talked about how all this would pass, that the government would have to go back to running a civilized society.

Vili's last hope for peace and the return to sanity died with his friend Pál Teleki, Hungary's prime minister when the war began. Both their families were old Erdély, both had attended university in Budapest and read law, both were Anglophiles — Vili because his father had been to Oxford, Teleki because he had enjoyed English literature. When Germany attacked Poland on the first of September, Teleki refused the German Army passage over Hungarian soil and opened the gates to Polish refugees. Some seventy thousand of them came, telling tales of savagery, of burning villages, of mass graves. When Britain and France declared war on Germany, Hungary still clung to its illusion of neutrality.

In 1940 most of Erdély was returned by the Germans.

Teleki had no cards left to play.

On the afternoon of April 2, 1940, Teleki was informed the Germans would march over Hungary to attack Yugoslavia. He argued, fought, shouted, slammed the phone down, paced his study, phoned again and shouted again. At eleven o'clock that night he demanded to be shown the telegram warning the Hungarian Parliament that allowing the German Army free passage over the country would lead to the end of diplomatic relations with London.

At dawn on April 3, he was found slumped over his antique desk, a bullet hole in the back of his head, another in his right temple. A third bullet was lodged in the flocked wallpaper of his study. There was a revolver, a large Browning, by his right hand.

In his farewell letter to Governor Horthy, he wrote, "My country has lost its honour."

True enough, but Vili didn't think Teleki had committed suicide. Teleki had been left-handed; how and why would he have shot himself with his right hand? And who had fired the second bullet? Vili believed that Teleki would not consent to Germans troops marching over Hungary and he was executed by Nazi agents. Teleki was too small a fish for Hitler himself to have given the order. It would have been Eichmann.

News of Teleki's suicide spread through the city, then the world. Churchill said that when the peace treaties were to be signed at the end of what had become the Second World War, Teleki's memory would be honoured by setting an empty chair for him at the conference table.

"Are you sure they did that?" I asked my grandfather when I read about the treaty in my New Zealand history book years later. "There is no mention of the empty chair here. No mention of Teleki at all."

"The man who wrote the book, was he there in Yalta when the treaty was signed? He wasn't?" Vili smiled triumphantly. "What does he know for sure? I know that Churchill announced there would be a chair for Teleki at the table. Why wouldn't Churchill have remembered that?"

Everything changed after Teleki died. Within days German troops overran the Bácska, using Hungary as their base; Croatia declared its independence and allied itself with the Germans; Hungarian troops were ordered into Yugoslavia. On the twenty-seventh of June, Hungarian radio announced that Russian planes had attacked the town of Kassa, and Hungary joined in the Germans' war.

"We were now led by Admiral Horthy, a man who fancied himself in dress uniform, his favourite the all-white outfit of an admiral, his chest dripping with medals, his pants tightly fitted into black calfskin boots, a red cape fluttering over his shoulders. He was Admiral Horthy, the only known admiral in the world with no navy, and he was Regent of Hungary, governing in place of a king who was no longer a king."

Horthy continued to imagine that he was providing a sanctuary for those escaping the Germans, though we were at war on the German side. He opened the borders to refugees; he set up safe houses for escaping Jews, even as he ordered that Hungary's Jews must volunteer for work camps.

In the national election that May, the far right won a third of the popular vote. In New Zealand, more than twenty years later, my grandfather was still trying to think of what might have been done to avoid it. "They used the ghost of Trianon to drive people toward the Germans. They had recovered from the humiliation of their 1918 defeat; if we joined them, we would do the same. My god, not a week went by that some chanteuse in Budapest didn't sing about the return of Kolozsvár."

"The far right?"

"The fascist anti-Semites. We should have taken them more seriously. They liked to dress in leather or some kind of military getup. Looked like toy soldiers. They were stupid, uneducated, small-minded, vicious, hideously arrogant. How could we have thought they would end up with power over people's lives?"

Endre Kabos was captain of the Hungarian fencing team. In 1936 his team won the gold medal at the Berlin Olympic Games. Kabos was Vili's friend. They fenced at the University Club and worked out in the Club's gymnasium in the evenings. In 1943 Kabos received the formal letter commanding him to a work camp. Kabos was such a star that they never thought he would be sent to work detail with other Jews. "Don't worry, Endre," Vili told him. "It's all a misunderstanding. We'll sort it out in a day or two, and you'll be home for New Year's."

He wasn't. Vili called the Swedish embassy. He knew that King Gustav himself had given Kabos a gold ring after watching him fence at an international sporting event in Stockholm. Perhaps he would help. The letter from the king arrived too late.

By November Kabos had died.

While thousands of Hungarians went to fight on the Eastern front, Horthy alerted British intelligence that Hungary was a safe place to land damaged planes. He sent men to London and to Russia to plead for a separate peace. He ordered the only home-based unit of his army to defend Budapest's Jews from deportation, but almost half a million Jews were sent to Auschwitz between May 15 and July 8, 1944.

"Hitler yelled at me about the Jews," Horthy said afterwards at the Nuremberg trial. "In Kleissheim, where I went to plead for Hungary's independence, all he wanted to talk about was his damnable 'final solution,' as if all of Europe hadn't been on fire, as if we hadn't already lost two armies on the Russian front." He said even Goebbels had been astonished by the Führer's temper tantrum.

Horthy had been certain the Allies would attack Germany from the Balkans, opening a corridor to Hungary, where his troops would have welcomed them. "Had they done so, the war would have ended two years earlier. And Stalin would not have ruled over Eastern Europe. There may not have been a Cold War. Churchill knew, but Roosevelt had made a deal with Stalin and he would not go back on his word. How many lives is the right price to pay for a man's word?"

In his final desperation, Horthy went on national radio to announce an armistice.

The German high command didn't like it. Their army marched into Hungary on October 15, 1944. They appointed a new "National Protector," the leader of the Hungarian Arrow Cross Party, a man who talked about racial purity, as if Hungarians had ever been a race.

There were long lines of people, four, five deep — old women with fur collars, men with long, white beards and side curls, men in business suits and overalls, pregnant women, little children clutching toys, some sleeping, their heads over their mothers' shoulders, women in dirndl skirts and babushkas, fashionable society ladies, their hair piled high, still wearing high heels as they marched towards the Eastern Railway Station. Some carried suitcases, as if it were just a journey. A few carried pets, dogs in their arms, cats in cages.

One of my mother's friends, now in her seventies, was a young woman when she was herded out of her home in Buda to join the forced march. "I never imagined we wouldn't be back," she tells me. "It never occurred to us. Or if it did, we wouldn't admit it even to ourselves. We were talking about things we'd left behind that we wished now we had brought along on the journey. A warmer coat or face cream, a waterproof hat for the rain. One woman worried she hadn't turned off the oven with her evening roast. At the station, a couple of the men got into the freight cars first and helped the women up. Some laughter about the tight skirts. A few of the children cried."

THERE HAD BEEN SOME DISCUSSION between the two sets of Great Powers who fought the Second World War that Budapest might be spared. There was talk that Admiral Horthy's pleas for declaring it a "free city" might find sympathy with both sides. Some said that Churchill remembered Count Teleki and his attempts to keep Hungary out of the war. Others were sure that when Horthy agreed to a bunch of patently crazy initiatives that sent Hungarian soldiers to certain death on the Eastern front, the Germans would be appeased. They hoped that when Horthy's colleagues in the terrorized room that passed for the country's parliament voted that all Hungary's production would go to help the war effort, let the people go hungry, that, surely, would impress the Führer. Surely even he would see how pretty Budapest was and spare it.

The talk in the few coffeehouses, where you could still sit over a single cup of espresso for an afternoon, was hopeful until the last moment. The big guns had already started their bombardment east of the Danube. There was rubble in the streets from British and American air raids, whole buildings had collapsed, the two main railway stations were destroyed, but it was Christmas. After all, if Vienna would be spared, why not Budapest? And didn't Vienna cheer the arrival of the Nazis with flag-waving and flowers for Hitler? Churchill would know that no one waved when the German Army occupied Budapest.

Vili was sure there would be a last-minute deal. In 1944, when he was pretending that his world was not coming to an end — at least not yet — and strutting along the Danube Corso as if he didn't have sixteen people in the basement of his house in Buda and another four on the estate in Penc, he argued with the other gentlemen in three-piece suits that the United States and Britain would remember that on October 15 just past, Admiral Horthy had declared on the radio that, in his view, Germany had lost the war. Even if the British and the Americans had forgotten everything else, they would remember that.

Budapest would be spared.

But it wasn't.

Hitler declared that Budapest would be defended street by street, building by building, and as the Russian Army circled the city from the east, the Germans ordered all the bridges destroyed. On the fourth of November, while afternoon traffic flowed from Pest to Buda, the Margit Bridge was blown up, killing over a hundred people. The next to go were the Petöfi (then Miklós Horthy) and the Franz Joseph (later, Liberty) bridges. The last to be destroyed were the Erzsébet Bridge and the Chain Bridge.

The city descended into its cellars. And stayed there while the battle raged.

As the Germans retreated, the Russians came. In a report filed by the Swiss embassy, the Russians are described: "Russian troops looted the city freely. They entered practically every home. They took away everything they wanted. They raped and burned, they took all the food they could find." When they opened the Jewish ghetto, they grabbed whatever small bits the Jews had saved. During the night, people would crawl out from among the rubble to find dead horses and hack them to pieces to take home a bit of meat. There were battles over one or two potatoes and a drop of lard. Under the light of candles and torches, in the snow and mud of the streets, people would appear, dark shadows in the night.

Later, the Russians would refer to those days as the days of our "liberation."

The joke was that "they had liberated us from the last of our belongings," Vili said. "Those things would never seem as important again."

The two Russian phrases everyone learned were *malenki robot* and *davay chasy*. The first phrase literally meant "a little work," but what it really meant was that they packed you onto a train to Siberia or to the mines on Lake Baikal, and you might never return. As for *davay chasy*, it meant hand over your watch, if you want to live.

One evening while the battles raged, Vili went up to the ruins of the Royal Castle, where he knew that what was left of the Hungarian Army still held out. He had to hide from snipers, crouching low under the trimmed bushes of the Promenade and up the steep steps of Castle Hill. Though Pest had been taken, there was still hope for Buda. He had known the last commander of the Hungarian Army when he was a major. Once when Vili invited a particularly aggressive young buck to duel for offending a woman at the University ball, the major had offered to be his second. As middle-aged men they had belonged to a dinner group that met once a month to discuss how the world was going. Dressed in black tie, the fourteen men in the group dined at the formal Tarjan Restaurant on Margit Island. They shared good wine, good food, cigars and conversation.

Now the major was a general. Vili met him under the old castle. There was a labyrinth of passageways and chambers, all lit by torches and candles, just as they had been since the castle was first built and defended against centuries of enemies.

General Ivan Hindy sat behind a big metal desk, a map of the city behind him. He was balding now, and his uniform was creased and smelled of coal dust and sweat.

They hugged each other.

"My dear Ivan," Vili said.

"I heard you wanted to see me," the general replied. "I told my men to give you safe passage."

Vili thanked him, then looked around. When he was sure they were alone, he said, "Have you been above ground, Ivan? Have you seen our beautiful city? It would break your heart. Pest is a ruin. Even the Russians say it looks worse than Stalingrad. Our women are raped. Our homes are wrecked. Have you seen the Russians? They can't be beaten. They can't be kept out. Why don't you let it go ... Save Buda at least. Let's save the little we have left."

General Hindy said that he was a soldier and he no longer had a heart. Soldiers couldn't afford to — they had commands to obey. Buda would be defended stone by stone.

"And if everyone dies?"

"Even if not one person is left alive."

"But Ivan, don't you remember ...?"

"I have no memory of peacetime," Hindy said.

When Vili left the general in the middle of his makeshift office, he was still standing in the centre where they had hugged. There was no expression on his face. Only Vili was crying.

"You were really crying?" I asked him.

"Really."

"And what happened to Ivan Hindy?"

"He was hanged. And I didn't shed a tear."

35

COMRADE SIPNOVICH NEVER mentioned his first name. Most of the other teachers would write their full names on the blackboard, at least once, when they introduced themselves. Not Comrade Sipnovich. He insisted on reverence and formality.

He was small-framed, bald-headed, stoop-shouldered, pinched-faced, but he had a strong baritone voice that carried all the way down the corridors. He had endless projects for his class, each one more time-consuming than the last: placard-painting, newspaper-clipping, flag-carrying, proletarian song-practice, folk-dancing, slogan-searching. He insisted that our time at school be spent as usefully as possible, since we would be the standard-bearers for the Revolution once we graduated.

The Sneaks started because I wanted to know his whole name. I made up the name of the group on the spur of the moment. Klara Toth had been hanging around Alice and me for a while; she had decided to be friends with us. She was pale and soft and, she let everybody know, a member of the wrong social class. "My father was a count," she told me. "One day we'll get back our half of the city." When I told Vili that Klara's family used to own half of Budapest, he said, "Of course." Then he advised that I stay away from Klara. "She exaggerates in dangerous ways."

Alice and Annie and I and a couple of other girls were planning a raid on the boys' end of the school on a Saturday afternoon. Klara asked if she could join our team.

"You what?" Alice asked.

"I want to join," Klara repeated.

Because I was the biggest and because the raid on the boys had been my idea, all the others looked at me.

"Hmm," I said.

"Can I?" she pleaded.

I gave that some thought. "There is an initiation thing, of course," I said at last.

"All right. Whatever." Klara was eager to please.

"It's about Sipnovich."

"Comrade Sipnovich?"

"You have to find out his whole name," I told Klara, while all the others snickered. "That's the cost of entry."

Klara looked pained. She had a habit of knitting her eyebrows into a straight line, wrinkling her forehead and squinting at you. "And you all know it already?" she asked.

I didn't reply.

"Even the Chipmunk?"

Alice said, "Don't call me that."

Two days later Klara came back with the name "Adalbert."

"That's ridiculous," Annie said. "No one is called Adalbert."

"He is," Klara said defiantly.

We were having this conversation in the alleyway next to the Corvin department store because we were too scared to talk inside the school in case the walls had ears there as well as in our apartments.

We all pondered for a long time, because I had told Klara that finding out Sipnovich's name was the price of admission to our group, but we didn't really have a group — well, not formally anyway. Here she was saying his name was Adalbert, and we were saying we didn't believe her. In the end, Annie and I said we'd let her know.

That night Annie and I waited for Sipnovich after the final bell had sounded and followed him. He didn't make it easy. He walked fast, his feet pounding the pavement, his arms whipping up and down his sides. Very military. He marched past the Post Office and onto Lenin Avenue, past the Children's Hospital and onto a short street near Petőfi Bridge where Annie and I had never been.

Suddenly he marched down some steps and disappeared behind a barely lit door. We were so out of breath that it took us some moments to notice the neon light over the door. Angel Bar.

We waited for a while, but it was cold and I was worried about my grandmother and about Jinny's evening walk. Annie thought her father might get mad if she came home after he did. He worked in the automobile factory in Csepel, and sometimes he hit her.

The raid hadn't been too successful either, because some-one — maybe Klara — had warned the boys. There was a large posse of them waiting on their side of the divide between their school and ours. I was the first over and they jumped me right away, three on one, with Alice yelling "Not fair! Not fair!" and her little hands hitting their shoulders and backs. Then Annie whacked the big red-haired boy with her rock-like fist, and the others jumped all over the rest of the boys. It was just a brawl, no winners or losers. Annie con-soled us by saying that there had been more of them than us and that girls usually get a big growth spurt around the age of ten. And Alice said we'd have to deal with the snitch who told them we were coming.

A couple of days later we were ready for Sipnovich again.

This time we had made up a story about how we all had to stay late at school for some Young Communist volunteer work, and five of us followed Comrade Sipnovich to the Angel Bar. We tried to peer in through the windows, but it was too dark inside to see anything. Alice had borrowed her father's derby and an old jacket, but she was too short to look like a man; the jacket sleeves almost dragged on the ground when she walked.

So after about an hour's wait and no Sipnovich, I put on the jacket and hat and snuck in through the door after a man and a woman who were too occupied with each other to notice me. I waited for my eyes to adjust to the darkness inside.

It was not in the least like the places where Vili had taken me.

There was a strip of red lights over a long wooden bar, cigarette smog, the smell of liquor; the floor was sticky and there was soft, thumping music, people dancing close together and huddling around small tables. There was a woman in red suspenders with a patch of red cloth over her pubic region. She gyrated on a small round stage in the far corner. She was singing with a microphone close to her lips, her voice all breathy and full of sighs. As she undulated, her dark hair swishing over her naked shoulders, she snapped the red suspenders over her breasts, this way and that, the breasts popping out as the elastic passed over them. Her big brown nipples and bright red lips took turns brushing against the microphone. They made a whooshing sound.

Comrade Sipnovich sat at the bar, his jacket slung over the back of his stool, his sleeves rolled up, his face sweaty as he watched the woman on the stage. There was a bottle in front of him, and a glass. His head shone in the red light. His feet were thumping against the bar to the rhythm of the music and the snapping of the suspenders. I crept a little closer. He was grinning, something I had never seen before, his eyes glistening with delight, and he swayed with the music, saying, "Yes, yes, yes, yes."

Then the man behind the bar yelled, "Get that kid out of here!" and the last thing I heard as I leapt up the steps was the same voice yelling, "Adalbert, is that one of yours?"

We all ran back toward the school, laughing and hugging one another. Oh yes, his name was Adalbert, and he liked naked ladies and drank just like Annie's father and Vili's brother Béla.

The next day we worried that he might try to ferret out which of us had showed up in his bar, but he never even mentioned it; he was the same severe Comrade Sipnovich as always.

Klara had to be admitted to our newly formed group. We called ourselves the Sneaks, in honour of our sneaking up on our teacher, and we made up a secret handshake. Our password would be "Adalbert."

36

"YOUR MOTHER," Vili told me, "has divorced your father."

"So?" The mention of my father always made me nervous. Or hostile.

"Nothing," he said matter-of-factly. "I thought you ought to know."

Why, I thought, is he telling me this? Then, with growing panic, I asked, "You don't suppose she'll want to do it again, do you?" They were flitting through my mind: Benny, Jenő, Peter, Attila the quiet one, the man with the feather in his hat-band who clicked his heels, the former grocer who had brought pickles, the little Rooster from Penc ...

"Why should she?" he asked. "No point in being saddled with a man twice, is there?"

I agreed completely.

For my birthday, Vili had given me the book he wrote on the rules of duelling. It was called *The Duelling Codex*, and it set out everything you needed to know about the challenge, the choosing of seconds, acceptable ways to begin, the designated places to pierce your opponent, even the ways of conceding defeat and enjoying victory. It had been published in 1928.

I was eight years old and trying to improve my fencing

technique in the basement of the old Piarist school, where the priests weren't allowed to teach real school anymore, though they were allowed to pray as long as they didn't mention the government in their prayers.

My grandfather used to come and meet me at the end of fencing class on his way home from the button factory. Though he was up earlier than I was and he had been lifting heavy stuff all day, he showed no signs of tiredness. He bounced down the stairs, three at a time, not even holding onto the rail as I did, his patched leather gloves hanging out of his pocket, his light wool coat flapping open like a cape. He never bothered to button up, even on the coldest days. He hadn't bought working clothes for the factory. He wore his old suits. "What's the sense of saving them?" he'd remonstrate with my grandmother. "When all this is over, they'll be too old-fashioned to wear."

By "all this" he meant the communist government, but he was too careful to say that out loud.

I had noticed that he had become more careful around his friends in the coffeehouses. They had stopped saying "communists" and "Stalinists" and substituted "they" or "those," and while the jokes about the Five-Year Plan went on, they had stopped mentioning government people by name. "They" had made the mistake of naming a brand of cigarettes after the Plan, giving Vili a chance to laugh at it going up in smoke or not catching fire. Five-Year Plan cigarettes rarely lit on the first try.

Some of his friends had stopped coming to the coffeehouses in the evenings. The others would explain that they had gone for Socialist Re-education or to learn class solidarity in Poland or to the countryside to learn how chickens were fed. A close friend who had been a writer and teller of short humorous stories had disappeared.

When he listened to "thevoiceofamerica" on the radio, Vili said there would be more Five-Year Plans because the

Russians needed our wheat and barley and coal.

I had wondered why Vili was less careful in the Piarists' gym than in the coffeehouses. Perhaps he thought it unlikely that "they" would bug an old, musty-smelling, underground gym. Perhaps it was because this had been Vili's gym when he was a boy fresh up from the Bácska, a rich man's kid wanting to be as sophisticated as the city boys. I think he figured that nothing had changed down here. All our outfits were the same, the baggy black shorts, the white shirts, the older kids with the padded chest guards, the priest in his black cassock.

When Vili bounded in, the priest would salute with his épée and grin. Sometimes he asked Vili if there was time to go a quick round, just the two of them. Most of the time Vili obliged him. But not that night in late February 1951.

That night Vili told him it might be a while before he came back for me again. "The nights are getting darker," he told the priest.

The old Piarist nodded as if that made perfect sense. Then he asked Vili if he had heard the one about the gypsy taking lifesaving lessons.

This is the joke he told: It was the duty of all good citizens building this haven for Stalinist ideology to be both mentally and physically agile at all times. That meant, among other things, that everyone had to learn to swim. The gypsy did fine in the theory classes, aced his exam, did fine even in the People's Pool. No problem with his demonstrating how he would save drowning men — whacking them over the head to stop their struggling, grabbing them by the hair and towing them to shore. Then it was time to take to the Danube and show his stuff. "Imagine," said the comrade instructor, "you see Comrade Rákosi flailing about in the ice-cold water as you stroll over the Chain Bridge. What do you do?"

"Simple," said the gypsy. "I take off my clothes, I jump off the bridge, I swim swiftly towards him, I whack him on the head ... then I swim to shore."

As they carried him off in chains, the comrade instructor asked him why he had forgotten what he was taught.

"Well, sir," said the gypsy, "I could hardly drag him along by the hair if he had none, could I?"

Comrade Rákosi, as we all knew, was completely bald.

The Jesuit shook with delight at his own joke. Some of the kids giggled, others stood about looking worried or indecisive. The older ones knew already that it was bad politics to understand jokes about the government. Vili laughed so hard there were tears in his eyes.

The tears were still there when we boarded the streetcar. Then he reached into the upper inside pocket of his grey worsted jacket, carefully pulled out his grey-white handkerchief and threw it out the open door. We were alone in the back of the car, just the two of us. I saw the handkerchief become a pigeon and flap its wings, lifting itself over our heads and up onto the ledge of the Apothecary near Rókus Church, and I realized that he had done this one for me alone.

Then I laughed at the joke and at my amazing grandfather.

37

THERE WAS ALREADY SNOW on the ground, packed and frozen; the wind was whipping more snow off the roofs and whirling it around as we descended onto the platform in front of the Corvin department store. Vili's coat was flying about him; he held onto his hat with one hand, my hand with the other. We crossed the street and blew into the wind tunnel of the taller buildings, past the boarded-up windows of the former grocery store and into the calm of the long entryway of our apartment building.

Mrs. Nemeth was cleaning the iron gratings of the elevator. "Doctor Rácz," she greeted him. She always called him Doctor — a German habit, addressing lawyers as doctors. "It's a rotten night tonight." She seemed unusually devoted to her task.

My grandfather tipped his hat to her, as he had always done, and repeated what he had told the Jesuit: "The nights are getting darker, I think."

Then she did something even more unusual. "Would you like to stop by for a glass of wine?" she asked.

To the best of my knowledge, he had never stopped in there for a glass of anything. "Thank you, Mrs. Nemeth," he told her. "Perhaps another time."

We took the stairs up slowly, not two at a time like we usually did. He continued to hold my hand and talked about the changing times — I was rather puzzled by this, because I certainly hadn't noticed any change in the times, still school every day, getting the morning coal, helping my grandmother with the cooking, taking Jinny for her walks. He said the government was looking for more enemies of the State to prosecute, and now that they were through cleaning their own house, getting rid of the old-style idealists, they would be getting around to more people like us. "You have to be especially careful now," he told me.

"How?"

"With everything you say. Never tell anyone that joke about the gypsy for example. You do understand that?"

I said I wasn't stupid.

"And everyone you pick for a friend. That they should be *safe*, no one you cannot trust, and no one you think might betray you if the going gets rough."

I was thinking of the man who had been in our basement and how he had cried about his own friends. I was very sure Alice wouldn't tell about that, not even if they threatened to kill her. "On Andrássy Avenue, do they use stakes?" I asked Vili, because I wasn't sure Alice would keep silent if they stuck one of those through her body.

We climbed past the piano tuner's floor. Vili's face was grim even from beneath, his mouth tending downwards, his bottom lip chewing on his moustache, a slight tremor in the soft skin just under his jaw. "No," he said finally. "They don't use stakes anymore."

The door to our apartment was ajar.

My first thought was: It wasn't me this time, no chance my grandmother could give me hell for leaving the door open, risking that Jinny would disappear. "It's because you hate to walk her, you'd rather she was run over by a streetcar." As if Jinny would give up her endless succession of free meals.

In our kitchen there was a strange man with a green overcoat and a large handgun. He had been rummaging through the upper drawer of my grandmother's spice and vegetables sideboard. He stopped when he saw us and waved his gun at my grandfather. "You better go and sit with your wife," he commanded.

"What the hell do you want here?" Vili demanded, striding through the kitchen door. There was a sharp edge to his voice, a tone I hadn't heard since we were at Leah's bedside in the hospital after she'd been raped.

The man straightened quickly and pointed his gun at Vili's chest. "You!" he shouted. "You want to be a hero? You still think it's going to be swords at dawn? We don't play those games anymore, Comrade."

They stood facing each other a moment longer, then Vili turned his back on the gun and marched through the darkened hall with the bookcases and the dining table and into the livingroom, where my grandmother sat, very still, on the arm of her favourite chair, Jinny in her arms.

I followed close behind him, but stopped in the hall, where another stranger in a long brown coat was pulling our books off the shelves, dropping them in heaps on the floor at his feet.

Through the glass doors of the livingroom, I could see my grandmother's face. Her too-thin eyebrows slanted up toward each other, her forehead wrinkled upwards as if surprised, the darkness around her black eyes was deeper than usual. One hand absently stroked the dog's head. A tiny strand had escaped the tightly pinned roll of her hair. She was staring at me but seemed not to see me.

Leah and Kati were with Laci, now Leah's fourth husband, the one with red hair who had driven the motorcycle from Szombathely when my mother was in jail. My mother was still somewhere on the Hungarian plains, measuring them for railroad tracks.

The third stranger, a big woman wearing a grey pleated skirt and bulky brown sweater, stood over my grandmother. Neither of them moved when Vili approached. Then my

grandmother said, "It's a search, Vili." Her voice was too quiet
for the woman behind her, I thought, because she repeated
what my grandmother had said, much louder and with an
edge to her voice, as if she expected to be contradicted. It was
the voice András, the boys' school bully, used when he told
me he was stronger and tougher than I was and would be really glad to prove it any time, any place — my choice.

"You have the search warrant?" Vili asked her.

The woman shrugged. "It'll be here when we need it." The
edge in her voice.

"You can't search a person's home without a warrant," Vili
told her.

"Why, Mister Publisher, you have something to hide?" said
the woman.

He continued toward her.

"Leave it alone, Vili," whispered my grandmother.

Then the man in the hall stepped past me, his gun pointed at my grandfather's back. "Sit in that chair, Comrade
Rácz," he commanded.

My grandmother reached out the hand that was not holding Jinny and pulled at Vili's sleeve with such surprising force
that he dropped into the chair whose arm she perched on.
To my even greater surprise, he remained quiet while the
woman went into our bedroom and pulled the duvet off my
grandparents' bed.

The man resumed tossing our books onto the floor, shaking
each one as he went. When he reached the art books on the
top shelves, I told him to be careful because there was something very precious behind them. I was sorry as soon as I spoke,
but it was too late to take it back.

"Oh yes?" he asked cheerfully. "Let's see what we have
here, then. Comrade Berecz." The woman stopped ripping
up our pillowcases and joined him. She climbed onto a diningroom chair and began to hand him the books carefully.

"It's not the books," I said.

"It's not?" The man smiled at me. "Behind the books?"

"Yes, of course," I said before I heard Vili's thundering voice telling me to shut up. But it was too late; the man had pulled out the roll of dark blue velvet and was already shaking it and waving it from side to side like a wand.

"What have we here?" he asked.

"Nothing that would interest you, Sir," Vili told him.

I wanted to tell him this man wasn't a sir, he was a comrade, but I decided, too late, to be quiet.

"We'll see about that." The two of them then pulled the dogskin out of its velvet casing, rolled it out and stared at the big, colourful Rácz family lion brandishing its ancient yellow sword, its hind paws firmly planted on a mound of greenish earth.

"It's just a family crest," Vili said dismissively, as if that crest hadn't been one of the most important secrets we had ever shared, as if it hadn't been won in the battle of Nándorfehérvár by a Vilmos even braver than he was.

"We won it fighting the Turks," I said proudly. I still don't know what had come over me. "Defending Hungary. And the Sultan's army was huger than anything you can imagine, just thousands and thousands of turbans and hundreds of ships and catapults and everything, but we won anyway. That's why Vilmos got the crest the next day on the flagstones, from János Hunyadi himself, and he even got to marry the beautiful Klara, and it's real dogskin ..." I wanted to tell them the whole story, but the man who had unfurled the dogskin had begun to laugh.

"It's really dogskin?" he asked. He was looking over my head at my grandfather.

Vili nodded.

The man who had been ransacking the kitchen came and joined in the laughter. They looked at it this way and that, then dropped it onto the floor with the books.

The three of them spread out once more. They flicked all

of Vili's papers onto the floor and emptied all the drawers and all the closets. They pulled all the paintings off the walls and tore the beige paper backings off the ones that still had their backings. They even pulled the painting of Christ on the donkey out of its frame, though Vili had told me once that this was the original gilded frame that the first buyer put on it when he got it from Titian. They searched under the loosened floorboards under my bed where the cockroaches lived and through all my mother's clothes, including the old pink and white ball gown she had kept in mothballs and stuffed up over the bookcases. They opened my grandmother's medicine bottles and pulled out her jewellery box. They emptied all her rings and bracelets and chains onto the bare mattress — they had already removed the sheets and flung them onto the floor. They looked in all her shoes and tore her neatly arranged dresses off their hangers. One of the men opened up my bear's belly and poked his finger into its innards, and he took a knife to Lightning's old wound to peer inside, then tried to tear off his head but couldn't. Lightning was carved from one piece of wood.

My grandparents hadn't moved from their chair, and though I kept following the searchers from room to room, I never said another word. Not even when I saw the woman called Berecz drop one of my grandmother's rings into her pocket or when one of the men took my mother's new nylon stockings and stuffed them into his jacket.

The last words Comrade Berecz said to us were "We'll be back."

I didn't start to cry until after they were gone.

38

WE WERE EXTRAORDINARILY quiet after they left. My grandmother made tea. My grandfather looked over his papers. Neither of my grandparents talked about the search. The strange thing was, they didn't answer my questions. Around midnight Vili went out to phone my mother and Leah. Then we spent most of the night putting things back in their places. My grandmother was so anxious to create order again, she did not seem to mind that one of her rings was missing.

Vili replaced the ball gown, the family crest and all the books. He took the longest time over the books. He had his own system, not any alphabetical order that I could discern then or later, but he knew where each one belonged. From time to time he would call out to me and read a bit of this book or that, usually the Hungarian poems or a bit of a story, a description, a scene. A bit about the warring children in *The Boys of Paul Street*, a long poem by Schiller about a boy and his father riding through the storm. The long Petöfi poem that was first heard on the steps of the Pilvax Café on March 15, 1848, the poem that inspired the people of Budapest to rebel against the ruling Habsburgs and declare themselves to be an independent nation.

He began to weep when he came to the lines "Dare we be free or must we be slaves? That's the question, the choice is yours ...," as I imagined most people who first heard the words must have wept. March 15, 1848, had been a cold day of continuous rainfall. At first there had been umbrellas, then Mór Jókai, a novelist and one of Petöfi's friends, challenged the crowd to withstand the rain. "If you worry about being pelted by a bit of rain, what will you do when you're pelted by Austrian bullets?" he asked them. By afternoon there were more than ten thousand wet people in the streets, and when Petöfi read the demands of the people on the steps of City Hall, everyone was euphoric. Everyone, that is, except the Austrians, who could see that part of the lands they had nabbed might slip away.

Two years later Petöfi was killed in action at Segesvár. He was twenty-six years old, one of the greatest lyric poets in history. He had been tall and slender, pale; a lock of brown hair fell over his forehead. He had piercing blue eyes and small, restless hands. He wrote love poems to a girl of eighteen with black hair who may have loved him just as much but who was no lyric poet so no one will ever know.

Vili read me the long poem Petöfi had written to his love foretelling his own death. "If you should give your love to another, come, lay your widow's veil on my grave, and I will come back from my shadowy world to take it and hold it dear, as I will still love you then, as I have loved you always." I could see Petöfi reaching up through the earth, a long white arm grabbing the black cloth and rubbing it against his muddy, ghostly face.

My grandmother had come in and put her hand on Vili's shoulder. "At a time like this, you read poems," she scolded, but I could tell she thought it was somehow marvellous.

"Petöfi died at the hands of the Russian troops who had come to assist the Austrians against the Hungarians," Vili said. "He was buried in a mass grave with the rest of the fallen."

When I first read Shelley, years later in New Zealand, I thought of Petöfi. They had both been great poets; they both died young, almost the same age. Both had been romantics, both in love when they departed, but how sad it was for Shelley to have had no cause to die for, only a silly notion of his own indestructible body, a fragile sailboat, some Italian wine.

How much more fitting for a lyric poet to die a heroic death.

My mother came home on the dawn train. On the prairie all the other members of her team were of similarly questionable political stripe, and they agreed to pretend that she was still there.

It was still dark, though Jinny sat, implacable, near the door. My mother dropped her small suitcase, didn't say hello, didn't take off her coat, but ran straight to hug my grandmother, who was sitting on her bed. They sat holding hands for a while, then my mother and Vili went out for coffee.

My grandmother grumbled that she was going to be excluded once more and that she wasn't a child, but all the same, she seemed rather restored by my mother's presence. She went about her morning routine, tidying the bedroom, lighting the livingroom fire, hurrying me off to school.

"It would be as well if you didn't mention the search to anybody," she said, buttoning my coat. "People could jump to conclusions."

"About what?"

"About us." She was impatient.

"Why?"

"It doesn't matter why. It's better for you to keep quiet. That's all."

"What were they looking for?" I asked.

"Nothing," she said. "They wanted to frighten us."

I had a rotten day not telling Alice about the search. When Comrade Sipnovich showed me his newest acquisition of a Comrade Tito-Comrade Stalin photograph, I couldn't conjure up sufficient enthusiasm to think of the perfect place to hang it.

I now qualified for the senior Young Communists League. They had been keen to have me as a flag bearer because I was tall and strong. The League captain was twelve. That day she gathered all the League members in the school quad, read a rousing portion of Lenin's letter about the class struggle and invited me to join her on the podium, where she shook my hand and told me how proud they all were that I would now be one of them. Then she whacked me on the shoulder and gave me my new red kerchief. Despite it being ten below, all the League members stood around in only their white shirts, displaying their red kerchiefs.

I took off my coat, put on the shirt over my sweater, pulled the already-tied kerchief over my head and tightened it under the stiff white collar. We waited while the League leader said a few things about how lucky we were to be growing up in a people's proletarian republic and how we would be the pathfinders for generations to come. Then we sang a song about Liberty and watched one another's lips turn blue in the cold.

Alice, who had been jealous that I was asked to join ahead of her, now said she hoped she wouldn't have to join until spring when it was warmer.

When I went home, the whole family was there, including Aunt Leah and Kati. Everyone sat around the dining table, eating scrambled eggs and Debreceni sausages with mustard and radishes. The air was so thin with anxiety, I wasn't surprised when the doorbell rang and Comrade Berecz returned.

She looked around the room, her face expressionless. Still, I think she must have been surprised to see my brand new uniform, because her gaze stopped when it reached me. "Well, now," is all she said about it. Not much, but more than my family had said. Not even Kati had remarked on my transformation into a full-fledged Young Communist.

Comrade Berecz wore a leather jacket with a turned-up collar, and her hands were chapped from the cold. She was accompanied by a young man in a khaki uniform who looked very much like the men we had seen lounging about outside number 60 Andrássy Avenue. He stayed near the entrance to the diningroom, but his eyes travelled all around, checking each one of us, then all the furniture, pausing over the book- cases, the gold-framed mirror and the painting of Jesus on the donkey. Then Comrade Berecz approached my grandfa- ther, who sat eating a green onion at the head of the table.

"It's going quite well for your lordships," she said. "Not a whole lot has changed for some since the People's Revolution, has it?"

"There are six of us in these rooms, Miss," my grandfather said, "not counting the couple from Csepel who occupy the room with the balcony that used to be part of the apart- ment." I thought it odd that he called her Miss when he had never called anyone else that.

"Some people," she said, her voice higher than it had been before, "live ten to one room and always have. Some places in this city have no water and no heat. This" — her chapped hand indicated the whole apartment — "is a palace."

My mother stood suddenly and approached Comrade Berecz. "I assume, Comrade," she said, very calmly, "you haven't come all the way here on a night like this just to tell us that."

"Who are you?" Berecz enquired.

"Maria Rácz," my mother said, ignoring the fact that she had a married name that we shared. "And I live here with my daughter."

"Are you going to return my mother's nylons?" I asked, encouraged by her lack of fear.

"Leave it ...," my grandmother said.

"And my grandmother's ring?" I went on.

Comrade Berecz didn't even look at me. "Perhaps your lordships need to find out how others live in this country." And she handed Vili a brown envelope.

Vili didn't open it until they were gone. He pulled out a letter, read it and handed it to my mother. I think everyone already knew what it said, because they all resumed talking at once.

I slipped away to look for Alice.

39

MY MOTHER TRIED to make it seem like an adventure. For a while I'd live with Leah, then I'd join my grandparents in Solymár for the summer. I'd love Solymár; it was leafy and green, never as hot as Budapest in the summer and there was a swimming hole where I could learn how to swim. (I had given up the idea of swimming when I almost drowned in the Gellért pool the summer before.)

My grandparents left the day after Comrade Berecz handed them the envelope. The State gave only twenty-four hours' warning to those it wanted out of sight.

"The government thinks some of the people in Budapest should live in the countryside and some of the people in the countryside should live in the city," my mother said. "It will be fine for the grandparents to have some fresh air. It's healthy." But she looked utterly miserable.

Kati explained, "They think we are class enemies. Especially our grandfather, because he had property and owned magazines. Class enemies should stay away from the centre of power. Budapest is the centre. Simple." I hadn't noticed before how tall she had grown. Not much earlier she had seemed much like myself — a little older, but still belonging to our common childhood. Now she seemed to be part of the adult world, much taller and thinner than before. Her face had lengthened, her forehead had become higher, her neck longer; her dark brown hair was swept back, and she talked to me slowly, as if I'd suddenly become hard of hearing.

She carried no bears with her. She seemed much sadder than before. Even sadder than she had been around the dinner table of her third father.

"Will I have to go home with you?" I asked tentatively.

"I doubt it," Kati said. "She'll want to come and live here." She nodded her head towards her mother. "Never quite settled in with Laci. The Raven is still flitting about the edges and there is another one, he is a bouncer at a nightclub. Big, bulging muscles. Not her type, really, but she doesn't listen to me. Living here will give her a chance to test how she feels."

"And Laci?"

"He'll wait for as long as it takes her."

"Why does she bother getting married?" I asked.

Kati shrugged. "Search me."

"Do you like Laci?"

"I don't care about any of them," she said.

Leah and Kati moved into the apartment the night my grandparents left. Nothing changed in the place, not even in my grandparents' bedroom. There was a sense that they would be back and everything would be as before. But it wasn't.

Leah left early for work and she was home late in the evenings, often when one of her men was already waiting for her. The Raven came with his chauffeur and brought ice cream and *dobos* cakes, white carnations for hope and red roses for love. He was very patient. He sat in Vili's big chair and gazed into space as if he were blind. The bouncer never brought gifts. He did pushups or paced. He checked himself out in the hall mirror. Laci brought bread, apples, eggs when he could find them. He tried to teach Kati and me gin rummy, but Kati never wanted to play.

Sometimes all the men arrived at once. They waited a while. If Leah didn't arrive, the bouncer left first, then Laci. The Raven had the Party connections; he waited. If Leah arrived while they were all there, she would laugh at the scene of three men waiting, each in his own style. I don't think any of them thought it was funny.

Then she'd say it was a silly mix-up, she had planned to spend the night at home with us. But that wasn't very often.

"Men," Leah would tell me, "are so damnably predictable. Lovable and sweet and fun to be with, but so terribly easy to figure. A pity, that. They all bore me after a while." She'd sigh in her throaty way and stretch. "Not a surprise in the lot of them. You'll find out."

She would come home in her grey overalls, grease on her hands, and she would change into her short, light cotton dress, her much mended nylons and the teetery high heels, cinch in her waist with a wide belt and brush up her hair. She was as slender as she had ever been. She wore crimson lipstick and her nails were a matching red. On the weekends she'd have her hair done at the salon, and when she had extra money, she had her nails shaped by the former manicurist who lived on the fourth floor of our building.

Kati made sure I left for school on time. She was three years older and had started at a new technical school. She said she was lucky to get into that, never mind the school she had really wanted to attend. People like us didn't get into good schools and absolutely never made it to university.

We cooked our own dinners. We had both learned from our grandmother how to make potato and hard-boiled egg casserole, spinach and sour cream, noodle soup, fried bread, marrowbone soup, apple fritters and, once, even, sauerkraut with pork bits.

I still brought the coal up from the basement, but neither of us washed unless my mother came home. She would arrive late on a Saturday evening, brisk, fake-cheerful, and try to pretend nothing had changed, that we were the same without our grandparents in the apartment.

Jinny was so confused that she slept in my bed most of the

time. Kati and I took turns walking her. I went to the Piarists for my fencing lessons, though I was showing no improvement.

I wrote long soulful poems and sent them to Vili. Vili's absence was a nightmare that wouldn't end. The place felt empty, abandoned. Even the streets had changed. Though I tried to avoid the places we had been together, I would some-times come upon a café or a street bench and find myself looking for him and feeling bereft. Men in too-large over-coats came to the door, asked for him and left, sadly. The maître d' from the Emke caught up with me on the street one day and asked, "Aren't you the kid who follows around behind Vili Rácz? Is he ill? Is it worse? Jail? Displaced?" He was bent over, whispering in my ear. His moustache tickled.

Kati and I stopped playing our story-games. I let Alice beat me at war even though I was Rákóczi and everyone knew I should win.

I punched András in the face one day on my way home from school.

No one ever hit András.

He had been waiting for me at the entrance of the Sneaks' peeing alley, and he told me that he knew all about what we were up to in there and that he and his friends had all seen my bottom. He stood with his hands in his pockets, his head leaning my way. Of course, he never expected that anyone would dare to hit him.

He fell back against the wall and slid down with a thump, his hands scrabbling to emerge from his pockets. I jumped on his chest and held him down just long enough to yell, "If you stay out of my way, I'll not tell anyone you were beaten by a girl." He nodded his red head. I got off him and ran home.

The peace lasted a few weeks, but András couldn't help himself. He was a fighter. He brought his whole gang to our alley one night. Alice was the only one to escape unscathed. She had hidden in the Corvin's sock department till it was over. She told me, "I would have been no use. I'm the small-est. And you'd have had to protect me, making it even worse for you."

I had two black eyes, a torn ear and blue welts all over my arms. I told Kati I had run into the wall during gym class. "Try something a bit better on your mother," she advised. "How about you fell off the streetcar when you went to your fencing lesson. Or you lunged into the priest's sword." Kati had always thought my fencing lessons were silly.

Leah didn't notice.

Klara Toth's family was told to leave Budapest as well. They had been expecting this for weeks and picked a pig farm col-lective near Esztergom, where Mr. Toth's estates had been before they were confiscated. The peasants in the area knew them and liked them, she told us.

I think Klara was just eleven when she threw herself into the Danube at Esztergom and drowned.

Before the end of March, Kati and I went to Solymár.

40

THE HOUSE WAS SET way back from the road, covered in thick-branched creepers, overhanging oak trees, acacias, poison-berry bushes, needle-leafed evergreens, long-armed yews that grew over the small windows shutting out the light. At first the house seemed to be a giant, shapeless mound. It was damp and dark inside, the ceilings low, the heat coming only from the single wood-burning stove in the kitchen.

My great-aunt Ilonka had moved into this place after she divorced Vili's brother Béla. She did not like to be reminded of Béla or of the fact that she had inherited a whole family by marriage, none of whom were of much use to her. She was a big woman with yellow, dry, flyaway hair, sun-crisped skin, big chin, prominent nose, rough, brown hands with chipped square nails and a permanent stoop she said was due to her silliness when she was a girl. We never found out what that was, but we assumed she was referring to her brief marriage to one of the wild Rácz boys. Now she raised goats.

Vili told me to make sure Kati and I didn't call her "Aunt," didn't remind her of Béla and tried to be nice about the goats. We were to pick strawberries, make jam, milk goats, plant things and generally make ourselves useful.

Kati chose household chores, assuming it would be somewhat easier. It wasn't — the goats were. I rose before Ilonka's lone rooster announced the day and went with her to the goatshed. She taught me how to milk the four nanny goats, how to lay my face against their bellies and murmur to them to keep them calm, how to make sure they didn't kick over the bucket when they grew tired of me and how to keep them interested by whispering stories while I pulled on their teats. When the sun rose, I would take the herd out for the day, let them graze from place to place, ever watchful that they shouldn't wander far. There were fifteen goats in all, including the big ram, who tried to take over the herd from me at least twice a day by butting me with his curved horns and bellowing at me to get out of his way. Ilonka called him Táltos.

"That's the ancient word for magician," Vili explained. "When the churchmen made it impossible for the *táltos* to exist, they changed themselves into magic horses. That way they could still keep watch over their people. During the time of Géza, the last great tribal leader, the ancients still walked among us. Géza allowed his wife, Sarolt, to pray each day at her Christian convent; he had his son, Vajk, christened as Stephen, so that the kingdom would have the blessings of Rome. But Géza himself made sacrifices to his primordial gods. And the *táltos* still cured the sick and guided the old to the spirit world. Though he could command all his people as he wished, not even Géza assumed power over the *táltos*. They roamed the territory inside the Carpathian Mountains at will. Only when Stephen, heeding advice from the Papist monks, outlawed their ways, did the *táltos* vanish from our land."

"If they were so powerful, why didn't they stop him?"

Vili smiled. "I have wondered about that myself. Perhaps the priests had become more powerful than the *táltos*. And the priests were fighters, they carried broadswords under their tunics and many of them rode their horses all the way to the Holy Land to kill the followers of Mohammed, just because they belonged to another religion. In Spain they killed the Jews who wouldn't convert and even when they converted, they killed many of the converts, because they were Jews. The *táltos* didn't want to see their people hurt. They were not fighters, they were spirit guides."

"Why do spirit guides need to have little goats killed?"

"The goats weren't killed for the *táltos*, they were sacrificed to feed the Earth, a god of the ancients' religion. You fed the earth much the same way you feed people, and you cared for it, never scarring it, never taking more from it than it would willingly surrender. That's why our ancients didn't plough the fields, they allowed them to grow wild."

Some mornings Vili came with me and the goats. We walked behind them, letting them find the way. "They always know where to find the juiciest leaves, and they will lead you to water when you're thirsty." I don't know how Vili knew so much about goats, but he was right. They did.

Although the swimming hole was just a muddy little pool of water, no higher than my armpits, it was cooling on hot days. The goats and I took turns splashing about in the mud. Vili taught me how to use a burning match to make the black, blood-sucking leeches loose their grip on your body, how to climb trees all the way to their tops, how to arm wrestle, how to stare down an angry billygoat and make him recognize you always by placing your hand in front of his snout and letting him lick you for the salt. And, as always, he told stories.

I remember the one about the old *táltos* who served Taksony, Géza's father. When Taksony said that he desperately needed a son who was both valiant in battle and honest with his people, the *táltos* sacrificed a goat on a round stone on top of the mountain near Visegrad. Géza was born in seven months, on the seventh day after the waning of the moon.

He was beautiful and brave. He defeated boys twice his size, and by the time he was fifteen, he was known as the best warrior in the land. He could kill prey with a single arrow though he rode his horse faster than anyone, and he went farther into the Germans' territories than the older warriors of his tribe.

One day he came upon a poor woodsman near the outskirts of his father's regal encampment.

"Help me," said the woodsman, his back bent double under the weight he was carrying.

"Why should I?" asked Géza, too proud to dismount. "You're just a woodsman, and I'm the king's son."

"Because," said the woodsman, "if I don't have help soon, I will die here, with no one to bury my body, no one to make sure I reach the other side safely."

Géza started to ride away. He was only a few paces past the old man when the earth opened up in front of his horse's hoofs and the two of them fell into a deep crevice. "Help, Help!" shouted Géza.

"But there is no one here except me," the old woodsman said from above, "And I don't see why I should help you, when you wouldn't help me."

"I promise to help you, if you help me first," Géza said.

The old woodsman peered over the edge of the crevice and grinned. "And why should I believe you, son?" he asked.

"Because I'm the king's son," Géza said.

The old man shook his head.

"Because I am the bravest and best in the land."

The old man only shook his head.

"Because I give you my word," the boy said.

In that very moment the crevice filled up with sand, but so slowly and gently that the young prince rose, unharmed, horse and all, to level ground again.

"Well, now," the woodsman said. "My bundle is there and it hasn't become any lighter."

Géza dismounted his stallion ("Why do princes always ride stallions?" "It's just the way this story goes.") and picked up the bundle of sticks. He followed the old man for an hour till they reached his mud-brick home deep in the woods. Then the old man told Géza he should come back in the morning and help carry another load, which Géza did. And the next day and the next, till seven days had passed.

On the eighth day, instead of the old man and his bundle, Géza found the old *táltos*. He was dressed in his long feather gown, his wrists and neck jangling with ceremonial bones. "Young man," he said, "from this day forward, your fortunes will rise just as the moon rose each day you helped with my load, just as the sand rose in the crevice. And just as you assisted with my burden, I will assist you with yours."

The *táltos* kept his word. Géza became the greatest of kings, he signed the peace treaty with the Germans and the Byzantines, he conquered his enemies and helped his friends. He let the pope baptize him and his family at Passau to pacify the Europeans. But the old *táltos* stayed with Géza until his death. Some say even longer.

His son, Vajk, who had become Stephen, was crowned King of the Magyars on Christmas Day, 1000 A.D. Pope Sylvester sent him a crown of pinkish gold with a cross at its peak. No one noticed that his new stallion had the eyes of the old *táltos* and that he never left Stephen's side.

August 20, as most Hungarians know, is St. Stephen's Day. It's the oldest holy day in Hungary, so old and so ingrained that the communists didn't dare abolish it. Instead they renamed it "Festival of the New Bread," and later, "Constitution Day," and allowed everyone to continue celebrating Stephen.

When Jinny died at Solymár, we gave her a formal burial. We dug a hole deep enough for her to stand in, since she expected to stroll into the world of her short-legged ancestors, and we filled her grave with things we thought she would like for the journey: her plate, her collar, a few choice bits of food and the winter coat my grandmother had knitted for her. Vili said a few words at the grave to speed her on her way. Kati and I cried. My grandmother said it was better for Jinny to be dead than to have to endure one more day of Solymár — the damp, dark house, the back-breaking work in the vegetable garden, the goats, and Ilonka, who never had a civil word to say to anybody.

Ilonka's preferred way of communicating was a guttural "hrumph" for no and silence for yes. Even when she taught me how to milk the goats, it was a matter of trial and error, hrumphing and silence, plus a few well-aimed kicks by the goats, that did the trick.

"She was once a pretty girl," Vili said. "Béla wouldn't have married an ugly woman. The son of a rich landowner in Bácska, he had a choice of all the girls. In those days the best a girl could hope for was to marry well. Girls had little education. Maybe they played the piano. They took dancing lessons and conversational French and German to attract a better class of man. Men were expected to provide, women to stay beautiful. You," he said once again, looking at me seriously, examining my face, "must have education."

"So what happened to Ilonka?" I asked him.

"It was the war," he told me. "Not the beginning, but later, when the Russians came. There were armies ranged over these hills, Germans blowing up houses, bridges, taking the livestock, carrying whatever they could on their backs. And then the Russians came."

Béla had purchased the house and the livestock from a peasant family who had decided to try their luck in America. He had chosen this spot for Ilonka because he imagined it was remote, not only from the troubles of war but also from his planned philanderings. His chauffeur brought Ilonka and her mother here after Béla remonstrated that the old lady couldn't endure the coming bombardment of the city. She was eighty years old, after all, and it was October 1944. The Germans were losing the war, and the Russians were moving fast towards Budapest.

As it happened, Béla never spent a single night under this roof. Instead he took his chances in Buda, where he had a villa, some provisions and a mistress who tucked him in on the sofa when he was too drunk to drag himself to bed.

The Russians arrived and holed up at this house and the other small farms that were not already destroyed while their high command planned the attack on Budapest. Ilonka and her mother stayed.

There was an officer with the men. He was a Marxist ideologue; he believed in the great Communist Manifesto, though Stalin had already imprisoned so many in the Gulag and more comrades were disappearing. Some say they went by the hundreds of thousands. In Russia they didn't even bother with show trials any longer; men, women, whole families vanished into the wilderness of anonymous camps where they perished. But the young officer hadn't changed his views, even when Stalin let the Ukraine starve and some eight or nine million peasants died. Who could keep count? Why would you bother? The young officer believed all the killing was for a great cause, one worth dying for. Great, sweeping change cannot take place without pain, he told Ilonka, and Russians had endured so much pain under the czars, what was another few years of agony if the next generation would inherit a brand new world full of justice and bread for all?

All the rooms in the house were occupied by his men, three or four to a bed, many more on the floor, except for the little bedroom I now shared with Kati. Ilonka and her mother had slept there.

In the evenings Ilonka sat in her kitchen with the young officer and they discussed in German and French the politics of greed and of the redistribution of wealth. Sometimes she played the piano for him. He was from a village near Stalingrad, he had never had a piano and he was enchanted. He told her about Papa Stalin, the fearless Georgian, and about the patron saint of the Revolution, Vladimir Ilyich Lenin.

The cook and the maid had fled when the Russians came, but Ilonka knew a bit about cooking and she made vegetable stew and bean soup in the enormous cauldrons the Russians had brought with them. When they ran out of pork and goats, the men machine-gunned the chickens, and they ate chicken. They emptied the larder and ate all the pork fat the Germans hadn't taken, and Ilonka made flat bread using a peasant recipe she got from a woman in the village. She showed the Russians the underground cellar where she kept the wine, and they drank it. One day when they were hungry, they shot the cow and ate it.

The young officer was called up to Újpest on Christmas Day. The siege of Budapest was beginning.

The men left behind in the house made a fire with the furniture. They took Ilonka's mother into the stable, sure that she'd tell them where the jewels had been hidden. They gave her an hour or two to show them, and when she didn't, they shot her. Then they all raped Ilonka before they joined the rest of the men in the siege of Budapest.

The young officer never returned.

4 I

I TIED LITTLE BELLS around the goats' necks so I could hear where they went. There was a narrow stream where they liked to play. The young ones would leap from side to side or chase each other or practise headbutting. The boys had tiny, itchy horn-buds on their heads that they liked me to scratch. Sometimes we played hide and seek. Usually I hid and they had to find me. The bells made it difficult for them to hide effectively. Once a day I would take them down to the salt lick near the swimming hole. Táltos stood guard, sniffing the air, grunting when he thought he smelled something out of the ordinary or someone coming.

Sometimes I heard a wild boar scuffling in the under-brush, but I never saw one. That's what I thought was lurking near the swimming hole one day when Táltos snorted and shook his head to warn me.

I told him to relax and went back to my thrashing, trying to lift my feet out of the mud while my arms flailed about in what I imagined looked like swimming. The next thing I knew, there was a huge splash and a pair of brown feet disappeared underwater.

A second later there was a head: brown face, curly, black hair, black button eyes, a big grin, white teeth, arms slapping the water. "Hello, how are you, a nice cool bit of water on such a hot day, and you're taking it easy with the goats, no sign of the old lady comes here with them mostly, good for you," he said in a breathless stream.

"Hello," I said and found I was already grinning to match his grin.

"I'm Rori, we're here in the wagons not far from here, and I've been watching you in the woods these past few days, wondering when you'd notice, but you never did, so I decided to come and talk to you anyway. Nice day." He had a soft lilting way of speaking that made most of what he said sound tentative, like a series of questions.

"You know Ilonka?" I asked him.

"Ilonka? Is that her name, well, nice name for a grouchy old lady, never thought she'd even bother with a name, that one, she's like a big rock, all edges and sharp, never get close, she'd hurt you all over, but my mother says the old lady's alright, only I'm to keep well out of her way, some just don't like to have people around. How come she let you stay? Where is your own mother? Don't you have a mother of your own?" He plonked himself onto a bit of muddy grass. He had thin wiry arms and legs, but big shoulders for such a small boy. He wore a pair of white underpants held up by a string. I thought he was about the same age as I was. There were tiny wrinkles from his nostrils to the corners of his mouth, slightly paler than his brown skin.

I told him my grandparents weren't allowed to stay in Budapest any more and that I did have a mother, but she was busy building roads on the prairies and that I had to stay where my grandparents were because my Aunt Leah didn't know how to take care of her own daughter, never mind someone else's.

"So she took you in, the old lady? Can't be as bad as the devil, then, can she? And the gent with the white moustache and the little lady who feeds the pigeons, she took them in, too? They are your grandparents? He reads a lot. Saw him trying to pick potatoes. Not too good at it. Does great stuff with cards. Never seen a white man do tops and balls so well. And he was doing some magic with a pigeon. Is he a magician?"

"Sometimes. He is also a great swordsman, and a publisher, and he ..."

"And the other kid?"

"That's my cousin Kati," I said. "Leah's her mother. She drives huge trucks and has lots of boyfriends. She is very pretty."

"Kati is very pretty, too, she picked strawberries near our place, kept whining about the work and the bugs, doesn't like it here much, does she?"

"We liked it better in Budapest," I said.

"Wouldn't if you knew this place better, we've been here for most of a year, longer than we usually stay in a place, and I love it, so do my mother and all my sisters, maybe you could come and make new friends? Can you bring her along?"

"Kati?" I asked, though it was obvious he meant her. "I could ask."

"When you put the goats in, sundown? I'll show you where we are. I'll see you near the big oak tree by the root cellar where *she* keeps her curdled milk and tubers." He hitched up his wet pants and took off through the woods before I even had a chance to say yes.

Rori was hanging upside down from one of the higher branches of the oak tree when we met him at dusk. He was still barefoot, wearing only the dirty white underpants and a gold earring. When he landed on his feet next to us, the top of his head came to about Kati's shoulder.

"You're even prettier than you were when I saw you with the berries, and what were you mumbling? You seemed so angry, and going on about Turks, no Turks hereabouts I ever seen, have you?"

She was staring at him. "Turks?"

I was really thrilled that Kati was playing one of our old games, though she kept telling me she was too old for those kinds of story-games now.

"Yeah, Turks."

She gave me a sidelong glance to let me know she'd hurt me if I told him, but I did anyway, and he laughed while she stomped on my foot. He had taken her by the hand and was leading her through the woods already, otherwise I think she might have killed me then and there.

It was a hot, hazy evening, buzzing with mosquitoes and grasshoppers, the sky still dark pink from the sun, the smell of white umbrella flowers, moss, branches whipping against our bare legs as we threaded our way around the trees and out onto a clearing close to the road where the bus stopped twice a day.

There were three fires, two big two-pole tents, horses, covered wagons, some tables and chairs close to the fires, and people milling around and talking. Something that smelled like roast pork was spinning over one of the fires, though it had been so long since we'd eaten roast pork, I couldn't be sure. There was some tinkling music and a great deal of loud talk. They stopped and we all stared at one another. Even the dogs raised their heads and stared.

All the women were dressed in long, layered skirts and sparkling shawls and had jewels shaped like big round coins hanging over their foreheads, around their necks and from their ears.

Rori was still pulling Kati by the hand, and I followed closely behind them. "Here," he called to them. "Come, meet my new friends."

They smiled and nodded and went back to what they had been doing, except for one woman who told us to come sit with her. "It's my mom," Rori said. "She is a real witch."

The coins dangling from her red and blue shawl caught slivers of light from the fires, sparkled and danced around her forehead. There were rings on all of her fingers. "I'm not really a witch," she said. "I'm a soothsayer. Know what that is?"

I shook my head.

"I tell the truth of things. Who you are and what you're thinking, your very own constellation."

"That means your stars," Rori explained.

"My stars?"

"Your own stars and what they say to you when you're not even listening." Her lips were soft and shiny; they quivered when she talked.

"We have to go now," Kati said firmly. She had pulled her hand away from Rori's. "They'll be looking for us."

"Don't you want to know about your stars?" Rori pleaded with her.

"No," Kati said firmly. "I don't."

Rori's mother nodded. "Maybe you'd like to come back another time, then." She was looking at me rather than Kati. "I could read your fortune in your hands. And in your cards."

"The old gentleman would like to come, too?" Rori asked. "It's not expensive, only one forint for each of you, never know how lucky you are till you find out. We have a big festival and people come from all over. And tomorrow, if you like, I could show you the Devil's Hole, we'll take the goats, give them something to do, they get bored, too, the goats."

"Will you show the young ladies the way home," his mother said.

HE WAS DISAPPOINTED that Kati wouldn't come along but we set out for Devil's Hole, anyway.

There was no path up the mountain, at least none that I could see. "This is called Rocky Mountain," Rori said, "and his cave is way older than even your grandpa." Rori said he could lead us to it directly, but that would be bad luck for us and no fun for the goats.

"My mother says you never walk straight into the home of the ancient ones, they don't want you to come if you don't know the rules and might even offend them, never ever offend the dead, you know, least of all the dead who have magic. They lived here back when everyone was a Traveller, hunting and picking, never in one place for long, like us."

Rori would leap ahead, disappear and reappear or whistle to let me know where he had gone — two notes, one low, one high. The goats seemed to know to follow.

He didn't mind or even seem to notice the stinging nettle that grew in big, aggressive bushes or the thorny plants with purple flowers that I had learned to avoid. But he stopped to give wide berth to a big oily black bird that cawed at us. "*Kalo chiriclo,*" he said, bowing to the bird. "Never cross a raven, they can bring bad luck, and not only for you, for your whole family, even your friends, and they can follow you and make your shadow grow shorter and put the sleep on you day and night, don't you know anything?" He picked up a couple of twigs and laid them down crosswise, then stepped over them. He told me to do the same.

When we reached the cave, I was surprised to see a sign confirming that it was the Devil's Hole. "Other people come here?" I asked him.

"Some," he said. "But you mustn't unless you know what you're doing. The ancient ones used to hunt the bear, the big flying dragon, didn't you know?"

Rori had a talk with Táltos, holding him by the ears and whispering, while he rubbed the whiskers under his chin. "The goats won't go away now," he promised.

I could hardly wait to see inside.

He flattened himself against the scrubby outside walls of the cave, approaching the mouth sideways, entering bent over, even though there was plenty of room to walk upright. "It's the only safe way in," he instructed. "Shows respect."

We descended into the belly of the mountain. It was damp and dark, but Rori had brought a candle. The walls were slimy. Strange rock figures oozing green and yellow appeared out of the darkness; some were short with blunt, washed out faces, others had pointy heads and stretched upwards, some dropped from the ceiling and hung motionless, dripping onto still others that seemed to grow while I watched. When Rori held up the candle, the whole cave seemed to change to white and orange.

"There," Rori said and pointed to the wall next to me. We were now deep in the cave. His voice echoed back and forth among the long shapes.

There were brown drawings on the wall — a standing bear, an antlered deer, a thing with wings, an arrow, stick figures.

"Did you make these?" I whispered.

Rori was poking the slimy earth under our feet. "Don't be silly," he said, echoing in and out of the cave, "It's the ancient people, their totems for protection, they were smart, not like some today." He took something from his pocket, dropped it into the thin well he had dug, covered it with his hand. Then he scratched some mud over it. "You got to give them your own gift, now," he told me. "Don't worry, I won't watch."

"My what?"

"You brought a gift, didn't you?"

"Why the hell would I have brought a gift?" I asked. I was shivering. The darkness, the gleaming walls, the drawings, the echo had made everything he said seem real.

He shrugged. "Might have to give them what you have in your pocket, then," he advised.

The only thing in my pocket was a tiny silver locket I had found in one of Ilonka's sewing baskets. I had been meaning to return it once I showed it to Vili and found out who the pretty young man with the black moustache in the oval photograph was.

Very reluctantly, I dug a hole with my fingers and laid the locket into it.

"Cover it up," Rori whispered.

I scratched some mud over it, just like I had seen him do.

He said something to the walls, then listened. He went on much louder: "Isn't this the greatest place? Don't you think they have the best home, better than the palace over the other side of the mountain and not nearly as cold, cozy in the winter, cool in the summer, wise they were to pick it for themselves, not that I'm jealous, it's their place not ours, it makes ours look so poor ..." He kept that up all the way back to the top, then he bowed towards the darkness and told me to do the same.

"Why did you say all that?" I asked. "It was cold and wet and ..."

"Shush," he interrupted, laying his dirty hand over my lips. "Never, ever insult your hosts, especially if they are on the other side. Got to treat them with respect, tell them their place is perfect and better than yours, you wouldn't want them to come and visit yours, now, would you?"

When I got home at dusk with the goats, I was still cold from the breath of the cave. Vili was waiting for me at the shed. He was in shirtsleeves, leaning against the door frame, cleaning his teeth with a long blade of grass.

"You make a pretty sight," he said, not looking up. "I hear you took the goats on a fine excursion."

Kati had ratted on me.

He helped me put the goats into their places, took the bells off and waited while I washed them down.

I told Vili all about the cave and what Rori had said about the people who used to live there. I told him how Rori was thanking them for their hospitality and about his little rituals outside and inside.

"His people call themselves the Rom," he told me. "Some say they have been travelling since before the time of Christ. From somewhere in India, maybe Rajasthan. Nomads, living from day to day by their music and their dance. They play wonderful violin, make things with their hands. A few of them can talk with animals; they used to take good care of horses. My grandfather hired gypsies to look after his pregnant mares. They knew when a mare felt her time for giving birth was near. She told them."

I asked why Rori had been afraid of the raven.

"Black birds can be terrible luck," Vili said. "Attila saw a raven the night he died. It hovered over his hide tent, its wings outstretched. When Attila's men tried to scare it off, it landed on a nearby tree and cawed at them. One of the young men put a fresh birch arrow in his bow and shot the bird for having the temerity to cast its shadow on the great one's tent. That night, Attila died in his sleep."

"Black birds were good luck for Hunyadi."

"Sometimes."

I think Vili was proud that I'd gone up Rocky Mountain. It fitted with his idea of my being insanely brave. "A true Rácz is virtually unafraid. That's our great strength. We cannot be intimidated. We are of the warrior class."

I felt a little guilty about the locket, but Vili said he knew how to get it back.

43

VILI DRESSED FOR THE OCCASION as he had dressed for our strolls along the Boulevard or for the old city coffee-houses. He wore his white shirt, grey suit, blue striped tie and grey-brown hat. It was Saturday afternoon, and he pretended we were on our way to visit family members by bus. At least that's what I think he pretended, because my grandmother said to give them her love, and I'm sure she wouldn't have been so affectionate toward the gypsies.

"Did you tell her a lie?" I asked him.

"Not exactly. I was somewhat economical with the truth. When she said you should try to see Gyula's daughter and grandchildren when you are in Budapest, I agreed that I would. Of course, we are not going to Budapest now. When we do, we'll be sure to visit them." With that, he considered the subject closed.

Gyula was Vili's middle brother. Vili barely mentioned him. My mother said there had once been a dispute between them about the Turkish baths they had bought in Buda.

We walked along the dirt road, not through the forest where Rori had taken us the first night. As usual, Vili led. He clasped his hands behind his back, pulled his hat down deep on his forehead to keep out the sun. The back vents of his jacket flapped open with each long step. The insides of the vents were frayed and mended, as were his elbows, where my grandmother had sewn square patches that blended in perfectly with the grey wool.

It had been a warm sunny day, swallows swooping over the fields of cut hay, the first big crop of the year. There were men making haystacks, women bent over long rows of potato beds. On the thatched roof of a whitewashed peasant house, a young stork tested its wings. We were passed by a horse and cart carrying corn to market. The driver tipped his hat to my grandfather, who waved. "Pretty day," they told each other.

The caravan was close to the road under a couple of broad-leafed chestnut trees. There were two wagons, unhitched, the horses grazing nearby. Something that smelled of burned hair was cooking over the wood fire. They had made benches with bricks and boards for a group of village folk who were watching a couple of men juggle bottles. A woman in a red bra and matching panties, kerchiefs hanging from her waist, was dancing around the jugglers, clapping her hands and hopping into the air making the bells ring around her wrists and ankles. The men wore black pants and white shirts open to the waist with no shoes.

There was a green table close by one of the wagons with a sign that said "Fortunes told."

"Is this the boy who knows about the caves?" my grandfather asked as Rori ran toward us, arms outstretched as if to hug us both. He stopped just short of leaping on my grandfather.

"It's Rori," I said.

"Great, great, great, you came," he shouted. "Want to see the jugglers? The dancing has just started. Look, that's my sister coming up now with the tambourine, and my brother is playing, he's the best on the violin here, maybe in the whole world, only a forint to see the show …"

Vili gave him the forint and we sat down among the village folk.

There were long swirling strips of iridescent colour as the girls danced and turned fast, this way then that, their arms swishing though the air, their black hair flying, their hands clapping, bells jangling. One girl beat a tambourine with her hand and snapped it against her hips as she danced. Two of the men played fiddles and another weaved in and out of the crowd of women, stamping his feet and clapping to the rhythm. All the men were shouting or singing.

My grandfather started clapping in time with the music. When the other people joined in, a young man leaped out of the covered wagon. He held two long, black sticks, one in each hand. As he danced past the fire, he thrust the ends of the sticks into the flames, lifted them, burning, over his head, then leaned back so far I thought he would fall. Slowly, his hips gyrating to the rhythm, he lifted his arm high over his head, angled the flaming end of one stick toward his face, opened his mouth and pushed the flames inside. There was a big "OOOhhh" from all around me as everyone leaned further in to see what would happen next.

He did the same thing with the other burning stick while rubbing the first one, still alight, over his bare chest. When he straightened up, the music stopped and everyone took a bow.

"The best forint I ever spent," Vili said. He was still clapping, his big hands making more noise than anyone else's.

Rori was already tugging at his elbow. "Come, come, it's not over, there is a fair with things to buy, or you might just look, you don't have to buy, and you will want to have your fortune read? Here is my mother and it's only one forint more, didn't she tell you?" He was directing us toward the green cloth-covered table where the cards had been laid out. His mother sat there, a little apart from the others. She wore the same blouse and skirt she had worn the last time I saw her, but now there was a black and orange shawl over her shoulders and her hair was swept back into a bun. Her hands were laid flat over the table on either side of the deck of cards.

"*Sarishan,*" my grandfather said, lifting his hat the way he did for ladies on Váci Street.

Rori's mother smiled at him. "*Sarishan.*"

"You must be the soothsayer," Vili said. "Or are you a witch?"

"Perhaps I'm both," she replied. Her lips formed the words slowly, shaping them, her hands stroking the table. "And you," she asked. "Are you the magician?"

Vili laughed. "Not one of the great ones," he said. "Your boy's been spying on me."

"What can you do?" she asked.

He reached into his pocket and took out a deck of his own cards. He fanned them out in front of her. "Pick one." He gave her the deck. "Now hide the card, don't tell me anything. Don't even look at me." She shuffled the deck and handed it back. Vili shuffled it some more, then he held it up toward her, palm up. "The six of hearts," he said.

"That's great, great," she said, her voice lightening. "Can you do one more?"

"And you will read my fortune for free?"

She nodded.

A few people gathered to watch. Vili loved an audience. He pulled up his jacket sleeves, showed he was hiding nothing and stared at the table with exaggerated attention.

He reached under the table, lifted it by one leg, completely still, over his head, turned around with it and put it down again. All the time, he was telling her not to worry about her cards, he would replace them with his own if they slipped off. They didn't slip off. When he put the table down again, they had disappeared. In their place there was a tiny grey mouse, crouching low under Vili's hand. It jumped off the table when he let it go.

For a second we all watched in silence. Then Rori's mother started to rise, and Vili reached out to keep her still.

"I need my cards," she said.

"These?" Vili asked, all feigned innocence as he pulled cards from the folds of her skirt.

"Wonderful!" she exclaimed.

Rori was hopping up and down, shouting that my grandfather was a master, the greatest, and begging him to do just one more.

"After you," Vili told the boy's mother. More people had come over from the performers.

Rori's mother laid her cards on the table face down and asked Vili to cut the deck in three places. When he was done, she turned up the first card from the middle deck. "This is your card," she told him. "The Knight of Pentacles. It's a lucky card, it has lots of dimensions, it can change things into new shapes, it can invent who it wants to be." She then turned the left deck over and laid another card in front of my grandfather. "This is where you come from," she told him. "The Seven of Staves. You've been a fighter, a soldier, no one has doubted your strength." She laid the top card from the third pile over the Knight of Pentacles. "This is where you're headed." It was a nine. It showed a figure sitting up in bed, his face in his hands. Above him there was darkness, and in front of him nine swords stood side by side all the way to the top of the card.

Quickly she laid out all the cards from the right-hand pile in a line facing my grandfather and studied them.

"Well?" Vili asked. "What do you see?"

She gathered up the cards, shuffled them and asked him to cut them again. She laid each of the three sections side by side facing our way. The middle card this time was the King of Swords and to his left there was a seven that she said was the Seven of Pentacles. He was leaning on a stave, gazing at seven circles with five-point stars inside them. "This crosses you," she said, picking up the card on the right and laying it over the King of Swords. "It's the card of Judgement."

Rori let out a sigh.

"And here is the Moon, and the Wheel of Fortune. It can still go either way, though you should not cross the paths of strangers, and stay clear of men in grey. Leave food on the table for birds, but beware of the crow, he may bring news you don't want."

"And this card?" Vili asked, pointing to the last one she had turned up. It showed a blindfolded figure, bound with white rope, surrounded by swords that had been stuck into the ground around him.

Rori's mother looked up at Vili with such sadness that everyone must have known it was a really bad card. But Vili, never easily intimidated, pressed on. "What does it mean?" He wanted to know.

"It means you should stay out of closed spaces."

"Like a gypsy?" Vili asked, still smiling.

"Yes. Just like a gypsy. Yes. That might be the thing to do," she said enthusiastically. "Come with us for a while. People will pay to see your magic. No one would think anything of it ..."

Vili was laughing now. "A wonderful idea. Much better than picking peaches. Trouble is, I have a big family." He stood up and thanked her both for the fortune and for the invitation.

"One last trick! A last one! You promised." Rori was jumping up and down again and shouting his little question-like requests.

Vili bent over the boy. "Okay," he whispered. "But this one is only for you. It'll be our secret. Agreed?"

Rori nodded vigorously.

"You know the magic words?" Vili asked.

Rori looked at his mother.

"Not magic words," Vili whispered. "Magicians' words."

"Abracadabra?"

"Shssh ...," Vili said. "Our secret, remember? On my command, you say the magician's magic words, and I will make something appear. It'll be old and precious, and it'll be your gift to my granddaughter. Well?"

We waited.

"How can I give her something I don't have? I have nothing that's old and precious," Rori protested.

"It's magic. Do you want to see it or don't you?" Vili whispered.

Rori nodded.

"Okay, then," Vili said. "The command: One, two, three, I will you to be. Now, you."

"Abracadabra?" Rori asked.

Vili reached into Rori's mop of black hair and, with a flourish, pulled out the silver locket I had buried in the cave. He dangled it for a moment for everyone to see, then laid it into my hand. "A very nice gift, indeed," he said. "Don't you think?"

"Oh," Rori said. "Oh." He sounded very disappointed.

His mother followed us to the road. "You're in danger, you know," she told Vili. When he didn't reply, she turned to me. "He is some man, your grandfather," she said. "Some man." She held his hand longer than I thought necessary for a simple goodbye.

He patted her arm. "*Kushto bokht.*"

"And for you too," she said.

She called after us, "Girl, one piece of advice for you, it's free."

We stopped and turned around. "Never, ever wear green."

44

"HOW DID YOU KNOW Rori had the locket?" I asked him on the way back from the gypsy camp.

Vili shrugged. "A lucky guess."

"What did you say to her?"

"I wished her luck."

"In Gypsy?"

"I learned a few words during the war. There were gypsies in Penc, near our farm, where that orchard of cherry trees grew.

"The Arrow Cross had been rounding up gypsies. They were going to have them killed. All of them. They called them vermin. I let them stay in the barn with the horses. When the Arrow Cross came, the gypsies hid under their hoofs in the stalls and the horses never made a sound."

"They survived?"

"Only five of them. The rest wouldn't stay. They hated being indoors."

Vili didn't notice the crow that had flown over his head while he talked, nor did he seem to hear its wild screeching and shouting when it landed on a low willow branch and all but disappeared from view among the thick leaves. I laid a couple of twigs down crosswise, but it was too late.

Two days later, on a warm summer evening, a group of men in grey uniforms marched into Ilonka's kitchen and arrested my grandfather. They manacled his wrists together and pushed him into the back of a truck where other grey men waited. They gave him no time to pack his clothes or even to say goodbye.

Though I buried the green sweater my mother had given me and threw away my green winter scarf, I wouldn't see Vili again for almost two years.

45

AT FIRST, THE CHARGE was going to be espionage, then it was changed to speculating in gold. He was kept at the State Security headquarters at 60 Andrássy Avenue while they decided what his crimes would be. *Szabad Nép* ran a story about the conspiracy to trade in gold, an illegal commodity, the source of the gold being an American industrialist. The people's paper was recommending the maximum penalty of five years.

His co-accused was a thin-faced man I had seen once in the Emke. He had been a terrible chess player, but Vili said it wasn't important to be a good player to enjoy the game. You just had to get used to not winning. *Szabad Nép* said that the man had already confessed and agreed to testify. They were waiting for Vilmos Rácz to do the same.

I pictured Vili in a dark cell behind the yellow facade of that pillared building. I imagined him being questioned by the lounging young men, his arms bound tight behind his back because they were afraid of his strength, piercing lights aimed at his eyes, shouted questions, freezing water thrown in his face if he tried to sleep.

During the night I thought of Vili not sleeping. I forced my thoughts away from their beating and starving him and maybe laughing at him the way they had been laughing at some shared joke that day we saw them. I imagined him with fingers like those of the man Alice and I had found in the basement. I grew afraid of the dark.

Every day I imagined how I would rescue him, but Lightning had lost his powers. I tried slicing my finger and letting the blood pour onto the parched earth, but the *táltos* of the ancients wouldn't come when I called. I went to the gypsy campsite to ask Rori's mother if she could cast a spell that would protect him, but they had already gone. There was nothing left of their magic but burned-out fires, horse manure, grass flattened where they had sat.

My grandmother wept. She would walk around Ilonka's strawberry patch, slowly making her way down to the last fruit tree, and she would stand there for hours, alone, even during the rain and after sunset, as if she expected him to reappear through the strawberry patch. When Kati and I talked to her, she didn't hear us. She stopped pinning her hair around her head; she didn't even brush it in the mornings. Despite the intense late-summer heat, she wore a heavy scarf over her shoulders. In the evenings she crawled into her side of the narrow bed and stared at the ceiling. She seemed exceedingly small.

I wrote short tragic poems and placed them in a cardboard box for Vili.

Ilonka went about her chores as if nothing had happened, as if in her world people came and went but nothing changed.

About a week after they took Vili, my mother arrived. She said we would all go back to Rákóczi Street on the train. Now that they had Vili, the rest of the family wouldn't count. She packed my grandparents' things into their brown suitcases, whisked their soap and toothbrushes into paper bags, cushioned their framed photographs among their clothes. My grandmother insisted on packing Vili's shirts herself. She laid them on the bed on their backs, one after the other, their arms flattened out, then folded them at the shoulders, the sleeves down straight, turned them and folded them into small packages with their collars up, their buttons down the front.

All the way to Budapest my mother tried to coax my grand-mother to talk, but all she would say was that there was no need to worry about her, we should, instead, think of a way to bring Vili back to her. She held her hands together in her lap, soft, motionless. She had buttoned her brown overcoat all the way to her throat. For the first time that I could remember, she didn't wear her stockings. "Therese," Vili used to tease her, "those stockings have been mended so often, you'd be more of a lady if you painted your legs like your daughters do. You still have the prettiest legs of them all."

She had always seemed shocked at the suggestion. In her world, a woman was not fully dressed without her stockings.

My mother had found a lawyer, she told us, but there was no sense in hoping there would be an effective defense. The People's Republic of Hungary wanted Vili Rácz in jail.

Leah came home and offered to return to the Raven if he would help us with the trial. Because Laci was there she insisted she'd do it even though she didn't care for the Raven now; in fact, she doubted she had ever cared for him at all. Laci went out on the balcony to watch the streetcars go by when she said that. When he came back, he had his hands behind his back and was leaning forward, as if against the wind.

"You liked what he gave you, that's what you liked," he told her. "It's all the stuff, the silver bracelet, the Russian fur jacket, the oranges, the bananas, the string of pearls. The big car." His face was redder than his hair. "You sell yourself like that."

"She used to sit on his knee in the back of his car while the chauffeur drove and I was sitting next to the chauffeur in front pretending to watch the road," Kati said.

"Okay, so I liked his car, and I liked to be driven by his chauffeur," Leah said, and laughed her high bell-like laugh. "Wouldn't you?"

Leah returned to the Raven's apartment and Kati stayed at Rákóczi Street.

Not even Alice could console me. She said that going to jail must be some kind of mark of distinction, because her father had told her the world must surely have turned on its ear if they dared to put Vili Rácz in prison. But her mother thought it would be safer if she didn't walk to school with me this term. Someone might think her parents were reactionaries, too.

Because I was so deeply miserable, my mother took me along to the Great Plains (Alföld) between the Danube and Tisza rivers, somewhere near Kecskemét, where she was putting down markers in the fields for a new road to Budapest. Comrade Rákosi had announced that we would have that new road finished by the end of next year to carry all the heavy equipment from Csepel to the Soviet Union. His Five-Year Plan called for a happy proletariat, enjoying its new wealth, singing, dancing and raising pink-cheeked children. In the village where we rented a room, there were placards of Comrade Rákosi's face over a jolly group that included a mother, father and two children marching down the road, holding hands, gazing into the future.

The future was painted as a red star over a bright light.

The white house where we stayed had a packed straw roof that smelled like Ilonka's cellar, of humid rot and wildflowers. Outside there was a plank fence that ran from one side of the house to the wall of the next house, which looked exactly the same as this one. Between them there was a courtyard, dusty on dry days, muddy when it rained. There was a brown barn in the back, a few bad-tempered chickens, two geese, a cow called Agnes that left at around five every morning with the other village cows and spent the day in the co-operative's pasture, and a heavy-set, yellow-eyed dog chained to a post.

All members of the family worked for the newly formed cooperative. The father and mother tended the animals, and the two teenaged sons were field hands. They left for work early in the morning wearing their black rubber boots. The woman's name was Marta. She was almost as wide as she was tall. She wore a red and blue kerchief over her hair most of the time, a heavy white apron and several layers of skirts, the bottom ones showing white embroidery. She was home the earliest, at around noon every day. She cooked potato soups, rice patties, sauerkraut, cabbage rolls with rice, eggs. On Sundays she stewed meat drowned in paprika. She baked brown bread. I'd never eaten so much.

My mother and I were in a room so small one of us had to sit on the bed when the other was dressing. Our window was the size of a book, with black wood frames; the walls were whitewashed like the outside walls, slimy, rough to the touch; the floors were packed earth, cold as the walls.

My mother said we would never mention where my grandfather was. I would start at the village school in a couple of days, get a sense of what everyone was studying, try not to draw attention to myself and not talk about Budapest. She thought the people here might have some unpleasant views of a big city and everyone who came from there.

Marta told me the co-op didn't mind if you had a few things going on the side, as long as you had never owned your own place before the war. Her husband, Feri, had worked for the landlord, who was still in jail in Debrecen. The landlord had been stupid enough to resist when the State took over his lands. Marta and Feri had saved a few of his chickens and geese when the big house was burned down and the co-op started. Feri had volunteered right away to be secretary of the local Communist Party. That way, he figured, they'd be able to keep the chickens and the geese. As secretary he didn't even have to attend the re-education classes.

Before the Russians, the Germans had come through here and recruited the young men, leaving the women to bring in the harvest. They had taken the gypsies from their wagon camp at the edge of the village. No one had minded too much, because they were always worried that the gypsies took chickens when the rabbits were scarce. Did I know they ate hedgehogs and moles and even cats and dogs when they felt like it? The trains had come through packed with Jews from Debrecen and Békéscsaba. Some gave them food, but most didn't. Marta thought the Jews had maybe been better off than the people around here. They were city folk.

The Russians left nothing. They ate even the raw potatoes, and they drove off the cows; a few weeks later they came back for some of the men and took a couple of the girls along to Budapest. None of them had ever been seen again, except for one of the girls, who was found by the side of the rails, naked and dead, her throat cut. Wasn't it smart of Feri to have hidden his family in the woods near the pasture? And wasn't it even smarter to have declared himself founder of the local Communist Party unit? Hadn't he flown the red flag right over their house when the Russians came and led them straight to the landlord's house? Wasn't he the one who told the other men they'd better volunteer to join him if they knew what was good for them? The Russians were here to stay. Hadn't they suffered enough when all the men joined Kossuth and the Austrians came and razed the whole village, leaving not one barn standing? This time they were going to be on the winning side, no mistake about it.

When Marta made bread, she let me knead her dough. Then I would watch it bubble and rise in the sun.

Feri said I should stay away from the dog. The dog ate city children. I used to skitter around the edge of his territory. He'd growl and show his teeth when I called his name. "Your job," Feri told me, "will be feeding the geese and the chickens. This is not Budapest. Around here everyone works."

The two geese were already fat. They ate everything left over from the meals. They even liked chicken bones and pork scraps, though Marta told me not to give them too much of that, it was bad for their livers.

"How come they don't have names?" I asked her.

She shrugged. "Geese don't have names."

On the first day of school everybody wanted to look at me. They lined up along the wire fence when I came and watched me walk along, my books under my arm. My mother had brushed my hair and tied it with a ribbon. "Nothing to worry about," she had said. "They are no different from the kids at your other school."

She was wrong, of course. These kids were bigger and tougher, and they didn't like city girls with ribbons in their hair. One of them ran up behind me and snatched the ribbon and threw it down; a couple of others ground it into the dust under their heels. "Big deal," I said. "I didn't like it anyway."

They crowded around and shoved me flying through the door. I sprawled on my stomach in front of the teacher, who had been waiting inside. He stood in front of the Rákosi poster, his hands on his hips. "Well, now," he said. "What a way to arrive. You like a grand entrance. Don't you?" He put me in the first row where everyone could throw paper darts at the back of my head. I remember smiling a lot at the girls closest to my desk, but they didn't smile back. They sniggered.

The next day the top of my desk was nailed shut, and there was glue on my seat. When I called them stupid bullies, one of the boys punched me in the face, and later the teacher told me to apologize to the class for calling them stupid.

I trained in the barn at night, punching the air. "I am tough, I am strong, I feel no pain," I kept repeating to myself. Agnes the cow watched in astonishment, the whites of her eyes showing in the dark. Vili had taught me to pull my head down between my shoulders and protect my eyes with my fists. Really good fighters could hop on the balls of their feet, keep their balance, dodge and weave with their bodies, shoot with their fists, keep relaxed. It hadn't worked too well with András, but that was before I was in training.

In the first real fight, I think I used all of Vili's boxing tips, dancing and ducking, feinting to the left and right, punching and jumping back, light on my feet all the time. The trouble was that when the boy's nose started to bleed, his friends joined in and hammered me from all sides. One of them pulled out a chunk of my hair, another stuck a bucket over my head so I couldn't see where I was punching.

It was the bucket that saved my face. The rest of me was black and blue, my knees and elbows bleeding, my clothes shredded. In the end, I think, the girls broke up the fight. I could hear high voices shrieking at the boys to stop, it was enough.

When I pulled the bucket off my head, I was alone.

After that Marta asked one of her sons to see me home from school.

In the evenings my mother and I would often go out to the local pub, the *kocsma*, with her troup of surveyors' assistants, and sometimes I was allowed to drink a little wine. "Poor kid," my mother said. "She's had her own battles to fight."

I think I was tired of my battles the second week, but I persevered till November, when the geese were readied for market. My job was to feed them four times a day, stuffing the mushed corn and milk-soaked bread into their unwilling beaks, smoothing it down their throats and into their gullets. The fattest goose would win the grand prize on a cooperative market day. When the geese were big and heavy, Feri made wooden crates in which they stood all day, their necks stretched through the space between the slats, their feet crusted in their own shit, unable to move. "That's how goose liver is made," he told me. "It's the specialty of the region," Marta said.

I have tried not to remember that he had nailed their feet to the bottom of their crates.

Every day I thought about the geese as I fed them. It was easier to think about them than to imagine Vili in his cage. I ran my palms down their warm, feathery necks, pushing the food down as Feri handed me more and more. The liquid spilled around their beaks and onto their gorged, dirty white crops, and I whispered to them that it wouldn't be long now, that it would be over soon. I turned my back to Feri, didn't want to let him catch me crying. "City girl," he had called me. "Useless."

They entered them in the regional contest, where Marta said they would win first and second prizes, and that wasn't only because Feri was Party Secretary, they also raised the best geese in the county. Everyone knew that.

The teacher asked that we write a composition about their family and read it in class. Mine included the first Vilmos at Nándorfehérvár, the second Vilmos who gave Lightning to king Mátyás, the Vilmos who looked after Rákóczi's horses. I ended with the last of the Erdély Ráczes, who was shot during supper. I wrote about Vili's wars and how he was now awaiting trial in Budapest on some charges that everyone knew were false. And I said I would never forgive Comrade Rákosi for that.

I remember the silence that followed my reading and how the teacher laughed nervously and suggested that I should stay after school. When we were alone, he told me never to mention Comrade Rákosi again, at least not while I was in his classroom. My kind didn't deserve an education. We should be made to pay for all the harm we had done to the people with our high and mighty airs and our wars. Didn't I know how much they had suffered here? Hadn't I learned anything in that fancy Budapest school about why the people had shrugged off the yoke that my people had forced on their necks for centuries on end? Hadn't I heard of Dózsa and the Peasant Revolt, and didn't I know what my people had done to him? Never, ever again.

Vili had told me that Dózsa led the peasant uprising against the Hungarian nobility in 1514. His forces were defeated at Temesvár (Timisoara), and he was executed in a most horrific way. He was chained on a scorching hot iron throne and crowned with a hot iron crown while the victorious lords praised the Peasant King. He died in agony.

No Rácz took part in that travesty of justice. A few, back from the crusades and nothing to do, had even joined Dózsa's ragtag troops. The teacher gave me a note for my mother, but I decided not to give it to her. We were almost ready to go home anyway.

Till then I spent my days in the barn inventing heroic tales that starred one or more of my ancestors and imagining how we might team up and spring Vili from jail. I wrote long narrative poems in pentameter with recurring rhymes about liberty. While Márta was at the co-op, I tried to make friends with the dog. I would sit in the dust for hours, waiting for him to come and sniff me. I would inch forward gently, still seated, presenting a small, insignificant target. I would whisper to him. I saved bits of bread and potatoes in my pockets and offered them to him. I was desperate for a friend.

In the beginning he barked and strained against his chain collar, snapping his teeth, ready to take a bite out of my leg. Later he just growled and didn't come near me. In the end he accepted the food offerings, but resisted all contact.

Still, it seemed to me that on our very last day, he favoured me with a wag of his tail.

46

I WAS NOT ALLOWED to go to the courthouse for my grandfather's trial.

My mother told me she had been shocked to see him so much smaller than he had been. His shoulders were thin and his chest hollow. But what upset her the most was looking at the back of his neck, wrinkled and vulnerable, his hair grown longer and whiter in the six months since she had last seen him. They had transferred him to the state prison at Recsk, northeast of Budapest.

The trial lasted only an hour. The man from the Emke described an elaborate scheme to smuggle twenty-five bars of gold out of Hungary with the help of two New Yorkers and claimed that Vili had been the mastermind. He said that he had gone along with the plan because he was venal, but now he repented and wished for nothing more than to serve the people. The Raven's lawyer said Vili didn't wish to enter a guilty plea, even if it meant a reduced sentence. He agreed with the judge that his client had exceptional connections with Americans, why wouldn't he? As a former aristocrat and publisher, he would have met a lot of them. But the facts were that he had no gold bars to smuggle, no money left, no hope of ever getting any. The judge asked him if his client had sold state secrets for gold. The Raven's lawyer said he had no doubt that his client would have been tempted to do so, but there were precious few state secrets to be found in the cof-feehouses, and even fewer in Solymár where he had been for a while now.

In the event, the judge concluded that Vili had sold gold bars and sentenced him to two years of hard labour.

When they led him out of the courtroom, Vili looked up at my mother and tried to smile. Then it was over.

Leah slapped the Raven across the face with the kid gloves he'd given her and returned once more to Laci, who had been waiting for her in the apartment. "That man has no pride," Kati said.

"Maybe not, but he is the best she's had," my mother told her. "He doesn't have a dreadful mother you might have to live with. He doesn't have a hole in his head. And he won't leave her for a prettier face."

"Nobody has a prettier face," I said.

My mother smiled.

It was the gloomiest winter. My grandmother was so quiet you would hardly know she was there. She spent most of the day in her bed writing long letters to Vili. Though she was away on her truck routes most of the time, Leah took over the household. She decided on everyone's chores, including mine. We were running out of coal. The fires would be set only every second day, and baths were to be shared, once every two weeks. Often we were hungry, there was neither enough food nor the money to buy it.

Laci lost his job at the glassworks. He had been a lawyer between the wars, but former lawyers couldn't practise law now. The money my mother sent back didn't seem to be enough anymore.

Snow piled up in the streets and froze. Kati and I wrapped our feet in newspaper, stuffed them into extra socks and wore old rubber boots to school. Some evenings Alice's mother gave me hot soup, though she was still strict about not letting Alice walk to school with me. Alice and I met in the basement and played some of the games we used to play, but I didn't enjoy them as much. With Vili gone, nothing seemed the same.

Vili had been moved to the east; the "Stoneworks," as they called the prison barracks. The men used big mallets to break rocks into small pieces for the cement factories.

"He is so strong, he'll do twice as much as anyone else," I told my grandmother. "And he won't even sweat. Never did when he lifted the chairs."

She didn't bother to reply.

I stopped volunteering for sign painting and often forgot to wear my Young Communists League red kerchief. One morning, when there was no one in the corridor, I drew a moustache on Comrade Rákosi and painted Lenin's head orange. The whole school, even the boys' section, was kept late for that.

We had progressed from the Russian alphabet to reading and conversation. The new Russian teacher, a woman with dyed blonde hair and hornrimmed spectacles, had spent the war in the Soviet Union and liked to tell us in Russian about the bravery of the Soviet people. "They have endured such horrors, such deprivation, yet they never succumb, never give up. They fought the Germans barefoot in the snow, firing their guns even as they fell." Stalingrad was the charnel house of the war. Did we know that more Russians had been killed than all the dead of the combined armies of all the other nations fighting in the war? She read Lenin to us and translated each word as she went.

She took the class to the top of Gellért Hill, where there is a massive monument to the Glorious Russian Army. "It's a monument to peace, to the victory of good over evil," she told us.

We huddled together against the devastating cold — few of us had winter coats — while she told us about the soldiers climbing up this hill in a winter much like this, looking back across the river, where there were no more bridges and most of the houses had been set on fire.

With Vili in jail, I had no sympathy for them.

The statue is bronze, at least fifteen metres tall, a broad-shouldered woman in a longish, clinging gown, holding an olive branch over her head. She started out as a boy. Vili had told me that the sculptor, a Mr. Strobl, had been working on the piece for Admiral Horthy. It was to have been an elaborate grave ornament for Horthy's dead son. When Horthy was arrested for declaring the end of the war and trucked off to Germany, Strobl tried to turn it into a garden statue for the German commander-in-chief, but there was simply not enough time.

Then the Russians came. G.K. Vorosilov, the Soviet commander of Budapest, commissioned Strobl to sculpt something impressive to celebrate Hungary's liberation by the Russians. Strobl took the angelic statue of the boy Horthy reaching toward heaven, put an olive branch into his hands, stuck him on a stone pedestal and added a greatcoated Soviet soldier with an iron flag. Vorosilov was ecstatic. Not only had Strobl produced the perfect monument, he had done it in record time.

Comrade Sipnovich singled me out for extra duties. He ordered me to continue the weekly newsletters, to replace the disfigured posters, to post new signs on the walls about loyalty, duty and the Five-Year Plan, and he told the whole class he would not tolerate reactionaries in his classroom. They all knew he meant me.

The Young Communists League's leader announced that counterrevolutionaries were working to destroy the Republic. Everyone had to be vigilant and prepare to make sacrifices if need be. Sometimes the enemy was in our midst, sometimes as close as our neighbours; not even our parents could be trusted. As communist youth, we owed our first allegiance to our country. We were visited by one of the League's stars, a boy of twelve who had told the State Police that his parents listened to "thevoiceofamerica" and Radio Free Europe and had meetings in their apartment at which people discussed politics. They were now in jail, all of them, and the boy was a Hero of the Revolution. He had even been invited to Moscow to speak at the annual Komsomol get-together.

I cannot remember what he talked about, except the part where he shouted "Long live Liberty! Long live our Land!" and raised his hand in a salute toward the huge picture of Stalin at the back of the gymnasium.

Alice told me that night in the basement that he lived in a state orphanage now.

I held a secret meeting of the Sneaks behind the Corvin. Not everyone came. I told them we should disperse the gang, that it was dangerous now to be in a gang with me. If they were found out, they might all end up in technical school, with no hope of university. But the six girls who showed up wouldn't hear of it. While I was gone, they had made Sneaks' badges and candlewax Adalbert figures. They had perfected a secret handshake and had challenged six of the tough boys to hand-to-hand combat and won.

I think the trouble was that they had all read the book about the boys of Paul Street. It is a wonderfully romantic book about boys in a gang who are willing to sacrifice their lives for one another. I had read it during our last few days in the village and thought that girls wouldn't be quite so devoted to a group. I remember thinking that girls were family people not group people, and now that I was angry at the world, I didn't want a group anymore.

The girls didn't mind that my grandfather was in jail. They said they all knew someone who had been jailed at least once, and two of them had grandparents forbidden to live in Budapest.

To celebrate my return, they lit candles and we watched the Adalberts melt one at a time.

A few days later a new teacher replaced Comrade Sipnovich.

It was done very discreetly, no announcement — no explanation. One day he was there, the next day he wasn't. I know the seven of us thought it was wax magic. Alice figured he had simply disappeared. It was not till summer that Annie admitted she had ratted on Comrade Sipnovich's late-night jazz habit. She had delivered an unsigned note to the principal. The note said she had been so impressed by the Young Communist who had betrayed his parents for the good of the Party that she could no longer keep Sipnovich's secret.

She felt she owed him for keeping her in late four nights in a row.

Comrade Sipnovich was sent away for re-education at a tobacco plant near Pécs.

⊰ ⊱

While Vili was in jail, his brother Gyula died. Though she hadn't liked Gyula, my grandmother sobbed through most of the funeral. She was thinking of Vili.

I have the vaguest memory of a young woman with long dark hair and big black eyes, a black shawl over her shoulders — cousin Edy, Gyula's daughter. There were two boys about my age, dressed in short grey pants with suspenders, white shirts and knee socks, sitting side by side on their livingroom sofa. My mother asked if they'd like to go play with me, but they shook their heads in unison. They wrote each other notes and snickered.

Edy talked about her father and how he had lost everything long before he died. Three wives, but none of them loved him. Her own mother thought he was a spoiled rich kid, suddenly without means, no realization that the world had changed around him. Bafflement, hurt. In the end, hopelessness. She was sure death had been a relief for him.

Then she went on about the Treaty of Trianon and how we had lost two-thirds of our country. She shared Vili's view that it was all because of the Paris International Exhibition. The space was booked for our exhibit but not yet paid for when we withdrew. A slap in the face for the French, and one not easily forgotten.

In the end, the pragmatic Austrians attended the Exhibition, and only the Hungarians abstained. That's why the only people who irrevocably lost the First World War were the Hungarians. Come to think of it, we had lost the Second as well. One day, she was sure, we'd get our country back and the whole lot of us would go back to Bácska.

The two boys rolled their eyes.

47

ONCE A MONTH my grandmother would reach under her bed, pull out the jewellery box, slip something into her hand and go down to the street. I was never allowed to go along. When she came back, she would have a letter from my grandfather. I tried to read over her shoulder, pencil scribbles on stained brown paper. She didn't let me read a single line.

The couple from Csepel fought all the time. They shouted and threw furniture and bottles at each other. The man dragged his wife out of their room by the hair and left her hammering on their door. Her face was bloody, her hands bruised black. When she locked him out, he used a cleaver to break down the door. He had bandages on his head and she had a broken nose. When she stuck a knife into his stomach, Laci escorted them into the elevator and down to the street so they could take a taxi to the hospital. "People in our situation," he said, "never call the police."

Even Leah admitted that it had not been smart to sell them her room.

When my mother came home, she raged about them and about the dirt and the cockroaches that had moved into the rest of the apartment. At night you could hear the cockroaches scuttling about on the walls and feel them dropping onto the beds from the ceiling. If you turned on the light during the night, they would duck under the pillow, skitter off the covers and slide under the beds. In the morning we were covered in red welts where they had feasted on our bodies, and there were bloody splotches on the sheets and the pillows. She shouted about that and about why my grandmother was allowed to stay in bed all day feeding the bugs and why Laci seemed to have no job.

One night she sat in the old rusty bathtub with her back to me. It was almost a year after my grandfather's arrest. I remember going in to tell her I had found some coal to heat more water — there was barely enough to cover her legs — and I was surprised at how thin she had become. With her hair piled on top of her head, her neck was white and bony, her shoulder blades a pair of brackets, her ribs like long fingers, and I could see every vertebra of her spine. Her thighs lay flat in the water, so narrow the knees protruded like red mountains, and her calves had all but disappeared. She was crying.

I had never seen my mother cry before. I had seen her angry, outraged, even gloomy and dark, but she had not cried.

I stood there with the half-full bucket, waiting. She drew up her pointy knees, cradled them in her arms and put her head down on them. Finally she said, "The water's getting cold," and I ran over to the heater and started to pile in the coal, making as much noise as I could. There was still a bit of fire going, enough to light the new bits.

"Is Peter coming to take you out tonight?" I asked. I thought it might cheer her up to think about Peter. He often brought her flowers and sometimes fizzy wine.

She shook her head.

"Adam?"

Adam was her newest man, tall, stoop-shouldered, with a thick mop of black hair that flopped over his forehead. He told me he only pretended to be an engineer, he was really an artist, and when I was a little older he might paint a picture of me. He used to sit with me and try to make conversation while he waited for my mother to get dressed. It was so pitiful I almost felt sorry for him.

She shook her head.

"Another one?" I asked.

She didn't reply.

I waited for a while, but my mother stayed in the bathtub. From time to time I could hear the water running as she filled up the tub with the water that had been heated by the piano tuner's coalpile. Then I went in search of Alice.

All Saturday night my mother cleaned the apartment, pouring turpentine into the corners where she thought the cockroaches built their nests, scrubbing the kitchen, scouring all the walls and windows. Early on Sunday morning she told my grandmother we were going to church and she would come with us whether she was ready or not. She helped her with her little round hair roll and dabbed powder on her face. Kati and Leah came because Leah felt guilty about the couple from Csepel.

We all sat in a row near the back of the narrow, gloomy Franciscan church, with its peaked arches, black-brown paintings of dying saints, chipped statues of St. Francis in brown habit and St. Therese in blue and dirty white. Not one of us took communion since no one had been to confession.

My mother said religion was a private affair. She went to confess from time to time, but there was not a whole lot she could do about going back to her husband. That had been the priest's main concern when he heard about her sins.

There was a lot of singing that day, and when mass was over, the priest led everyone in the long version of the anthem. It starts with "God bless the Magyar," and most people got so choked up they had to stop singing.

Afterwards we went to the restaurant called Apostolok, the Apostles. It was dedicated to the twelve apostles, who were framed in fake gold on the walls. There were long, dark oak tables and benches in separate compartments, each big enough for at least eight people. The partitions were wood and green mosaic. If you were little, you could stand up on the bench and peer over the top into the next booth. It was 1955, and I was too big to stand. There was a wrought-iron chandelier in the centre, with six branches and a big light in the middle. The waiters glided along the ceramic floor between the booths, they wore black tie, their aprons were gleaming white. They brought tall glass pitchers of frothing beer and salted pretzels and *pogacsa*.

When we entered, everyone stopped eating and drinking and looked at my mother.

⋈ ⋈

When we returned forty years later, nothing about the place had changed. And all the men still put down their forks and watched my mother.

⋈ ⋈

Laci told her she was beautiful.

She gave him her withering look.

Leah said something about her getting a job in a café. She was tired of the trucks. Kati asked if she could drink some beer. I had raspberry soda.

All the talk settled into a hum. I tried to kneel on the bench, unobserved, and peer at the couple in the next booth. They were kissing. He slid his fingers up and down her bare arm.

Suddenly there was silence.

"What did you say?" Leah asked.

"I said I'm going to marry him," my mother replied. Her voice was quiet. She poured more beer into her glass. We all watched as her arm strained and shook, holding the jug by its ear. Her glass filled with froth.

"Let me do that," Laci said.

"You're going to do what?" Leah's voice was rising.

"You heard me," my mother said. "There is no other way to get our father out of jail."

About two weeks later, in a registry office near the Eastern Station, she married Jenö, the Party man who had made sure she would get her job back when she returned from jail.

I HAD NEVER REALLY looked at him before. There was no reason to look at the men who drifted in and out of my mother's life. They had no claim on her, no permanence. Vili had explained that there would always be men about her, and that was that. I didn't have to like them, I didn't have to be interested in them. Though it would probably be helpful if I didn't treat them with downright disdain.

But unlike the others, Jenö moved in with us. He would sit in the livingroom/my mother's bedroom in the evenings and read *Szabad Nép*. Vili had told me that *Szabad Nép* reported nothing of interest to the ordinary citizen, that it lied about even the most commonplace events: harvests, the weather, sports scores. Even its name, "freedom for the people," was a lie.

Jenö put on his half-moon glasses and read the paper from the first page to the last. His hands were blackened by newspaper ink and so was the bridge of his nose, because his glasses kept slipping down and he continually pushed them back. He wore brown suits in various shades, white shirts, blue ties, short black socks.

He was balder than my grandfather. The few bits of short brown hair he still had were assembled at the back of his head in a neat line near his collar. His face was round and tanned or yellowish in colour. He had tiny blue eyes, and he squinted a great deal. I didn't think his glasses were strong enough. He had a short nose and slightly puffy cheeks, a thin neck that wrinkled under his chin and long, thin fingers with soft pads and finely shaped fingernails. He said he had been born with a sculptor's hands. He would have been a sculptor, but his family was too poor to think of such a profession. He had to earn a living already at twelve, working in a machine shop with grease all over his artist's hands, saving up fillérs toward his education. One day he severed a tendon in his right hand when it got caught in the drive shaft of a truck. The doctors hadn't sewn it back right. In those days there was no public medicine and poor people couldn't afford good doctors. He showed me how his hand couldn't be straightened anymore.

His father had worked on another man's land, giving the landlord more than half of what he brought in. There had been years of hunger, and during the winters it was never warm enough in the one-room house they shared with their two cows. His mother hadn't gone to the balls my aunts had attended. She took in other people's washing so that her son could become an engineer.

A few weeks after he moved in, he told the couple from Csepel to go back to Csepel, and they did. Now he and my mother had a separate bedroom all to themselves. He brought in fumigators for the cockroaches, had the walls painted blinding chalk-white as his own home had been when he was a boy. He purchased a nearly new bed from the couple on the fourth floor, who were being deported to Havas.

What the country needed was increased industrial production, Jenö told me. Lots of heavy machinery, new roads, rails, boxcars to carry all the produce to markets. Luckily the Soviet Union needed all that. He thought Comrade Rákosi's Five-Year Plan was grand. The people had a purpose, and it was good to keep an end in sight. Five years was not so long that people would get discouraged and not so short that they would think they couldn't achieve what was expected of them.

My mother told me not to argue with Jenö. It was advice she tried to take herself, but she failed from time to time. She told him that in the old days, there had at least been a few people to envy, but now we were all equally poor. Only the Party élite had cars and houses.

Jenö drove a small Skoda that made a great deal of noise when it started and smelled of rotten eggs in the back seat. He was proud of his membership in the Communist Party. He wore a Party pin in his lapel. It had a large red star in the centre and a bit of the Hungarian flag over the top.

Leah, Kati and Laci had moved into their own place. Only my grandmother remained in the apartment with us. She was very still most days. She fed the pigeons on the window ledge, and now that my mother was home more often, she had started to cook again. When she didn't, Jenö brought home food and beer. We were never hungry now. For the summer he bought fans to cool the apartment, and he made sure there was enough coal in our cellar for the winter.

"He is a good man, really," my mother told me. "He has a kind heart. You could try to be pleasant to him. Or civil, at least. And there is no sense in your mentioning Peter and Adam and all the others. He knows about them and he doesn't care."

"Not even Benny?"

"No. Not even Benny. Besides, Benny died."

Sometimes Jenö gave me money to go to the movies with my friends or to buy everyone ice cream. He said I should stay with the Young Communists League because they might teach me something about cooperation and humility. The class system doesn't teach those things, he said. And there are few people more conscious of the class system than the bourgeoisie.

He liked to be alone with my mother in the evenings.

Alice and I explored the city that summer.

We ran the length of Margaret Island and made up stories about the ruins of the Dominican nunnery where King Béla's daughter spent her life. She had been only nine when she was brought there. We imagined her screaming and begging to be returned to the palace, tearing at her scratchy nun's habits, wanting the brocade and silk she had worn before. Béla had promised her to the Dominicans if the Tatars went home, and much as he had wanted his beloved daughter back, he had to honour his word. It had been hard to argue with the logic of it, God had clearly intervened: the khan had died, and his hordes — the Tatars were always referred to as "hordes" — went home. And that was that.

It was the thirteenth century. Her long, golden hair had been shaved, and she whipped herself about the shoulders with leather straps each night. During all the long twenty years she had spent here, according to Vili, she never bathed. She believed that bathing was immodest and possibly insulting to the Virgin Mary, who wanted the nuns to be pure.

Alice and I had her fall in love with the groundskeeper's son and had the two of them holding hands through the bars on her window. Alice, being smaller, insisted on being Margaret, leaving me the role of declaring my everlasting love outside the ruined walls. I never noticed how she stank because of the wall between us. Once we tried to elope, but the nuns came and beat me to death.

Now that I was out of the way, it was easy for Alice to be canonized.

We roamed Budapest's squares, from Liszt to Vörösmarty, and I recited Vili's favourite poems and told Alice about Franz Liszt being the greatest pianist ever and about his affair with George Sand, who was a woman but dressed like a man and didn't care a whit what anyone thought.

We scaled the wall to the Gellért Baths, stripped to our underwear and tried to teach each other to swim. We were thrown out when Alice lost her panties in one of the artificial waves of the wave pool.

We teamed up with the remaining Sneaks and fought the last battle of the Empire in the ruins of the Roman amphitheatre in Óbuda. Vili had told me that Attila, being quite proud of his role in the fall of Rome, had put his main fort here, on the site of the old military amphitheatre where Roman soldiers used to march in excellent formation and with much pomp. It's from here, in Óbuda, that Attila terrorized the more settled and sedate Europeans. Pope Leo the Great decided to try to buy peace by offering him Princess Honoria with all her estates. Attila already had a bunch of earlier wives, but no matter, God's Emmissary on Earth was willing to make the sacrifice of Honoria. Needless to say, no one at all asked Honoria's opinion about the matter.

We were all quite pleased to have such a nasty, violent, fearsome ancestor as Attila. It was delicious to contemplate being the aggressor rather than the victim.

49

Jenö said Vili would be home in late August 1955.

We were all there, Leah and Laci, Kati and my grand-mother. We waited, leaning over the balcony, not quite believing that he would be home again. Jenö and my mother had driven to pick him up in Recsk, where he had returned for the last month of his imprisonment.

My grandmother cooked for three days. There were dishes of fried pork, chicken *paprikas*, liver dumplings, cheese noodles, marinated tongue, schnitzel, sour beans, dilled cucumbers, *rétes*, cream-filled cake flutes, even a dish of chestnut purée. She had stood guard over them all when my gang tried to sample her food. She was so excited her hands shook and there were stewed cherries in sugar syrup on the floor. She had gone to the hairdresser on Barát Street and come back with her hair dark brown, beautifully curled at the ends into an even roll below her ears.

Then she went to her bed again, prepared for disappointment.

"He might think he has greased every government wheel," she told me, "but there is always that one last little rusty one that everyone forgets about." Her voice was jagged, as if she had a sore throat.

I knew she was talking about Jenö because she never mentioned his name. He was always "he" or "him," no matter how hard he tried to please her. She had left the chocolate mousse cones he bought uneaten on her bedside table, and she played solitaire with her old sticky cards rather than open the new cellophane-wrapped card package he had given her.

The Skoda stopped right in front of the building. Jenö got out and went around to open the door for the old man with stooped shoulders and white, bald head who had been the strongman hero of my early childhood. Jenö offered him his arm, and for a moment I thought he would take it. He didn't. Bent over, he walked slowly toward the entrance.

We all ran through the door and down the steps, reaching him as he was about to enter the elevator. He turned.

He had shrunk in the twenty months he spent in jail. He seemed no taller than Jenö. His grey jacket was loose, hanging in waves down to his hips. His loose, baggy trousers were tied with a rope at the waist, the cuffs touching the ground. I remembered this suit. The black trousers he said he had worn to the Parliament Buildings, the 1930s jacket that used to have a matching vest. It had been his best impress-the-world suit. He had been proud of the way it had fitted him after twenty years. Not an extra bulge; the creases perfect. Now the jacket was hollow in front.

You could see the bones in his skull and the fissures where the bones met. When he turned, slowly, and looked at us, his eyes were small granite pieces in dark hollows, his forehead jutting out over them. His cheekbones were round, the space under them deep and long. His lips had become thin and his moustache was gone. "It's been a very long time," he whispered. He kept his lips together when he talked. His voice was soft.

Kati and I had been racing to be first to jump on him, but we were stopped by his appearance. He didn't seem to be my grandfather, my Vili of the one hundred sword fights, the hussar captain, the magician. He was an old man with barely the strength to lift his feet as he walked. My mother and Leah were standing a few inches from him, their eyes watery, their faces pale. I had never noticed any resemblance between them until then. Now they looked alike in shock. Leah reached her hand out but seemed afraid to touch him.

Jenö had closed the car door and leaned against it, his eyes closed.

Only my grandmother seemed unshaken. She threw her arms around him and held him, cradling his face between her hands, stroking his back and his arms, saying how wonderful it was to see him again.

The two of them went into the elevator together. The rest of us walked up slowly, making each step last.

Still, we were in the apartment at the same time as they. He stopped at the kitchen door, looked at my grandmother's special-occasion real Herendi plates all laid out with the meal in his honour, put his hand on my grandmother's back. Then he went on to the room where the couple from Csepel used to be and now Jenö and my mother slept, gazed up at the painting of Jesus entering Jerusalem and ran his fingers along one of the dachshunds in the bottom right-hand corner. He walked slowly through the middle of the livingroom, looking at the worn Persian carpet, its strands flat where we had marched towards my grandparents' bedroom. He held onto the door frame of his bedroom and nodded, as if to confirm some memory.

Then he lay down on his bed, crossed his arms over his chest and went to sleep. Kati and I watched his chest rise and fall, waiting for him to snore as he had always done when he slept, but he didn't snore. My grandmother put her forefinger to her lips to tell us to be quiet and pushed us out.

"Let them rest," my mother murmured.

Jenö said that Vili hadn't known he would be coming home until they opened the door to let him out. When Jenö picked him up, he was still in his prison uniform, the brown paper package with his old clothes under his arm. "He didn't know who I was," Jenö said. "Thought he was going in for another round of questions."

Leah and my mother were still crying.

"It would've been so much easier for him had he admitted to the gold scam," Jenö said. "What the hell difference does it make once you're convicted?"

"He didn't do it, that's what," Leah said. She was red-faced and angry now as well.

"So?" Jenö said. "It doesn't matter about the gold. He was guilty of something, it might as well have been the gold. Weren't for his pride, they would have put him back into the prison. Men his age don't have to break stones with a hammer if they admit their guilt."

"What guilt?" my mother shouted. "What guilt?"

Jenö shrugged.

"What the hell guilt are you talking about?" She had come close to him, her face angled up toward his. She was spitting as she shouted.

"Bourgeois guilt, if you must know." Jenö seemed rather calm, though his bottom lip was twitching and his little eyes were half closed. "Those hundreds of years your lot lived off the land, never giving anything back, taking and lording and not giving a damn about the rest of us, that's what. The gold is symbolic. Don't you see?"

My mother turned on her heels and ran out of the apartment. She slammed the door so hard that my grandmother's special dishes rattled in the kitchen and the big tin pot with the noodle soup fell off the sideboard.

We ate the meal in silence, Leah, Jenö, Laci, Kati and I. Laci said our family really knew how to thank a guy for doing us a favour. No chance the old man would have come home without Jenö's influence.

My grandmother stayed with Vili in the bedroom.

My mother didn't return till after midnight. Then she slept

curled up on the couch. Her breath smelled of sweet red Eger wine.

I spent the night with my back propped up against the wall, listening to my grandfather breathe. I could see him fairly clearly in the moonlight. He still had his arms folded under his head, the muscles still bulging where they had always been, only his shoulders were smaller and his chest had caved inward as if he had been pushed by a giant hand. His pillows were piled up high, his knees raised under the blue eiderdown. His cheeks were hollow under the high cheekbones, there was another hollow below his temples, his eyes were so deep in their sockets I couldn't see them at all until first light. His chin had become more prominent, and his Adam's apple stood out. His neck had become thinner; the big muscle that had connected the back of his neck to his shoulders now seemed more like a pair of ropes, taut even when he slept.

He didn't make a sound all night.

Early in the morning, when the pigeons started to move around on the windowsill, his eyes opened, but he remained as still as before. He didn't move till my grandmother got up and asked if he wanted his coffee.

50

A COUPLE OF DAYS LATER, when I was leaving for school, I found a woman in a dirty pink coat sitting on the top step near our door. Her hair hung in long, blondish strands.

"You live there?" she asked over her shoulder, barely glancing at me. "Must be Leah's kid."

"Puci's," I told her.

She stood up and smiled at me. Her two front teeth were missing. "That would make you my niece," she said.

Her hands were chapped red, though it was summer still. Her coat was too short and unnecessary on such a warm day. Her stockings were of the same beige variety as my grandmother's, wrinkled.

"I don't think so," I said.

She nodded. "You don't know, do you? Doesn't surprise me much. He wouldn't talk about us around the dinner table, would he? Ever mention Amelia? Ever talk about her?"

"No."

"Well, then," she hesitated. "We'll just have to go and ask him ourselves, won't we? The old man is here, isn't he?"

"Jenö?"

"Vilmos Rácz, your granddaddy, dear. My father, that's who."

"No," I lied firmly. "He left early. Working in a shirt factory."

"We'll see about that," she said and pushed past me, moving fast down the passageway and into the diningroom, where she ran into my grandmother dusting the bookcase.

They stared at each other for a while.

"I'm Irén, Amelia's daughter," she told my grandmother. She got nothing in response, not even a nod. "I need some money right now," the woman went on undaunted. "She is ill. TB. So is my sister. Amelia can't get stage work any more. Too old. Nobody wants her. She has no strength for factory work. And I can't take enough home for all of us. Since *he* stopped paying, we don't have enough to eat. It's not fair," she added, looking around at the room with its big oak table, the pictures of horses and dogs on the wall and the bookcase that ran from one end of the room to the other. "It's not fair," she repeated.

My grandmother dug into the pocket of her knitted brown cardigan, extracted a handful of coins and gave them to her. "It's all I have," she said gently.

"Not enough. You tell him from me: Not enough." She smacked her hand against the bookcase. "We've waited for over a year and a half. Now he's out of jail, he has to bring us something again. He has obligations." She turned and grabbed some books off the shelf nearest her, tucked them under her arm. "Maybe I can sell these," she said. Her voice had lost some of its fight. I thought that if someone touched her, she would cry.

She tried to look through the glass doors into the living-room, but my grandmother stood in her way. "You don't know what it's like," she told my grandmother. "Three of us in one room and no food. Tell him Irén was here. Tell him Amelia is dying. Or doesn't he care at all?"

She and my grandmother let the question hang in the air. The woman picked up a framed photograph of Vili and tucked it under her arm with the books. Then she left.

"Amelia?" I asked my grandmother.

She sighed. "A poor demented creature off the streets. She needed help." With that, she went into her bedroom and banged the door shut in case I thought of following her.

"Who is Amelia?" I asked my mother.

"Why?" She had been playing chess with Jenö and losing, which was usually a good time for interruptions.

"Her daughter was here today, wanting money. And she took your Maupassant, the François Villon and two of grand-father's Dumas's."

She slid her rook back to the king in an obvious feint at defense that was really an attack on his queen. "Must be a student of French literature," my mother said.

"Grandmother gave her our shopping money and let her take a picture of Vili. Her name is Irén. She claimed I was her niece. That she is Grandpa's daughter."

"What an idea," my mother said and swept all the remaining chess figures off the board into Jenö's lap. That's what she usually did when she was about to be checkmated.

"Do you know of an actress called Amelia?" I asked Leah. I was becoming smarter.

"Of course. She was a singing and dancing star, early 1930s. Played in Lehar's *Gypsy Queen*, I think. She must be dead by now."

"She isn't." Then I told her of Amelia's daughter's visit.

"Why don't you ask the man himself," Leah suggested. "And while you're asking about Amelia, you might enquire about Gizi and Frannie and Zsuzsi and all the others. And *their* children. Could be quite an education for you." She laughed. "Think of all the shit your grandmother has had to put up with."

I didn't ask him. Not then.

51

THAT WINTER OF 1955, Vili stayed as quiet as he had been in the first few days after his release from jail. He spent hours looking out of our bedroom window, watching my grandmother's pigeons. He was smoking smelly Five-Year Plan cigarettes, the tobacco sticking to his lips and fingers; Jenö brought them home for him from a Party place where you could buy them at a discount. He drank sweet coffee my grandmother poured for him into tiny Turkish cups.

One day he brought up his old medals from the basement and polished them all with vinegar.

He didn't talk much. He told no stories. He didn't go down to his favourite coffeehouses, though Jenö had assured him they were still there.

I watched him watching the pigeons on the window ledge, smoking, thinking. I waited for him in the evenings, hoping he would come and sit on the side of my bed as he used to and start telling some old story about another Vilmos or a Hunyadi or Rákóczi. He didn't.

It was a quiet Christmas. We had all given up on Baby Jesus and no one bothered ringing the bells when the tree was ready. Vili gave me a leather-bound volume of Madách's *The Tragedy of Man* and promised to take me to the National Theatre one day to see the play. He had started to write in his notebooks again. Jenö gave me a pair of green socks that I quickly exchanged for Kati's grey ones. "Never wear green," the gypsy had said.

The summer of 1956 Jenö thought it would be educational for me to spend a few weeks on a tobacco farm. My mother agreed that I should be out of the apartment while Vili was recovering. Jenö told her we had to get the next generation ready for the system. Whether Vili liked it or not, communism was here to stay, and why would he want me to lurk outside the system as Vili had? Would he prefer the prospect of my following the family tradition of jail terms and menial labour?

All Vili said was that there were things worse than menial labour.

Since his time in jail, Vili was no longer careful around Jenö. I think he figured there was no point in his pretending any longer. Some evenings he even listened to "thevoiceofamerica" while Jenö and my mother retreated to their bedroom.

The tobacco farm was a Young Communists League venture, intended to ignite sympathy for rural folk in the city dweller's heart. It was one of the final steps in qualifying for the next level of the League, one that came with a badge. It would make me a full-fledged member of the international army that would soon take over the whole world in the names of Marx, Engels, Lenin, Stalin and our very own Mátyás Rákosi.

There were about twenty of us from Pest; the rest of the pickers were local and actually knew something about tobacco. They showed us how to take the leaves off without damaging the plants. Then they sat in the shade of the surrounding ash trees, chatting, smoking and watching our progress. We were all more or less the same age, twelve; a couple of the boys had begun to sprout ugly pimples, the girls had started to have breasts and I had a bit of both. We spent the days bent over, sweating, our hands covered in tobacco-leaf goo with cuts around the fingers and palms. In the evenings we strung the leaves up to dry. The smell was pungent, the music loud Russian working songs, the food chewy fat.

I deeply regretted whatever passing kindness I accidentally might have shown Jenö.

Fortunately, I developed ugly puss-spewing welts on my
hands and had to be sent home before the rest of the unhappy city crew. "Five more days and you could have earned your
red star," our group leader told me regretfully.

I grinned. "You can have mine, too, if you like," I said.
"And you know where you can shove it."

52

Vili didn't tell stories about his time in jail. I don't know how he survived the cell at Andrássy Avenue, the interrogations, the work detail. Years later I heard about a man at Recsk who entertained the other prisoners with magic tricks. He had used tiny stones and bits of paper fashioned to look like cards, and he asked them to guess what he would turn up next. He had made them laugh.

The only time Vili mentioned Recsk, he talked about the darkness inside each of us, darkness so fathomless it has depths best left unexplored. But that was later.

My mother told me Jenö had helped secure my grandparents' release from Hungary. "He's had to use his Party connections, and everything we had left from 'peacetime.'" When she looked at my face, she added, "You do understand, don't you? If he stays here, they'll kill him. It's only a matter of how long it'll take them to fabricate new charges."

"But he's already served his time," I protested.

"With men like your grandfather, they will not be satisfied until he's dead."

It was during Vili's last week in Budapest. Sunday morning, early September, the trees turning yellow, clear blue sky, a hint of winter in the air. He had thrown open the door to the balcony, looked down Rákóczi Street toward the Danube and announced that it was a perfect day for a walk. Thanks to my grandmother's tireless cooking of the food Jenö supplied, Vili had regained some of his weight. His moustache had grown back completely white and he had been experimenting with some sort of dye to turn it brownish again. Instead it had developed a faint blue tinge that I rather liked, but I think he found it embarrassing. He hadn't been going to his cafés in the evenings.

That Sunday was the first time he suggested we go out together since he came home. I was ready and waiting by the door before he found his brown felt hat, its brim dusty and warped from the long humid summer.

We walked along Rákóczi Street, past the Rókus Hospital with its plaque for the victims of the 1838 ice flood, past the Naiad fountain on the Franciscan church square. We stopped in front of Pilvax Place, where the old Pilvax Café had once stood and where Sándor Petöfi and his friends wrote the words that inspired a whole nation to rise against the Austrians in 1848.

"Petöfi," Vili said, "is the greatest poet of the nineteenth century. Had he written his poems in English, he'd be the most famous poet in the world."

We stopped at the bronze statue of the young poet in the small square named after him. "Our only hope of survival as a nation is our language," Vili said. "And it's our greatest tragedy. No one but Hungarians will ever know the greatness of Ady or Jókai, or Madách, Arany or Vörösmarty. And it's the best we have to offer the world. Lehár is no more than salon music, and what will they make of Bartók and Kodály without a sense of the people who first sang those songs? All they can see is our movies, the Kordas, Cukor, maybe Molnár, or hear our music, but the best of Liszt fades beside the grandeur of Petöfi's *Ode to a Nation* or his *End of September*."

He stepped into the Inner City Parish Church, where the priest in his yellow and white robes had just faced the faithful and raised his arms in benediction. "It's nine hundred years old," Vili whispered. "Bishop Gellért was buried here in 1046. The red marble is Mátyás's marble. The Turks made it into a mosque and prayed here in their own *mihrab* next to the altar. Did you know your mother was married here? I gave her away. She wore a long white dress trailing halfway to the door. A bouquet of angel's breath. Two flowergirls in white, six bridesmaids in light pink taffeta, six ushers in hussar dress uniform. Only one of them survived the war."

The congregation recited the Lord's Prayer in Latin, and Vili joined in. He dipped his finger into the shell-shaped holy-water font as we left. "Puci was radiant. That day she was the happiest I've ever seen her."

He stopped at the old building where I had come for my fencing lessons, the Piarist Secondary School where Vili had first come some fifty years before, a boisterous Bácska boy. "I didn't know how lucky I was. Barely opened my books, looking for ways of escape. My poor father had to travel to Pest, seven hours by train, and sit in the upstairs waiting room while the Piarist brothers compiled dossiers of complaints about his son."

He rested for a while on a green park bench facing the white marble statue of Mihály Vörösmarty reciting his long poem, *Szózat*, an admonition to all Hungarians to remember who they are or risk extinction.

A woman came toward us, smiling. Vili stood, bowed slightly, lifted his hat, smiled, and walked on briskly. He waved to a man hurrying along on the other side of the street. "If we stay here, I'll have to talk to someone," he said. "I'm not ready for that." We headed toward the Vigadó concert hall. He stepped under the battered arches, climbed the marble steps, still broken where shells had hit them in 1945. "They used to feel the swish of long gowns as the beautiful people came to the balls, the music — schmaltzy Viennese waltzes, French minuets, risqué Spanish tangos — chandeliers trembling overhead, champagne flowing, a desperate hope for peace even as armies gathered."

We hurried past an outdoor café along the Danube Corso, gypsy musicians in Hungarian peasant garb played sad songs for the few people seated at the white cloth-covered tables. One man stood up and saluted Vili, started to come toward us, but Vili didn't stop. We turned onto the Chain Bridge and crossed the river toward Buda.

Of all the Danube bridges, Vili had loved this one the most. When I was little, he had lifted me up onto one of the giant stone lions guarding the entrances, and held me yodelling with delight over the Danube from the balustrades. When the Germans blew up the Chain Bridge, the whole city went into mourning. When the Chain Bridge was rebuilt in 1948, the city rejoiced.

We climbed the steps and narrow winding paths toward the castle. He pointed to the place where the executioner's block had stood, seating for the spectators on three sides only to allow the royal party easy access to the site. Some say they also kept it clear for an easy escape should the crowd turn ugly. This is where young László Hunyadi was slaughtered.

Vili stopped now and then to look across the river, pointing to this or that building, the cupola of St. Stephen's Basilica, the tip of the Market, the remnants of his publishing office. The gothic towers of the Parliament Buildings shone gold in the noon sun. "If only it was a parliament of dunces, it would be easy to forgive them. But it's a parliament of the fervently corrupt. Their weapon is terror. They kill with conviction."

We passed the wreck of the Sándor Palace, where Count Pál Teleki had shot himself; passed the ruins of blue and yellow medieval houses where the haute bourgeoisie had thrived and joined the Habsburgs in their last hurrah, the First World War. A few of the houses had been restored for the new bourgeoisie, the Communist Party bosses.

We stopped in front of the Russwurm's window, where two generations of the privileged had indulged in chocolate confections and where even now there was a tour bus of Russian sightseers descending into its cavernous rooms.

"All those coffeehouses," Vili said. "There has to be something worth preserving in a people that can sit over tiny cups of espresso and write great poems, foment revolutions, elect leaders, declare independence, argue the cause of liberties and lose, while never leaving their perch, not even to order a second cup. It's one of the wonderful things about us."

We reached Szentháromság Tér (Trinity Square), the centre of life on the hill. Across from us was the old town hall, where Vili had once represented a few thousand of Buda's souls. He had joined the Liberals and shrugged when many of his old friends abandoned him as too pink.

On the east side, there is Mátyás Church, started under Béla in the thirteenth century, rebuilt by Mátyás in the fifteenth. His coat of arms is still displayed on the winged altar under the black baroque madonna. It was dark inside, the red globe lit on the main altar, a few supplicants' candles at the Loreto chapel. "In 1301," Vili said, "when Béla, the last of the great Árpád kings died, some of the nobles decided they wanted Wenceslas to succeed to the throne; others supported the pope's choice: Charles Robert of Anjou, the Neapolitan. The Wenceslas faction met here — in those days it was called the Church of Our Lady — and excommunicated the pope." His laugh echoed through the church, from one ornate end to the other, until it disappeared into the darkness near the confessionals. "Isn't that so typically Hungarian? They actually excommunicated the pope!"

"What did the pope do?" I asked.

"Being a smart guy, he ignored them. Some seven years later his candidate was crowned here with St. Stephen's crown and solemnly presented to the worshippers as if they hadn't been the very same people who had chosen Wenceslas. I heard that the crown was too big for his head; he hired two men to help hold it up during the ceremony. When the communion bells rang and they dropped to their knees, the crown slipped down over the eyes of the would-be king. It was his nose that saved him. Had his maternal grandmother, not blessed him with a rather prominent Habsburg nose, the crown would have slid all the way to his neck and the ceremony would have dissolved into cheap farce."

"Mátyás was married here. A splendid occasion. Beatrix, the great Renaissance beauty, Mátyás, the last of the Hunyadis, the most beloved king of Hungary. Four hundred guests, each with his own pure gold place setting for the feast to follow the wedding ceremony. There were kings and queens, emperors and princes, the wealthiest landowners from the kingdoms of Europe and even a goodwill emissary from the sultan. Did I tell you the sultan himself had sent a letter of condolence to Erzsébet Hunyadi when János died of the plague? His letter said he was much grieved to lose such a worthy adversary."

Over our heads there were the deep red and black frescoes that Vili had told me were left over from the time the Turks converted Mátyás Church into their main mosque in the city. Our teacher, who had brought us here after a long visit with the Statue of our Liberation on Gellért Hill, had informed the class that they were folkloric motifs, showing that the peasants of Hungary had found a way to make their presence felt even in this landmark of their oppressors.

Vili stopped in front of the Trinity Chapel, where King Béla and his third wife, Anne of Chantillon, had been reburied, and told me he had passed through here on the day after the Siege of Budapest and found two dead horses lying side by side next to the marble tombs. "The city was full of corpses. Some had been killed by bombs and were barely recognizable as human, some simply shot, some hanged, some frozen — it was the coldest winter in years — but there was something about these two horses that made the horror real. More real than the body of my dead friend, a journalist, I had just gone to visit.

"In those days the only way to discover if your friends were still with you was to walk the abandoned streets of the ruined city.

"I had found him slumped over his desk in his old study, the rest of his house blown away. The roof had caved in, his books were scattered over the street. Only this one part of the house remained, attached to the only standing wall. Only fragments remained of his wife and teenaged daughters. I took his dachshund home with me. The little guy was still sitting under the writing desk, cold, frightened, but unharmed."

A woman in a black dress and shawl walked from the side chapel, genuflected toward the main altar and settled on the far side near the confessionals. "Little Margit," my grandfather said. "She'll be there for a very long time. It's one thing to sleep with your enemy; it's quite another to spy for him."

"That woman," I asked, "she is a spy?"

"Shsssh," he said.

I thought this might be a good time to ask him about Amelia. "Amelia," I said as we left the church through the side door. "You remember Amelia, don't you?"

Vili strode in the direction of the Fishermen's Bastion, the long, white, turreted confection of terraces and arches where the stone statues of the seven tribal chieftains observe the Danube from above. He climbed the steps to the southernmost turret and sat on one of the stone seats that form part of the wall. "This stuff" — he indicated the rest of the Fishermen's Bastion — "is almost new. When I first saw the castle in 1901, it was not yet here. There were only the moss-covered ramparts of a bastion left over from Turkish times. It all but disappeared again under the siege, but the Republic must like it, because it's been rebuilt ahead of other parts of the city. Perhaps it's because of the view."

We could see clearly across the Danube, the Chain Bridge, the Elizabeth Bridge, the Corso, the houses of Parliament, the top of the Academia, the round tower of the Pest Market, the empty space where the last emperor-king of Austria-Hungary had sat on his white stallion, wearing the red mantle of power, the crown and sword of Saint Stephen, and saluted the four corners of the Hungarians' kingdom. In 1914 he took them into a war that cost two-thirds of their country.

"Amelia," Vili said at long last. "A sad story that. She was a princess, daughter of the Duke of Hessen, only fifteen in 1694 when she married Prince Rákóczi. An arranged marriage, of course. Yet she claimed she loved him, even helped him escape from Leopold's prison, she bought off the guards and paid for his passage to Poland. She was kept hostage in Vienna, her two sons immersed in the German language just as her husband had been. When she came to him years later, in a glass carriage, she was sent by the emperor to negotiate peace with the Hungarians. But no matter how beautiful, no matter how great the inducements, Rákóczi stood steadfast. He would not give up his people for personal gain ..."

"Not that Amelia, the other one. The actress."

Vili took a deep breath. "Another time," he said finally.

As we walked back down through Watertown, Vili stayed silent. When we reached the Danube, he turned to me. "Look," he said, his voice barely audible over the rushing of the river. "I had thought I could stay here and wait till this madness, too, was over, just as I stayed through the last one and waited. I thought I could maybe help some people or just walk the streets and let them see I was still there, some kind of resistance against the terror. I could sit with my friends in the cafés and talk, write but not publish, make buttons or bricks in a factory, and I would remain hopeful. But I know now that I cannot. That barrier between us and them has blurred. I no longer know who we are.

"It happened one night at Recsk. I was alone in the darkness of my cell, listening to the carefree chatter of the guards and the howling of the tortured. And for the first time in my life, I was afraid. Not of the pain, or even the certainty that I would be there for a long time, nor of the loneliness, the hunger, the loss of dignity. I was afraid that my sense of who I am would be altered forever. I was suddenly afraid that all that" — he threw his arms up as if to embrace the city across the river — "is a sham, that the enemy is ourselves. That we all share the darkness. That the men with those carefree voices, those boys who swagger about with their rubber truncheons, their whips and chains, gun barrels at the ready, that they are also us, to a man. You see, if I stay here, I will be complicit in their game or die in their cells. We live in times when silence is not enough."

That night my grandmother took her jewellery box out from under her bed for the last time and gave it to a man who looked very much like the man who had come to search our apartment a couple of years earlier. A week later my grandparents left for New Zealand, where my aunt Sari, her husband Kálmán and my cousin little Sari were living on a horse farm. Kálmán, who had been a cavalry officer, was training New Zealand's equestrian team for the Olympics.

Once my grandparents were safely out of the country, my mother asked Jenö for a divorce.

I WAS TWELVE YEARS OLD and very angry without Vili.

Once Jenő was gone we lost most of the apartment to a government lawyer named Toth and his mother, whom he beat most evenings with a ruler or a strap. She told me he had broken both her ankles. He said he treated her too kindly, considering she was utterly mad, and made up terrible stories about him and everyone else whom she had ever met. If I thought that what she said was true, I was a simpleton and I probably still believed in Baby Jesus and the angels bringing me gifts at Christmas.

My mother and I had moved into the room where the couple from Csepel had lived. We had the old tile stove, the Titian with the dachshunds, my grandfather's books piled on top of my mother's books in bookcases along the walls, the green standing lamp with the tassled shade from the old house, a small seventeenth-century table and the bed. I slept on a mattress in the bed's pull-out drawer. The rest of our old furniture had been bought by the lawyer.

He thought he would make a perfect new husband for my mother, then we could move back into his part of our apartment and use the kitchen again. He tried to give her silk stockings and pearl earrings. She told him he was the most repulsive man she'd ever met and what possible need would a government that does not believe in law have for lawyers?

Leah advised my mother over beer and pretzels at the Százéves Restaurant that she should reconsider. He wasn't the worst choice she'd ever made, and he could make life more comfortable for us. "He is no uglier than Jenö, and Benny was no beauty, Peter drank too much, and he isn't married to one of your sisters."

My mother stood up and left the table. I stuffed the pretzels into my pockets because I hadn't eaten that day.

Alice and I put a dead rat into the lawyer's supper stew. I don't think his mother noticed.

The homeroom teacher recommended me for art and craft school. I had no chance for university, given what they knew of my parents and grandparents. At craft school I might learn something useful. She thought I had shown aptitude in my early Communist Party posters. One night soon after, I geared up a string at the top of the stairs leading down to the gymnasium and watched her cartwheel to the bottom. I was deeply disappointed that she didn't break any bones.

I delivered an invitation to the boys' end of the school to pick their best six and come to fight the Sneaks. We lost. I told them all I was sick to death of them and I disbanded the group.

I didn't greet the new men who came courting my mother. If she wasn't there behind me when the doorbell rang, I would tell them she didn't want to see them and slam the door.

I wrote long poems in which large women did brave battle and died. I was so angry, I stopped dreaming of Vilmos and stopped wishing I was alive at his time. I put Lightning down into the cellar with the rest of our old garbage.

The twenty-third of October, 1956, was cold and wet. We were in Russian class. I was writing an essay about the Cossack hero Taras Bulba when the Revolution started. Annie had just come back from an expedition to buy ink at the Corvin. She whispered to me that there was a demonstration along Rákóczi Street, maybe we should check it out. I thought it was weird that nothing had been announced, planned and organized like other parades. It wasn't even a parade day, no anniversary that I knew of, nothing to rejoice about until the seventh of November and the anniversary of the Glorious Bolshevik Revolution.

We handed in our essays (though I liked the poem, I had done my best to make Taras seem silly. Both he and his author were Russians) and went out to the quadrangle for gym class. I kept going, through the quadrangle, out the front door and on toward Rákóczi Street.

At first it didn't even seem like a parade. There was no music, and people weren't marching in step. They were talking and hurrying towards the river. Some were shouting, but I couldn't understand what. A young woman near the Franciscan church told me they were heading towards Petőfi's statue, and that they had been shouting "Down with Rákosi." Why weren't they afraid?

I saw one of them tear up a poster of Comrade Rákosi and two men cut the hammer and sickle out of the Hungarian flag. Then there were more flags, all with holes in their centres, and I stopped to watch someone climb up to the lower balcony of the building just past the church, pull down the red Russian flag and throw it onto the sidewalk. The crowd pressed on, trampling it under their feet. A shout went up, and we slowed to watch another man cut one of the big red stars off the top of a restaurant. He used a hammer and some sort of wire cutter, and people scattered as the heavy metal star fell and cracked in two. There was clapping and cheering. The man with the hammer took a bow.

There were so many people by then, I couldn't get close to the speakers at Petőfi's statue, and none of us at the Erzsébet Bridge could hear them. The crowd was pressing forward, I couldn't have turned around and gone back home. They were waving and yelling, greeting one another as new waves of people joined. "Here come the university students!" "A big cheer for the textile workers!" "The guys from the ironworks!" There was a sense of jubilation about it. Laughter. Excitement. People were asking one another if anyone had heard what the speakers were saying at the Petőfi statue, and no one cared much that they hadn't.

The people in front began to sing the first lines of Petőfi's poem "Arise Hungarians, your country needs you, the time is now." Some knew the tune, everyone seemed to know the words. We surged forward toward the Parliament Buildings. They were shouting for a man called Imre Nagy, then someone yelled "Russians go home" and everyone joined in.

"Who is Imre Nagy?" I asked the woman whose shoulder was in my face.

"Don't you know?" she yelled back at me. "Everyone knows Imre Nagy."

The people around me began to chant "Nagy for leader! Down with Rákosi! Down with Gerö!" Vili had said that if we lived in normal times, Ernö Gerö would be in jail for robbery. He had even robbed the Hungarian people of their time. Not only was all that they produced floating off to Russia, he had come up with a plan to have them work extra days without pay. These "Stalin Days," or "Peace Days," were designed to pay off the endless loans from a generous Soviet Union.

I was somewhere in Sas Street, moving so slowly now that mostly we were standing. I had joined the shouting for Gerö's demise, calling for Imre Nagy, though I wasn't sure why he would be such a great idea for leader. He was, I knew, a Party man. A loudspeaker spluttered on, and people started to hush one another, "Nagy is going to speak," "Imre's at the microphone," and in the quiet that followed, I could hear a voice, but not the words. Those farther back tried to push forward, grumbling that they couldn't hear.

I peeled off at the corner of Zrinyi Street with a bunch of kids around my age. "I heard they are bringing down Stalin," one of the girls said, and we headed across Saint István Square towards Városliget. Andrássy Avenue was full of people, a huge crowd near the number 60 block. Angry women held up photographs, yelling "Down with the AVO" (State Security Police), though the AVO headquarters had moved by then. Vili, I thought, would love this. I skirted the edge of the big crowd and joined a group running towards Heroes' Square. There was applause and hooting, just like the days we had marched here for May First celebrations. There was shouting, becoming louder as we ran, and whooping and more hollering as more people ran forward. Flags with jagged holes in their centres hung from windows overlooking the street. A man in overalls was taking apples off the end of a horse-drawn cart and handing them to passersby; a young boy had climbed up a lamppost and yelled that they were cutting him off at the boots.

Then the earth shook; the buildings groaned as a thunderous sound reverberated all around us. A man in a black funeral suit turned to me and screamed, "The son of a bitch is down!"

When we reached the square and looked up to where Stalin had stood above the podium on those special days, there were only two giant boots, still taller than the statues of the heroes. From inside one of the boots, a man was waving a Hungarian flag.

"Take that from your grateful Hungarian people!" a woman shouted. Stalin's body was so huge it took up most of the parade ground. There were people with chisels and blowtorches trying to carve pieces off him as he lay, beached, still with that benevolent smile under his moustache.

When I reached home, my mother was standing on our balcony in the darkness, smoking. She wore her utterly exasperated expression. Her arms flapped in anger. "I've been waiting for two hours," she said. "A stupid time for you to be hanging around with your friends, don't you know what's going on? I had to go see Alice. She said you'd left school early."

I told her I had been waiting around in Heroes' Square to get a piece of Stalin for my grandfather, but that only made her angrier.

"There was shooting at the radio building. How in hell can I be sure you're safe?"

"Safe? Why wouldn't I be safe?"

My mother stared at me. "You really don't know what's going on?"

"Nobody was shooting. It's more like a New Year's Eve party, everybody's happy. Maybe you heard firecrackers."

"What a dummy," a man's voice said. I hadn't noticed him before. My mother's friend Adam sat cross-legged by the tile stove. His hair was damp, his overcoat dirty.

"Look who's talking."

"Enough of that." My mother stomped her foot. "We'll see how it's going tomorrow." She unpacked her net bag and put salami, bread, green peppers on the small round table. Adam uncorked the wine. It occurred to me that I had been right. Even here, it was a celebration.

He splashed wine into my mother's glass and waited for her to taste it before he poured some into his glass and mine. Although we could now all hear the popping outside, the atmosphere in the apartment had lightened.

I toasted my grandfather's health.

54

MY MOTHER INSISTED that I change into my nightshirt while Adam stayed, his back to the room. On the radio, the announcer said there were counterrevolutionary rabble outside, but order would soon be restored. They played a lot of music. There was still some shouting in the street below and popping sounds in the distance.

I had trouble going to sleep that night, thinking about the toppling of Stalin's statue, the flags, the ruined pictures of Rákosi — and that nothing would ever be the same again. I saw Petöfi shouting his verses from the steps of the Pilvax and Kossuth, his chest gleaming with medals, speaking in the National Assembly. I wished Vili had stayed with me for this. Today may have restored his faith in Hungarians. Maybe he'd live here again now. I would go back to Heroes' Square the next day and break off a piece of Stalin for him.

It was still dark when I woke up. My mother and Adam were on the balcony arguing about whether they should go to work that day. In the end he convinced her that it was safer to go. The Russians were going to get behind the AVO, and the whole thing would be over by noon. Good jobs would be scarce for people the Party thought might have been involved in the events of October 23.

"You'll stay inside," she told me. "No school today."

I was dressed and out the door a few minutes after they left.

The piano tuner's daughter asked if I could help her carry buckets of soapy, slippery water and splash them over the street. "The tanks will be coming this way," she explained. Alice helped us, and later so did the doctors' sons Alice had thought were informers. In the pink dawn the pavement glistened silver and the streetcar tracks turned polished gold.

When the tanks came, they seemed smaller than I had expected. Certainly smaller than the German tanks in the Russian Second World War movies. You could tell they were Russian from the red stars on their sides. They slid around on the wet paving stones, hit the sidewalks sideways, bounced back and skidded to a halt at the National Theatre, where they bumped into one of the old gaslights. There were only three tanks. One propelled its long gun down Rákóczi Street, the other two pointed along the broad, circular road, the Körút, one in each direction.

It was quiet when they stopped rumbling.

People returned to the street. A man on a bicycle went by shouting "Russians go home." A Hungarian Army Jeep came out of the side street, five uniformed soldiers and a girl in a short skirt and tight blue sweater. They all carried guns. When they saw the tanks, they retreated the way they had come. The girl's laughter echoed between the tall buildings.

The thing about the tanks was that they didn't do anything. They sat there, their turrets swivelled this way and that, the machine gun in back didn't even move. They were like three grey bugs, checking the surroundings with their antennae. They didn't budge even when the street filled with men in blue overalls who carried placards saying they were auto workers from Csepel. Some were riding brand-new motorcycles from the factories. "These aren't going to bear any Russian arses," they taunted the tanks. "No Russian arses for our brand new bikes!" "Hey, Comrade, take your arse home to Mother Russia!" They shook their fists or lifted them in "up yours" salutes. But they kept their distance from the tanks. And the Russians didn't move.

There were more tanks heading toward the Danube, a few rambled along the Körút, their snouts aimed at the windows above, black-helmeted heads in the back where the machine guns swivelled slowly from side to side. I took Vili's hammer from the kitchen drawer and followed the tanks toward Városliget.

A few people in the streets now carried guns, slung over their shoulders as casually as if they were string bags of groceries. On one corner there were two Hungarian Army trucks with men in uniform talking to the people on the street. It had started to rain.

A small green tank with the Hungarian emblem painted on its side had positioned itself at Stalin's head. Its barrel pointed away from the people climbing over the fallen statue, taking pictures of one another, waving and smiling for the cameras. There was a man wearing an old red hussar tunic, gold braid, copper buttons, tall cap, his sword aloft as he stood on Stalin's chest, a movie camera whirring at him. A girl was giving him stage directions.

I tried to knock a piece off the thigh cavity, but it held firm. "Like this," a woman said, brandishing a chisel and taking my hammer in her other hand. "You put the chisel in a crevice, hit the head with the hammer ..." Her voice echoed inside the statue.

After a while a couple of small pieces flew off. I slipped one into my pocket and felt along its rough ridges. It was about an inch thick, shiny on the outside, deep black and scarred on the inside.

"Sic transit," the woman said when she pocketed her own piece.

⚜ ⚜

In the late afternoon one of my classmates, a girl called Zsuzsi whose one distinction was that she could swear as well

as the men in the ice carts, came striding across from the
Corvin with a bouquet of red and white flowers, went straight
to the nearest tank, ignored its swivelling in her direction
and placed the flowers into its turret.

Everyone applauded.

55

IT WASN'T UNTIL the next day that the tanks began to fire.

Zsuzsi, Alice and I were coming out of Garibaldi Street, eating vanilla ice cream from a street vendor who was giving it away. We were following a bunch of people on their way to the Parliament Buildings. Despite the rumours, we hadn't seen any fighting, and Zsuzsi insisted that the Russians wouldn't fire. If they were going to fire, she'd already be dead, she reasoned. There was still a carnival feel to the day. It had even stopped raining.

Suddenly there was the sound of machine guns, louder and faster than the popping of the single shots the night before. When the screaming began, the people behind us pushed forward into the retreating crowd. Nobody believed that soldiers were firing. "The army is ours," someone said as he rushed on. "Maléter came over." Pál Maléter was commander of the Hungarian Army. Zsuzsi said it must be the AVO; everyone knew they would screw their own mothers if they got extra for it.

The firing continued and people began to run: a man with a gash over his eye, a woman carrying a child, another with blood all down her front, two men supporting her. I thought the firing came closer. We turned toward Vörösmarty Square, but it was hard to run with all the people hurtling forward, many with flags and placards, some shouting "Don't shoot" into loudspeakers, a few more now with guns. I pulled Zsuzsi in behind one of the pillars of the Ministry of the Interior. We'd wait there.

I couldn't find Alice. The gunfire continued. Looking up to where I thought the sound was loudest, I saw two men in khaki uniforms on the roof of another government building, their guns pointing down at the people below, the rapid rat-tat-tat of their guns sweeping the street from side to side. "Sons of bitches," I said to the woman next to us. She had a black scarf over her head. Her shoulder was bleeding.

"I think I need help," she mouthed, looking at me to see if I understood over the deafening noise. The patch of blood spread to her chest and down her arm and dripped from her fingers.

"Can you walk?" I asked her.

She was leaning against the pillar, her forehead on the stone. She draped her injured arm over my shoulder, and we took a couple of steps to the back of the arcade then slid along the wall to the doorway, where there were others. "She needs a doctor," I told a man with a young boy behind his trouser legs. The boy glanced at me and shrank farther back into the shadows.

The sound of sirens now mixed with the rat-tat-tat. A man in a long raincoat took the woman's other arm. "Come," he commanded. She was still clutching my shoulder, her hand dripping blood down my shirt front. I remember thinking how angry my mother would be about the stain.

The man propelled us both toward the river. He sat her down on a green wooden bench and started to peel back her sleeve to see where the wound was. She lay back, her neck over the back of the bench, her eyes closed, her other arm flopped onto the ground.

"She'll be all right now," the man said. "Run along home. Nothing you can do here." When he saw me still sitting there, he said, "Your parents will worry about you."

Zsuzsi was there tugging my sleeve. "Come on. Let's go."

There were stretcher bearers, some with white armbands, others wearing white coats, running towards the Parliament Buildings. Tanks came hurtling down the Széchényi Embankment. A boy with cropped hair who looked vaguely familiar shouted for us to duck behind one of the old chestnut trees. "Watch out for the machine guns in the back," he yelled. The guns were swivelling quickly, firing short bursts at the lower windows of the Ministry building that we had just come from. The man on the bench ducked under the seat. The woman didn't move. Three more tanks arrived, their guns aimed high over the buildings, shooting as they went. Someone shouted that they were shooting at the AVO men on the roof.

A little girl came running out of a doorway and stood bawling in the middle of the street. The tanks went around her, but they ran over a man who had stopped in their path. I thought I heard a crunching sound over the screaming and firing, and after the tanks had passed, all that was left of him was a flat smear of blood and meat and dark-stained clothes. I heard the high shriek of a woman over the noise of the guns.

The boy opened a sack he carried over his shoulder and handed Zsuzsi and me bottles with paper corks. His fingers were sooty. "Here," he said. "You light the cork and toss it at the tanks ... They go up like big whooshy firecrackers ... You got matches?"

I didn't.

"You can have this," he said. "I'll use my mom's lighter. Now watch," and he ran out next to a racing tank, tossed the bottle at its side, then he raced back. "Missed," he yelled as the machine-gun turret swung our way. I pulled Zsuzsi down next to me. Earth splattered over our faces and hands. We were lying flat on the ground, our cheeks on the wet pavement. There were soggy cigarette butts under my lips. The boy sprang up and shouted something then flopped on his belly beside me. The tanks careened past the corner and rumbled down the next street. I looked up to see if more of them were coming.

"He goes to the boys' school," Zsuzsi whispered. She had to tell me again, louder. My ears were full of the sound of guns.

I wanted desperately to be home.

There was silence. In the distance, sirens, a male voice on a loudspeaker, a car revving its engine. A young woman ran out of the shadows and bundled up the child from the middle of the street where she still stood crying. The stench of gasoline and blood.

I got to my knees. Zsuzsi was already standing. Only the boy remained lying down behind the tree, his face turned to us, his eyes open. "We're going now," I told him. There were five or six more bottles leaning against the tree. "We could maybe take one," I suggested, to appease him. "Perhaps there will be more tanks along the way."

He didn't move.

I prodded him with the toe of my shoe. He still didn't move. "Here," Zsuzsi shouted to a woman in a white coat coming from where the tanks had gone. "Will you please look at him?"

It was so quiet now that Zsuzsi's voice rang loud as a school bell. I could hear a crow up in the tree over our heads. When the woman reached us, she bent over the boy, lifted his arm and turned him over on his back. Only his head stayed the way he had lain. It didn't turn with him. There was too much blood around his throat. "He is dead," she said.

I don't remember how I went home, not even which streets I had to avoid. And I don't remember when Zsuzsi said goodbye or whether she ever did.

But I was alone when I stopped at the piano tuner's apartment and asked if I could clean up before I went upstairs. He shook his head with disapproval, but he let me in anyway. He didn't ask where I had been or whose blood had stained my clothes. He was tuning his own piano, his eyes fixed on the keys. I washed my shirt in his bathtub; the blood coloured it pink. I put it on wet, but when his daughter saw me, she gave me one of her knitted sweaters.

I noticed that they had moved the grand piano to the back, near his kitchen, away from the windows.

"My father," she said, "has bad memories from the war. He hates the sound of gunfire. The Russians used his family for target practice." She mixed a glass of strawberry drink for me and we sat near the window, listening to her father's scales.

I was so tired I crawled up to the fourth floor and waited outside Alice's door until I heard her voice inside telling her mother we had been playing in the cellars all day. Then I went home.

That was the day, they said later, that the real Revolution began. Until then it was just an uprising.

⤳ 56

ON OCTOBER 26 at around five o'clock in the morning, Radio Kossuth announced that school was cancelled. My mother, who thought I had spent the previous day playing in the apartment building with Alice, suggested that I do the same while she went to see if Leah and Kati were all right.

It was my mother's birthday. She thought we would all spend the evening together. She had a bottle of wine and there was still salami, ham and hard-boiled eggs. She would find bread on the way home.

We hadn't slept much that night, and she seemed tired and disoriented. But she didn't want me to join her on the journey up Rákóczi Street. During the night people had dug up the streetcar tracks and laid them across the street to slow down tanks coming this way. A crowd was piling up paving stones and building barricades. There were Hungarian flags flying from all the windows of our building. A lone woman with a black armband and a machine gun patrolled the National Theatre. An army truck had blocked off the entrance to the Corvin. The soldiers were handing guns to people who reached up for them.

As soon as my mother left, I hung out our flag.

There were airplanes over the city. From the balcony you could see them dive down along the Körút. The doctor upstairs said he was sure they were Russian, but the piano tuner, leaning out of his balcony and looking up at the sky, insisted they had Hungarian markings.

His daughter said we would go to the barracks and see what was happening and she asked if I'd come along. "My father," she told me, "was a flyer in the last war. We still have his medals in a bag in the cellar."

"My grandfather," I told her, "was a hussar in the war before that. His medals are in our trunk. Must be over a hundred. Some of them are for bravery in battle, but a whole bunch more are sports medals. My grandmother used to keep them upstairs, on velvet, under glass, and we used to shine them every now and then. Then we hid them in the basement." I hadn't mentioned the medals to anyone in a long time. My mother told me the government didn't like you to have won medals in the wars. It felt great to talk about them now.

"Vili will be so sad to have missed all this," I added.

"Perhaps," she said. "My father doesn't think it will make much of a difference. The Russians are still here, and Nagy is the man who asked for them to stay. He is a Communist like the rest of them." Her name was Eva, and she had been friendly with Kati. She had long thin fingers with blue and red woven metal rings. I don't think she had ever noticed me until I came home with the bloody shirt the night before. "The only hope we have is Pál Maléter. If he really came over to our side, we might win this war."

I followed her past the barricades and around the corner to the Körút, where there were crowds gathering and someone shouting that the AVO building still hid the bastards who had shot people in Parliament Square. "More than five hundred died," Eva told me.

We were moving through the crowds, snaking right and left, trying to follow where people were going. You couldn't see where one street ended and another began, the crowds were so thick, people walking and biking or walking their bikes. There were a few Jeeps, trucks with men in army uniforms waving flags, women and children holding hands, a few men with kids straddling their shoulders and more men and women with guns. The noise was loud, like shouting inside a well, ricocheting off the buildings, swelling to fill the inter-sections. There were shots in the distance, then closer, and when we reached the space that I thought might be Republic Square, the shots were louder, there were the long booming sounds of the tanks, guns and rapid machine-gun fire, but the crowds seemed to pay no attention. "The army's on our side," they shouted. "The army is ours."

I saw the first one of the hanging men some two or three feet away. At first I thought it was a store dummy, but there was blood on his face. He hung from one of the trees where the edge of the street used to be. As the crowds pushed on, I was almost level with his waist. He wore leather boots and a belt, unbuckled, his fly unbuttoned, the pants hanging just over his hipbone, hands hanging by his sides, his throat cut. His chin was lifted by the rope around his neck, blood caked over his face, eyelids puffed part-closed, blue watery eyes, mouth open and something bloody and oozing protruding from between his lips. I didn't want to be close to that, I shouted for Eva, but she couldn't hear me and I was close enough to smell him — sweat, shit, stale piss. I pushed against the people near me. One of them spat on the dead man's belly.

The second one was hanging by his feet. His hands lay on the ground. A boy not much older than me was grinding his heels into the palms of the dead man's hands. His belly was exposed, soft, white, hair parted on either side of a central white line. He wore white underpants soaked in blood. His khaki britches were also caked in blood, cut open where his penis had been. His face was horribly disfigured. Mouth wide open. His genitals stuffed into his gaping mouth. Eyes staring. Black.

A small boy was passed overhead from hand to hand, his pale face turning this way and that, as if searching for someone. "The son of an AVO man!" they were shouting. "Death to the bastards!"

I wrenched free of Eva.

I don't know how long it took for me to reach home.

Somewhere along the way a man leaning out of a Jeep gave me a heavy gun with a long snout and a handful of long black bullets. I don't remember carrying it into our doorway or trying it on one of the Corvin's windows. What I remember is the sharp pain in my shoulder where the gun kicked back and smacked me against the wall. I sat there for a long time, wanting to think about Vilmos and King Mátyás, Hunyadi and a bunch of other heroes, while some of our neighbours came and went.

Nobody talked to me.

After a while I went down to the basement, stuck the gun into the closet with the ball gowns, closed the door and climbed up to our room.

Using bits of cardboard, scissors, watercolours, Vili's flat-tipped quill pen and inks, I made a card for my mother's birthday.

57

I DON'T KNOW WHETHER the lights had stopped working or if we were just too frightened to turn one on. There was worry about providing targets in the dark. We sat around the yellow candle Kati had brought as my mother's gift. It had a very faint, flickering flame that paled everyone's face, made our shadows grow, turned the room into a darker and less familiar place. I was thinking of Vili's fathomless darkness and trying to make sense of what I had seen that day and the days before. I held my knees close to my chest and shivered in the damp cold.

Laci said there was a curfew. Nagy wanted order in the city. No one was allowed in the streets after six, but he was going to join in the fighting. A man couldn't sit by while others took the initiative around him.

Leah laughed at him. "You don't know one end of a rifle from the other, let alone a machine gun. All they need out there is someone like you loose in the crowd."

Adam had found a bunch of flowers for my mother and stuck them in a wine glass. We ate the salami and bread. Leah had brought a piece of hard butter she said she had saved for just such an occasion.

Radio Kossuth announced the restoration of peace in the city. Radio Free Europe said the Revolution had been successful and they extended the "free world's" heartfelt good wishes to the Hungarian people. Gerö and Rákosi had fled, the Central Committee of the Communist Party had handed over power to a new group headed by Imre Nagy. The Voice of America assured us that the AVO had been disbanded. Soviet troops were withdrawing from Hungary.

Late that night Jenö arrived with an armful of fresh bread for my mother's birthday. At first Adam told him he wasn't wanted inside. "You belong with your kind in the Party," he told Jenö. "And don't you know about the curfew?"

My mother offered Jenö a glass of wine.

"The Party isn't the enemy," Jenö said. His coat was rumpled and dripping rain, his moonface had become thinner. He shook the water off his hat and tossed it by the cold stove. "Nagy is our only hope and he belongs to the Party."

"So do Rákosi and Gerö and the rest of the bastards," Laci said.

Jenö said there was no hope for the Revolution without the Party and there was no chance for anything but compromise. Only idiots thought the Russians were going to leave. And who the hell else but the Party could hold people together? Surely they weren't going to bring back the tin-pot admiral and his Nazi friends. Surely that's not what the Revolution was all about.

All the same, I had noticed that Jenö's Party pin was missing from his lapel.

During the days that followed we went to the Road and Railway Company's cafeteria for lunches, because even though they had suspended work on their usual projects, the staff provided food for the workers and their families. We walked the length of Rákóczi Street each day, stepping around the piled-up stones, mangled streetcar lines, burntout tanks and shells of cars. There were unclaimed bodies on the sidewalks and bits of other bodies on the street where tanks had run over and squashed them into pulp. Some of the bodies held crosses in their hands, some had their faces covered, some had been covered with blankets. Some were missing arms or legs or only their boots. Some looked as if they were sleeping.

By All Saints' Day most of the bodies had been claimed. That night the city was lit by thousands of candles as the people mourned their dead. In Kerepesi Cemetery there were thousands of new graves with hastily carved markers. Farmers did a great business selling white lilies from their horse-drawn carts.

The only bodies left in the streets now were those of Russians and AVO men whose families were too scared to claim them.

I wondered what had happened to the little boy.

I still think about him sometimes.

On November 3, 1956, the newly renamed Radio Free Kossuth announced that the world was returning to normal. The streetcar lines would be repaired. Schools would open. To prove their determination for all things "normal," a few of the city's cinemas opened.

In the afternoon my mother took me to see a French film with Hungarian subtitles. It was called *Pique Dame*, "the Queen of Spades," and it featured darkness and menace, messages from beyond the grave, identifiable evil, desperate, unsullied good and a man who was willing to gamble his soul for the chance to attain his desire. It took place in czarist Russia. It was so long ago and far away that you could sink into every moment without fear of losing your way. I thought it was the best film I'd ever seen.

That night Radio Free Kossuth said Russian troops were still gathered at Debrecen and Nagy was still negotiating for their withdrawal. Radio Free Europe talked of support for the Revolution. Adam, who had been visiting every day and often came with us for lunch at the Road and Railway Company, said that was nonsense. Western Europe was going to be busy with Suez. I had no idea where Suez was, and my mother hadn't even heard of problems there until Adam told us.

After that she began to listen more carefully to "thevoice-ofamerica."

A few minutes after midnight on the fourth of November, Jenö arrived with the news that the Russians were on their way to Budapest. There were long armoured columns from the Ukraine, and fresh regiments of soldiers.

Jenö sat on the bed, cradled his face in his arms and cried.

A little after five a.m. we listened to Imre Nagy telling the world that the Russians had attacked Budapest. He called on the Hungarian Army to resist and on the Russians to stop.

The Russians ignored Nagy.

The rolling tank columns were firing at buildings; the sound of their booming guns drowned out everything else. Though machine-gun fire was almost constant, what I remember most about that morning is the steady, relentless booming of the big guns, their metal armour clanging and crunching over the barricades. And my mother suddenly telling me to pack a small bag — we were going to the basement, the guns were coming down our street. There were a few people down there already: Mrs. Nemeth, the Fothys, the piano tuner and his daughter. Toth, the government lawyer who had moved into our old apartment, was there without his mother. He said she had insisted she would stay. The doctors said their apartment had been taken over by the army, or the Revolution, or both. They had set up a command post for counterattack on the tanks below.

We ventured upstairs at around noon to survey the damage. There was a big hole where our balcony had been, our bed was destroyed, books were scattered all over the floor, some stove tiles were shattered, there was a line of gunshot along the ceiling and everything was covered in plaster dust.

Only the Titian seemed untouched.

My mother and Jenö tried to put things back where they belonged, but they gave up after a few minutes and we set out for Leah's apartment with a suitcase each and the remnants of our bread and sausage. Jenö kept insisting that he would make sure we were safe, and my mother kept telling him she would rather he left us and went to his own home. She reminded him that they weren't married any more.

The tanks had passed on to the Körút. There was still a great deal of gunfire and yelling, but the great booming sound came from farther east. We kept close to the walls and inside the colonnades of the older buildings. There were dead and wounded in the doorways. There were bodies draped over the barricades along Rákóczi Street. I saw András with one arm in a sling, his head bandaged, the other arm holding a shotgun at waist level. He waved at me with the gun.

I remember waiting at the Rókus Church for some tanks to pass; they kept firing up at the buildings, and the machine guns in the back sprayed the sidewalks. There were people firing at the tanks from empty shop windows, from balconies, from doorways, and lying on their stomachs behind makeshift barricades.

The firing never stopped during the night or the next day. Sometime late at night I left Leah's place and, ducking in and out of crowded doorways, made my way toward Marx Square, where they said the fighting was still heavy. There were young kids, some younger than me, filling bottles with gasoline or turpentine, corking them with paper, lighting them and throwing them at the tanks. What I remember most from that night is the noise of gunfire and screaming, the smell of burning rubber and of corpses. A Hungarian soldier in army uniform offered to teach me how to fire a gun.

The morning of November 6, I met Zsuzsi near the National Gallery. She had a machine gun, and a belt of bullets was slung over her shoulder. The gun's muzzle was pointing up in the air. "Do you want to see how it works?" she shouted over the noise, pointed the gun at a burning tank and pressed the trigger.

Later that day she was dead.

I retrieved my too-heavy gun from the basement.

That same afternoon, I met the enemy. He had come out of the wreckage of his tank, crawled into the doorway where I had been standing with my shoulder to the wooden frame. I had learned how to endure the gun's recoil. The enemy's whole face was bleeding. His leg dragged behind him and there was blood all over his chest. He pulled himself into my doorway, but he made no attempt to live. He asked me in Russian to help with his leather helmet. It had big, round ear-pieces that would have made him deaf. He had white-blond hair, and when I wiped his face with the back of my hand, I saw that his eyebrows, too, were almost white. He said he hadn't thought he was going to die like this. His mother would be really angry. I thought that was amazing, perhaps our Russian teacher had mixed up the words for "upset" and "angry." He was twenty. He had a girlfriend in a place with a long name that sounded like Nizhny-Novgorod.

He died very quietly with his head on my knees. I think I was holding his hand.

58

MY MOTHER INSISTED that we had to leave Hungary. With all the fighting, the chaos, the borders weren't well guarded. This could be our last chance. Besides we had nowhere to live now. When I protested that the Revolution would be won and we'd live in the family house in Buda again, she said it would be a long time before this world put its pieces back together. Too much had been broken. I wanted desperately to stay. She said she would leave without me. When I asked Leah if I could live with her, she told me she would leave, too, if my mother left. Kati said I was stupider than usual and anyone with half a brain could see that the Russians would win. There was nothing to stay for unless I fancied going to jail for a long time. Someone was bound to have seen me with the gun. She was the only one of the family who knew about my gun in the cellar. Eva must have told her, I thought.

"Vili would want me to stay," I said.

"Your grandfather wants us to come," my mother told me. "He's been waiting for us in New Zealand, worrying what you might get up to in this mess. Look, if I'm wrong, you can return. If I'm wrong, the borders will stay open. You'll be able to come and go as you please."

We went back to Rákóczi Street to wrap the Titian into a blanket and hide it in the cellar. She sold the few remaining pieces of furniture to Toth; our clothes and the rest of the paintings went to the Fothys for safekeeping. Their apartment had remained unscathed.

We sat at their kitchen table, Toth, Mr. and Mrs. Fothy, Moci, my mother and I. Toth produced some legal paper, in case we ever came back, he said, so we could retrieve our things from them. He tried, for the last time, to persuade my mother to marry him. "It'll all be fine for you then. You'll have a place to live, I can get the kid into a decent school. University later."

Fothy wasn't so sure. "With so many dead, there will be retribution. She'd be best out of the country. When this is over, we'll want to know where everybody was from October twenty-third till the end."

I thought he had been looking at me. He had put on weight during the Revolution, his small eyes were even smaller, squeezed up by his cheeks. There were beads of perspiration on his forehead. He had definitely said "we."

Moci was examining the bag of clothes.

Both Toth and Fothy reached for their wallets and gave my mother two hundred forints each. "We'll consider it a loan," Toth told her, smiling benevolently, "not payment for your things." But he had her sign the papers in case there would be questions later. "For your own safety. If you get caught, they will grab everything. This way the room, the paintings, your clothes will still be here for you. Even the Titian. You do understand, don't you?"

She didn't, but it was the twenty-second of November. Imre Nagy and Pál Maléter had disappeared during a meeting with the Russians to discuss mutual disarmament. János Kádár had declared that a new "worker-peasant revolutionary government" had been formed. Theirs was the real revolution, and it had begun back when the Communist Party first took power. This other revolution was not a revolution but a counterrevolution fuelled by the old bourgeois elements who were determined to oust the real worker-peasant leaders and take them back into the dark ages of their slavery. Jenö said there was still some hope for the country, because János Kádár had spent years in one of Rákosi's jails and the AVO had yanked out his nails. All of them, one by one. A man like that can't be a fan of the old régime. Can he? Tanks were patrolling the streets. People were tired and grey. There was a hush over the city, waiting for the end. The corpses had been taken away. The borders were closing.

I couldn't say goodbye to Alice. Their apartment had been dark for several days.

This time I wasn't angry with my mother. I wasn't angry with anyone, not even at the world, the way I had felt when my grandfather was jailed. I was longing for answers to questions it would take me years to phrase and I felt a great sense of grief that not even the promise of seeing Vili could assuage. I wrote long, sad, unrhymed poems about dying.

The train was filled with people heading for Austria. They carried the oddest things — small dogs, birdcages, chickens, framed family portraits, gold brocade curtains still attached to their rods, feathery hats, a cuckoo clock, a standing lamp with a pink silk shade, a big bottle of dill pickles, a suitcase full of books, a spindly-legged table. The path from the train station toward the border at Andau was strewn with belongings. There was an antique chest of drawers someone had abandoned in the snow, a couple of Persian cats that serenaded our passing, their voices piercing, plaintive, astonished at their fate, a parakeet shivering on a fence post, open suitcases, kitchen utensils, albums, boxes, shoes.

My mother wore her old ski boots. She wasn't going to make the same mistake she'd made the last time we had come this way. We both had put on as many clothes as we could wear, and we carried small bags that wouldn't weigh too much for the twenty-kilometre hike. The only things she said she regretted leaving behind were Vili's medals.

When I asked if she thought my father was still hanging

around in Vienna waiting for us, she snorted. "Wait?" Then she looked at me as if to say she was sorry. "Didn't I tell you? He has remarried. Moved to Australia. Not a word from him since I signed the divorce papers. Besides," she said, "we're not going to Austria, we're just passing through. We are going to New Zealand where your grandparents are."

Our group included Leah and Laci, Kati and a guy with round spectacles and small feet, my mother and two of her friends, including Adam. He tried to shove his hand down the front of my jacket when no one was looking. I elbowed him in the ribs and stepped on his foot so hard he was still limping when we were surrounded by Russian soldiers three or four kilometres from the border and told to keep our hands up.

The man who did the talking was Hungarian, very thin and very young. At first I thought he was close to my age, but when he stopped in front of my mother to check under her arms for guns, I realized that he must have been older. The skin was stretched tight over his face, frown lines, downy whiskers, blue eyes to match his uniform, hat too big for his head. "What the hell do you think you're doing bringing a kid this young?" he demanded. His voice, even when he wasn't shouting as he had been when he told us to get our hands up, was fairly loud. He spoke with a country accent. When my mother said she didn't have anywhere to leave me, he said that was no excuse. "Kids this young shouldn't be dragged into the line of fire. Don't you know that?"

At the time I thought he was talking about himself as much as me.

We spent the night in an open field. The Russians let the women gather wood for a fire. They formed a loose circle around us, their short-barrelled guns aimed at our midriffs. The ground was hard, already beginning to freeze for the winter. There were a few trees nearby, but we weren't to go toward them. When a woman tried to go there to find privacy for a pee, the Russians levelled their guns at her head and waved her back to her space near one of the fires. In the end she asked everyone to turn away and she peed at the edge of the flickering lights, her bare ass toward us. The Russians guffawed.

I looked to find out how much you could see of her when she squatted down. In the end I decided to pee in my pants while I sat. For a minute or two it was pleasantly warm, but for the rest of the night the backs of my woollen pants froze. In the early morning I stood over the fire and worked on trying to dry them. Oddly, the Russians didn't make me sit down again till the trucks came to cart us to Györ, the closest town with a jail big enough to hold the hundred-odd people they had rounded up with us that night.

I was still wearing the pants — a lot drier now — when they ushered us in to meet the Russian commanding officer. Thick brown hair, moustache, fat lips, narrow eyes, big shoulders, stiff khaki uniform with epaulettes, gold stars on the points of his collar, buckled leather belt with a holster attached. His gun was some kind of revolver, small, fat-nosed. It lay on the table next to his hard-rimmed cap, the handle toward him, the muzzle toward us.

"Landowners," the young, sour-faced Hungarian told him in Russian. "Rich reactionary mother with Western connections. Americans. Gold buried on their land. Might tell you about it if we ask her nicely. Shall we?"

"And the girl?" the Russian asked. I liked the way he said *ghevoshka*, all soft and breathy.

The young Hungarian shrugged.

"We're from Budapest," I said in the best Russian I could muster. "Our apartment's been destroyed, nothing left at all." I repeated *nyechevo* a couple of times for effect and looked even sadder than I felt. "And we don't own any land. My mother works laying down railroad tracks, and I am in the Young Communists League. We were hoping to meet up with my father, who went to Vienna. We have nothing at all. Two hundred forints that Fothy and Toth lent us, and they are keeping our things."

"She is lying," the young Hungarian said. The Russian motioned for him to be quiet.

"How old are you?" he asked.

"Please tell him to leave," I asked, trying unsuccessfully to squeeze a tear from my eyes.

The Russian motioned with his arm. "Take her with you," he said, and the Hungarian grabbed my mother by the shoulder and propelled her out of the room.

"Twelve," I said. I could hear my mother yelling outside.

"Come closer," he asked, a small smile spreading under his moustache. "You learned Russian at school?"

"We all did."

He nodded appreciatively. "*Harasho*." Good. "Is it true about the apartment?"

"Yes, it's true about the apartment. Even our bed is gone. The wall collapsed. It was one of your tanks."

"Lucky you weren't in it," he said, smiling openly now.

I was standing next to him. "Sit," he said, slapping his knee with one hand. The other stayed close to his gun, and he glanced at the door from time to time as we talked. "Sit." He undid the top brass buttons of his jacket and pulled out a stained leather pouch.

I lowered my bum on his left knee, the one nearest the table. He smelled of Five-Year Plan tobacco, sweat and gasoline. I was hoping he couldn't smell my pants as well as I could smell him.

He opened the pouch and took out a faded photograph of a young girl with pigtails. He laid it on the table and flattened it with his palm. "Look," he said, and his voice was soft. "My little girl." He whispered the word for girl. "She is about your age now. Eleven. I haven't seen her in two years."

She seemed a lot younger than eleven, shy, her head tilted down, the eyes looking up, a round face like mine.

He said something long about the world being a rotten place and how it was going to be better when his little girl and I grew up, then he took a sheet of paper from the far end of the table, scribbled on it and gave it to me. "This will get you and your mother through the next lot of Russian troops, if you meet any. After that, you had better give up and go back to Budapest. There are worse places, you know."

As it turned out, we didn't need to use the paper. Two hundred forints got us a ride on a wooden cart all the way to the border, and except for a strange moment when we had no idea which way to run and a couple of bullets whizzed past our ears, we reached Austria without being afraid.

59

AUNT SARI SAID her husband, Kálmán, had some Turkish blood. That explained his frequent slips from grace. It wasn't that he intended to go against God, it was that he didn't always remember the difference between right and wrong. Since leaving Hungary, Sari had become somewhat religious.

We were sitting in her king-size bed surrounded by peach-coloured pillows and a peach-coloured duvet with white lace trim and pale peach-coloured walls and heavy peach drapes that floated over the white shag carpet. Her bay windows opened onto a garden of roses, azelias, rhododendrons and shorn lawns. Her house was on the east coast of New Zealand, near Hastings. There were blood-red, long-tailed birds in the garden calling to each other in high-pitched whistles.

Kálmán was as tall as my grandfather but slimmer. He liked to wear riding britches and soft leather knee-high riding boots with star-shaped spurs. His hair was still black though receding a bit from his forehead. He often ran his fingers through it, from front to back, as if to reassure himself that it was still there. He had blue eyes with dark fringes, a broad, low forehead, small, white teeth, a wide jaw. His nose had been broken and remained a small protuberance spoiling the symmetry of his face. He had learned to ride when he was four years old, become a captain in the Hungarian light cavalry and rode horses as if they were part of his own body. He never seemed to make the slightest movement to control them, yet they did exactly as he wished.

"When I met him, I thought he was the handsomest of men," Sari said. "It turned out I wasn't the only woman who thought so." She put peach-coloured polish on her finger-nails and asked me if I thought Kálmán was still as handsome as in the old picture on her dresser.

It was 1957; we were newly arrived from a refugee camp in Salzburg, Austria, where we had spent several weeks eating chocolates and cheddar cheese. The Red Cross seemed to think that was what we needed most. They gave us bundles of warm clothes, none of which fit, so I was still wearing my peed-in pants when the Flying Tigers disgorged us in Auckland — three planeloads of dirty, puke-covered refugees bundled up in cast-off evening clothes, long winter coats, moth-eaten fur caps and mittens. It was the tail end of the New Zealand summer, the tarmac steaming with heat.

We were strangers in a country that was too far away for me to imagine my being Gergely and making my way back home to Eger in the dead of night. There was too much water in between. I didn't tell Sari that I thought Kálmán was too loud, his nose too small and snuffly, or that I was afraid of him. I said that I thought he was dashing.

"Your mother's always thought so," Sari whispered. She held up her tiny hands for me to admire the peach-coloured nails. Her skin was beginning to parch dark brown in the New Zealand sun. "Or hasn't she told you?"

I shook my head, eyes focused on my cousin little Sari — Carla, now, renamed for New Zealand — practising hand-stands on the lawn. She was not pleased about my being in her mother's bed, even less pleased that she would have to tell her friends we were related. She found me profoundly embarrassing. Cloyingly foreign. No doubt she thought the same of our grandparents, but they were ensconced at the farm, with little chance of showing up at her school.

"Do ask her sometime." Sari looked at me. "Ask her about 1946 and why we left Hungary. You ask her," she repeated emphatically.

My aunt's peach-coloured, feathery felt slippers stood like soldiers at the foot of her bed.

I did ask my mother, a few days later when she was packing her bag to leave for Wellington. Because she could see I was anxious, she tried to make light of it. "At least the packing takes no time," she said. "Used to be so boring. Making lists, making choices. Worrying about the weather. Do I take boots? Or sandals? Will I need my sunhat?" Everything she owned fit into the brown plastic handbag the Red Cross had given her in Vienna right after they decided we were refugees.

"Sari said I should ask you about 1946," I said.

"'46," she mused. "Not one of my better years."

I didn't want to press the point. There had been too much shouting earlier that day in the big house. Sari had smashed a bowl of flowers.

My mother would take the dawn train.

It was Leah who told me the story. In 1946, it seemed, my mother had fallen in love with Sari's new husband, Kálmán. "I can't imagine what she saw in him. But there is no sense trying to understand why people fall in love. She left with him for Vienna. The whole dumb thing lasted about two weeks. Can't imagine why Sari has to make such a fuss."

Leah was working in a coffeeshop in Hastings, making espresso the way Hungarians liked it. The locals thought it was adventurous. A few of them, including a sheep farmer from upcountry, came back often.

VILI LOOKED DIFFERENT in New Zealand. He had put on weight, he was bronzed by the sun, his arms still bulged in his short, striped shirt-sleeves, and when he embraced me for the first time, I thought he would never let go.

"A person is as strong as his dreams," he told me when we walked to the paddock with the horses. "Sari lost her dreams somewhere. She may also have lost her memory for truly important history. Could be because she is trying so hard to fit into a new country." In New Zealand Vili had taken to sighing when he talked about things that mattered to the two of us, and his eyes clouded over as they had never done before, not even when the two men manacled his wrists and carted him off to jail. On Saturdays he wore white pants, a white fedora and a blue blazer, like so many of the elderly bowling gents around Hastings. I don't think I ever saw anyone in Hungary wearing a blazer and fedora, and bowling had never made much of an impact in Budapest.

And he kept telling his stories. Many of them took on an aspect of might-have-been.

"Sigismund's daughter did fall in love with Vilmos — who could have resisted such a beautiful boy? — but he was called to battle against some Czech rebels, and while he was away, the Emperor ordered her to marry Albert Habsburg. Our family," he admitted, "had rather a mixed experience with the Habsburgs."

The Habsburgs spent most of their time, generation after generation, amassing vast fortunes in land and turning the local population into serfs. A couple of them made reasonably good kings and a few of my ancestors liked to hang around in their courts, but nothing ever made up for their 1849 slaughter of the martyrs of Arad.

The whole world would have gained had Vilmos married Elizabeth, Vili told me. The Austrians by our side, we would have beaten the Turks before they had a chance to move in. Rákóczi would have been emperor. We would not have joined in Kaiser Wilhelm's losing war. When Ferdi Habsburg was shot and killed by the Serb student in 1914, no one would have paid the slightest bit of attention; it would have remained a private Habsburg family tragedy. There would have been no Treaty of Trianon — there would have been no reason for a world war in the first place. With no German connection, Hungary-Austria would have joined the winning side in the unlikely event of a Second World War. With Hungary-Austria strong and occupying the middle of Europe, the Germans would have been contained within their own boundaries. And we would have remained a powerful bulwark against the Russian bear to the east of us.

"So why didn't he marry her?" I wondered.

"Like you, he was too young to think of the consequences," Vili said earnestly. Before getting into the possibilities of a revised history, we had been arguing about my attempting to bicycle to the local school the next morning.

He had taken most of a day trying to teach me to ride a bike. We were both bruised and exhausted, and I was planning to take the next plane back to Hungary. Overall I thought it was a whole lot more attractive and easier to be a freedom fighter than a refugee, and it had taken less effort to learn how to use a gun than to learn how to ride a bike. Vili's was an old-fashioned man's bike, and I simply couldn't master the art of braking and hoisting my right leg over the bar at the same time. The choice was this: brake and fall sideways, or hit a tree.

I told my grandfather that the whole thing was undignified and I would never go to school if I had to ride a bike to get there.

I wasn't going to cooperate about Vilmos. "Elizabeth must have been a bit of a dog," I said.

Vili reluctantly admitted that she was no great beauty — overweight, a double chin, a long, flat nose — but she was funny and a great raconteur. Besides, she was to be queen of Hungary, and anyone she married would be king. Hence Albert. He was a true Habsburg. Did what was expected of him.

Like all the Habsbugs, he married well. "Already in the sixteenth century, there was a Latin saying: *Bella gerant fortes: tu, felix Austria, nube.* Meaning 'the strong make war, the lucky Austrians just marry.'" My grandfather still spoke fluent Latin. He believed that all civilized people should speak Latin and that an education without Latin would not produce a literate man. He insisted that this was also true of Rácz women, but he was willing to overlook that Leah and Sari hadn't learned. Their beauty had defeated their Latin tutor, who couldn't get past declining the Latin verb "to love." Now, so many years later, they resented the fact that my mother's convent school had given her the Latin advantage.

The thing about the school in Hastings was that they taught, Vili believed, tolerable Latin.

Once we were together again in New Zealand, Vili and I talked a lot about ancient history. He told me new stories and some new versions of stories I had heard before. What we didn't talk about was the Revolution he had missed. Being Vili, he never pressed me to tell him anything I wasn't ready to tell. Likewise, I held on to the tiny piece of Stalin I had brought for him in the corner of a handkerchief. I thought I would hand it to him one day when the time was right.

There was a drawing of Hunyadvár in my grandfather's history of Hungary, a hardcover book with a black binding, silver lettering stamped on the cover and spine. When he left in 1955, it was one of the few possessions he took on the journey to the other side of the globe. It was next to his bed in Hastings, New Zealand, where he could always reach it and make sure he still remembered the stories he was afraid to forget. He once told me Hunyadvár was full of men in armour and a terrible place for women. I told him it could not be as bad as a school full of English-speaking strangers that could only be reached by bicycle.

My cousin Carla's bike was pink. It had gently curved handlebars and no bar connecting them to the seat. It had some fluffy pink things in the wheel spokes that went around rapidly and very prettily when she rode out the gravel driveway past our grandfather, who made a face at her back and gave me an encouraging shove to follow. All the way to school I tried to keep my mind on János Hunyadi and the Turks. My bottom was sliding forward on the slippery, hard seat, my eyes focused on the side of the road, not straight ahead where Carla's white-socked legs pumped confidently, her blue skirt spreading around her, head held high, ponytail bobbing.

I followed her all the way, but at a distance. I knew where the school was because Sari had brought me there a week before to tell the teachers they would be taken up on their publicized offer to accept a refugee.

I stopped by riding the bike directly into a tree behind some bushes, where I was reasonably sure no one could see me and wheeled it the rest of the way to school. Vilmos, who was already in full battle gear at the age of thirteen, would have laughed at my plight. And no doubt all of my ancestors, for whom Latin came easily and most of whom learned to speak an astonishing number of languages, would have been greatly amused to note that I was the only person in first-year secondary at Hastings Common School who could not speak more than two words of English.

Hastings C.S. was a low-slung, white-painted, wooden building at the far end of a fenced-in asphalt quadrangle with basketball hoops at either end. There were green wooden benches lining the walls, green metal bicycle racks along the fence. Carla and a group of her friends were hopping up and down under one of the hoops. They were laughing and shouting, flapping their arms like a bunch of colourful birds. I knew that Carla had already decided that her best bet was to pretend that I hadn't been following her all the way from her house and to feign surprise and unleavened gaiety at my appearance.

We were about the same age, an awkward twelve. I recognized the desire to blend in with the group. In Budapest it would have been easy. But on that hazy, early summer New Zealand day, wheeling Vili's rusty bike towards the bike rack, I knew there was no hope I'd be able to follow her example. Apart from the fact that we were all girls, there were no similarities. Carla's golden-tanned friends wore pretty clothes, full skirts cinched with wide belts, pristine white blouses with lace collars, frilly ankle socks, barrettes in their hair, ribboned ponytails, two-tone running shoes or silver-buckled sandles. I, on the other hand, wore navy blue men's overalls donated by the Viennese Red Cross and the blue lace-up shoes I had chosen for the long journey from Budapest to the Austrian border. They had been my favourites and may once have been a perfect fit, though I doubted it now. I was still proud of the fact that they had survived the twenty-mile trek, the rain, the envious glares of the young Russian guards and five months of refugee camp. None of me had seen the sun since tobacco picking the previous year. Europe had just been getting over its winter.

To make matters worse that first day, I hadn't had a particularly easy landing behind the rhododendron bushes, had torn my sleeve, had scraped my chin and was covered in dust.

A middle-aged woman came out of the building and watched as I crossed the seemingly endless yard. I expect that she could see right away what was so funny that Carla's friends were convulsed under the hoop. To her credit, she quashed her own urge to laugh and, instead, addressed me in rapid English. At first she was unperturbed by my lack of comprehension, gesticulated energetically, pointed at the now-calming group of girls, then continued at a greater pace, and louder, searching my face for signs of understanding. There were none.

Assuming that she was the teacher, I offered up a smile.

Accepting this at face value, she grabbed me by the elbow and propelled me through the double doors, down a white corridor and into an airy classroom, all the time speaking to my shoulder, convinced that I was waiting for the right moment to respond.

I remember debating whether to try "yes" or "hello," and settling on "yes." Thus encouraged, she steered me to a desk at the back of the classroom under a six-foot-high wall map of New Zealand. She talked with great enthusiasm, stabbing repeatedly at the map, particularly at the northeast area where my mother had assured me Hastings was. Indeed, we managed to locate a big red-headed pin through the word "Hastings," and green-headed pins through Wellington and Auckland, also on the North Island. The South Island, which the teacher didn't bother to point out, had remained unpinned.

I nodded.

She turned triumphantly on her heels and marched to the front of the class. Meanwhile, Carla and her friends and acquaintances had appeared at their various desks and snickered with glee at my first lesson in New Zealand geography.

I had only the vaguest notion of what their morning lessons contained. I looked at the pictures of warlike dark-skinned people with body paint and face art in the book the teacher had left me and copied them into my exercise book to take home to my grandfather.

At lunchtime, I sat alone on one of the green wooden

benches and unwrapped the damp ham and cheese sandwich my grandmother had fixed for my first day at school.

In the afternoon the teacher put a Latin textbook on my desk.

During the five days that followed, the only week I spent at Hastings Common, I learned to decline Latin verbs in Vili's honour. In the evenings he told me what the verbs meant. By the end of that week I had broken the chain, the spokes and one of the pedals of my grandfather's bike and, as Carla was eager to report, I had elbowed her best friend in the stomach, sending her home in tears.

I refused to return to school.

At first Vili was deeply disappointed. "An uneducated woman has no options but to marry," he told me, "and marriage does not work for everybody. Particularly not for women." His mother, Jolán, had studied with her brothers, and she was smarter even than Vili's Oxford-educated father. "She read Latin and Greek, she could have been a university professor, but in those days, young ladies had few choices," Vili said reprovingly. "In the nineteenth century it was pinafores and piano lessons and waiting for a man to come along." Jolán was different. She married late and married the man she wanted. Vili was sure that she made the right decision because she had been wise enough to seek to be educated.

When he saw that no amount of cajoling was going to work, Vili called my mother. She had found a job in Wellington cleaning house for a Catholic family who thought they were all gaining points in heaven by allowing her to scrub their floors and do their laundry. She was disinclined to be sympathetic to my grief over the school and the bike. "Tell her," she told my grandfather, "to dream about something else while she goes to school. God knows, you've told her enough stories to fill her mind. The trick is to go through the motions while in your mind you're really somewhere else. It's how I get by."

The Catholics gave her pocket money, a room in the basement, three meals a day, but they wouldn't hear of my living
there as well. I hadn't been part of the bargain when they
took her in.

I followed Vili on his daily rounds. He took the horses into
the paddocks, mucked out their stalls, readied their feed.
Sometimes he would help Kálmán exercise them by running
them around a grassy knoll, holding on to one end of a long
rope tied to their bridles, flicking the tail of a whip at their
butts to hurry them along. Now and then he rode them
around the paddocks. Kálmán ran a riding school for young
girls who wanted to learn show jumping. I used to listen to him
shout at the girls in a wild mixture of English, Hungarian and
whatever else while they tried to manoeuvre their horses over
the wooden jumps my grandfather had helped him build.

Naturally, Carla was a perfect show jumper.

At first she had been relieved about my decision to stay
away from her school, but as the days went by and she would
come home to see me hanging around the horses with Vili,
she grew less tolerant. "While you weren't here, Grandfather
used to tell me stories, too," she said one evening at supper.
"It's not fair you should be with him all the time when you
had him for so long. It's my turn."

I was sure that's why Sari concluded that I should go to
school on the far side of the North Island.

She found a bunch of nuns in Wanganui who were
inclined to take in a refugee kid from Hungary. They were
the Sisters of Saint Joseph in the Sacred Heart Convent, on
Saint John's Hill. "It's a wonderful school and you're a lucky
girl," she assured me. "We couldn't afford a convent education for you, and there you'll be getting one for nothing. All
you have to do is keep your nose clean and don't shove any
of the other children. This is a peaceable society."

For once my mother agreed with one of her sisters. "All
you have to do is survive," she said on the phone.

Vili was ecstatic. I would be educated after all.

When we said goodbye, I gave him my gift of Stalin.

When the wrought-iron gates of the convent clanged shut behind me, I was suddenly very understanding of my mother's willingness to do just about anything to get away from her boarding school. Had there been a balding man willing to marry me on the spot, I would have seriously considered it.

I was received and accepted in the rectangular parlour by two nuns in black habits who kept their hands hidden in their sleeves and could glide along the shiny wooden floors without so much as a ripple in their skirts. During the year and a half I endured on Saint John's Hill, I don't think I ever saw their feet.

In the beginning they were keen to turn me into a pious soul, but I showed little aptitude. Tired of teaching me Latin and catechism, they let me smoke in the washrooms and hide in the attic studio, where I drew forgettable charcoal images of grand battles won and lost and of corpses propped up against city walls.

I wrote to Vili every day, and Vili wrote to me almost as often.

When I graduated, he wore a red rose in his lapel and gave me a whole armful of white oleander flowers — for hope, he said, and in memory of his mother.

VILI CAME SECOND in the Hastings Bowling Club cham-
pionship. Everyone clapped enthusiastically when he
received his small gold-plated figurine, and one man even
shouted "Attaboy, Willie" as he returned to his seat between
Sari and me. He rode Kálmán's horses in the early mornings
and never complained about cleaning out the stalls. "All
Hungarians love horses," he told me, and I didn't argue.
Kálmán was training the New Zealand Olympic team again,
and Vili felt excited to be involved.

He spoke a basic, somewhat courtly English, and most
people addressed him as "Doctor." In Hungary lawyers call
themselves "Doctor," and Vili saw no reason to give that up,
particularly after the greengrocer took him to the back of the
store and told his wife to get undressed so the doctor could
see what was wrong with her.

When my mother married again, Vili and my grandmother moved in with her in Christchurch, on the
South Island, where Vili immediately joined the bowling
club and made it to the playoffs in the first year. He rode
his bike to the bowling green almost every day, tall and
straight in the saddle, his white wide-brimmed hat at a
jaunty angle. It was an old-fashioned bike, like the one in
Hastings, with oxhorn handlebars. He had to stand on the
pedals to stop. He could still beat Laci at arm-wrestling and

ran faster than I did. He organized races along the Avon River where we lived.

He corresponded with old friends, writers, historians, former parliamentarians, poets. He was still trying to understand what had happened to his country and why. He read Hungarian newspapers published in the United States and Canada for the new immigrants still interested in what was happening in the "old country." He read books of history and analysis and new novels by writers now living in the United States, Canada, South America, wherever refugees went. Sometimes he would be jubilant, discovering that an old friend he had believed killed in Auschwitz or Birkenau had survived or when he read a new book by a writer he loved, Sándor Márai, for example. He filled thousands of thin airmail-paper sheets with his small handwriting and posted letters all over the world.

In the evenings he still told me stories, but most of them were now about his magical childhood in Bácska.

One day when he thought I was old enough, he asked me to join him and a "special friend" for coffee at her apartment. She couldn't have been much older than forty, though she wore too much makeup for me to be sure. She made thick Turkish coffee and dreadfully sweet Viennese cakes that she served with a flourish on a silver tray. I could tell that he was thrilled with her attention to detail. She talked constantly — about New Zealand politics, recipes for Viennese cakes, how she had bought her Herendi porcelain set in the most expensive store in Wellington and what else she was going to purchase there. When she said goodbye, her hand rested like a small anxious mouse in my hand. He must have told her that she should impress me.

"Well?" he asked when we left.

"She is very pretty," I told him after a while. I didn't ask him about Amelia or the others he had loved and abandoned, I already knew as much about them as I wanted to know.

"Of course, you won't tell your grandmother," he said.

"Of course," I said. "She'd be heartbroken." I was thinking about Therese and how beautiful and frail she had been when they first met and made the promises to each other about loving and protecting. And how often her heart had been broken. But in some deep recess of my mind, I was proud of him having a girlfriend when he was eighty.

I told myself I would never marry, and Vili, always reading my thoughts, said, "Promise me you'll never marry."

I didn't have to think twice about the promise.

I worked my way through university and left New Zealand for England and, later, Canada.

When we said goodbye in 1968, I think Vili knew we would not meet again. He gave me one of his big hugs that took away my breath and told me to go back home one day and see his Erdély and his Bácska. He was sure the communists were losing their grip on his country, and he wanted, more than anything, for me to share his sense of place, his histories.

New Zealand had been kind to my grandfather. But he never thought of it as home. It never changed who he had been. He didn't apply for citizenship. He didn't even see himself as an immigrant. When he talked about the great Rákóczi in exile to the end of his life, never able to return home, I know he was thinking of himself.

My grandfather died in 1975. Sari said he was shaking her doors and rattling her windows long after he was dead, and Leah's bed lifted some five or six inches off the ground a week after the funeral. They thought he was unsettled, angry about something, but neither of them knew how to talk to the dead. He is buried in the churchyard at Hastings, where he was later joined by my grandmother.

One day, I think, I should dig up his ashes and take them to Bácska where they belong.

IN 1972 I BROKE my promise to Vili. I got married. My mother, whose third marriage had dissolved, was an enthusiastic witness to the occasion. She flew to Canada to help choose the gown and to remind me that not all marriages have to be disastrous. Of course, she was not speaking from personal experience.

I have two extraordinary daughters. They are true Canadians. Unlike their grandmother and me, they never question their identities. Still, the old stories that filled my childhood have made their way into theirs.

When Catherine, the older of the two, was eighteen, she surprised me and her father by announcing that she wanted to be presented at the annual Toronto Helicon Ball, a grand Hungarian affair that resists all efforts to adapt to modern times. A girl whose favourite garb was blue jeans and sweatshirts was now dressed in a flowing, off-the-shoulder gown and insisted on tails for her escort. She pinned on a blue-pink orchid and wore sparkling white high heels as she walked, tall and slender, down the red carpet on the arm of her still-stunned father, curtsied to the ball's honorary sponsor and whipped up her skirts for the obligatory opening waltz. For her birthday my mother had given her an exact replica of her great-grandfather Vili's ring, the one with the lion brandishing a sword over the ramparts of Nándorfehérvár.

When Julia, her younger sister, turned eighteen, she announced that she wanted to come with me to Transylvania, Vili's Erdély. I had been planning to visit the birthplace of our stories, a journey to my grandfather's heartland.

"Why?" I asked her.

"I think it would be cool," she said after some serious thought.

It still seemed to be "cool" in the spring of 1998 when we crossed the Romanian border at Gyula, heading toward Arad. I had been going on about 1848, the War of Independence, Rákóczi as a kid separated from his mother, the courageous Ilona Zrinyi, Munkács Castle, the Habsburgs, the Turks, and I wondered what Julia was thinking as she looked through the glass at the grim countryside of smoke-spewing factory chimneys and gas-belching cars, approaching a city that seems to begin nowhere and takes in visitors with such reluctance that it has failed to put up signs to its centre. The fashions were Stalinist era; the men still wore the brown suits mass-manufactured by the Russians, the women's thick stockings were rolled down their thighs.

We drove past the vast railway station, along the Boulevard Revoltei ("Which revolution?" Julia asks. "The last one. The Romanians threw out their communist dictator"), past the huge, incongruously cake-like city hall, past the imposing state theatre with its Baroque trimmings, down winding streets with giant potholes and, after several passes, to the Hotel Park. The room was postwar Eastern Europe, paint peeling, thick rust in the bathtub, narrow metal cots, blankets like emery boards, smells of stale liquor, sweat, stagnant cheap cologne. A lone cockroach crawled toward the balcony.

The women at the backlit reception desk had never heard of the battlefield nor of the executions of 1849, but an old man collecting broken bottles in the parking lot, pointed across the river. We took off on foot.

The bridge is narrow, with a single lane for pedestrians,

trucks speeding by in the centre. There are bullet holes in the stone barrier and wide gaps where the iron girders barely hold.

I looked down at the slow, brackish water meandering between the muddy shores, and suddenly I felt as if I knew this river, that I had known it for a long, long time. I could almost see the bodies it has carried, its current sluggishly spilling over the flatlands on its way to the Black Sea. Some of the bodies became stuck on the protruding rocks. After the battles were lost, the women and the crows would come down here in the morning to claim them.

The generals had wanted to wear their red jackets when they were hanged ...

"There were thirteen," I told Julia. "Nine were hanged, four were shot by firing squad."

"You've already told me."

"Did I tell you that the two tallest generals took almost an hour to die because the gallows had been built too low?"

The monument stands by the side of the road leading to Timisoara (our ancestors' Temesvár) no more than twenty kilometres from the battlefield of Világos where General Görgey laid down his arms at the feet of the Russian General Rudiger on August 3, 1849.

It isn't much of a monument, a pile of stones no more than twice a man's height, off the main road, hidden behind a football field to the side of a rutted dirt track that wanders on toward a quiet village. If you didn't look for it, you'd never know it was there.

There were chickens pecking at the sparse grey grass, a couple of low, lye-washed houses. An old chestnut tree towered over the houses and the stone pile. The sound of children reading in unison through the concrete building behind the monument. A huge red and white canvas sign hung over the entrance: *Global Sportiv Scolar Gloria Arad*.

The monument, like the giant football field, belongs to the school.

Three stones are arranged like a set of tall steps over a concrete footing that slants down and outward. The names of the thirteen generals are etched into the stone, as is the date: October 6, 1849.

Their bodies were left hanging for several days.

It had been raining that day, as it was now.

"If they had already won, why did they hang them?" Julia asked.

"The Austrian general, Haynau, wanted everyone to remember what happens to people who resist."

"Or it could have been revenge."

We headed back past the gates of Arad Castle, once a convenient jail for the hundreds the Austrians suspected, now a training camp for young soldiers. They eyed us warily. "They are so young," my daughter said, and I was so glad she had grown up in a place not given to sacrificing its young.

That evening we left the Hotel Park in search of food. The Palace of Culture was dark, as was the Boulevard Revoltei, a bus, a man on a bicycle, a couple of cars going by slowly. The only lights came from a McDonald's. The radio blared Sting.

In the hotel bar it was *L. A. Law* with subtitles.

63

THE NEXT MORNING we stopped to greet the storks nesting on telegraph poles along the road under Déva Castle. It's high on a conical mountain, the stronghold of ancient spirits between the mountains and the plains. In 1849 the Austrians blew it apart. Now only a few of the walls remain. The road to Hunyadvár (now Vajdahunyad Vára) seemed to be a smog-belching, rust-eaten, foul-smelling, Dickensian hell. Coal dust and broken windows, grime-encrusted, cracked concrete walls, the screaming, deafening noise of machinery, oily mud between buildings where grim, bent-over men marched in black gumboots carrying iron rods on their shoulders.

And suddenly, like a painted backdrop, a stage set, there it was. Exactly as I had imagined it: Hunyadvár. High on a green hill, seven red turrets rising from stone towers, long slits for the archers' arrows, narrow windows overlooking the valley. The Hunyadis' stronghold. It was already two centuries old when King Sigismund gave it to János. It was in the southern region of Erdély the king was sure the Turks would want. It was a gift no one would miss because no one had lived in the castle for God knows how long and no one was brave enough to try living in it now that the Turks were coming and going as they pleased.

When János Hunyadi and his wife were finished with it, Hunyadvár was exactly what castles were supposed to be. A tower at each corner, battlements in between, a drawbridge, a moat, a central, stone-paved courtyard, a family chapel and winding stairs leading to living quarters in the turreted upper chambers of the towers. Underground corridors connecting all. A dungeon for dangerous enemies. Tapestries celebrating great moments in other people's battles. Everywhere dark and damp. Moss on the walls. Small, deep fireplaces that could not have kept the cold out. Stark, chiselled stone tables where men in armour could decide who was friend and who was enemy. Walls with lances, swords, iron stands for armour, heavy candelabra, torch holders.

We climbed up from the small car park, past the ice cream and sandwich stand, across the bridge over the moat. The tallest of the turrets flew a triangular flag, the Hunyadi raven in a blue field.

Inside a guide offered tours in Romanian.

We were the only visitors.

In the high-vaulted rooms there were tall terracotta fireplaces, remnants of marble statues, hidden passageways, broken friezes of battle scenes. In János Hunyadi's chambers, a massive oak table, ravens engraved at each place setting. In Erzsébet Hunyadi's chamber, a ten-foot, cream-coloured ceramic stove, ravens etched into the tiles; in the corner, a deep, carved-stone windowseat where she might have sat waiting for János to come home.

In the hall of the knights part of the tile floor remained, raven shields on the walls, crossed spears, a chain-mail shirt, fragments of tall vases and decorated plates. This is where the argument with Count Ulrich Cillei began. It's where Vilmos waited with the other knights.

Julia took photographs of the ceramic floor. "Do you think this is where he was killed?"

The ceramics were surprisingly clear, the colours hadn't faded. Leaning over them, I thought I could see something that looked like blood. But that's not what Vili had said. "No.

It's the chamber above the hall. His dagger killed Cillei and saved László Hunyadi's life."

László Hunyadi's body had been laid out by his mother on the stones in the Hunyadi chapel, in front of the altar where his father had offered up mass to a vengeful Lord whose help he needed to defeat the Turks.

"Have I told you about the faithless young king who had László beheaded in Buda, and that László's long hair almost saved him?"

"Yes."

"And that his mother cried for forty days and nights and the ravens all came and cried with her, their black bodies forming a dark wall around this castle?"

"Uh-huh."

"But have I ever told you about Vilmos's great black stallion, Lightning, who ran so fast its hoofs barely touched the ground?"

"Yes, but go ahead anyway."

⤜ ⤛

Our house had been somewhere near the village of Tövis, north of Arad, four days' journey on horseback from Hunyadvár, two days and nights if you are in a hurry to be near your friend's son to protect him from his enemies.

⤜ ⤛

Tövis is called Teius now. It's a collection of run-down, flat-roofed, low-slung houses. No one here speaks Hungarian anymore.

An old woman with a cane pointed out the Catholic cemetery. "Iancu Hunyadi," she said. The iron gate had rusted shut. We climbed over the chipped spikes into a jumble of tall weeds, gnarled trees, wildflowers, grass, brambles, stinging nettle and a few old mossy stones.

The names of the dead have all but disappeared. A few of the most recent stones have dates of birth —1820s, 1830s — but no dates of death. As if the owners had meant to die here but hadn't succeeded.

In 1849 the Hungarians in Tövis were slaughtered by their Wallach neighbours. The story has made its way into Romanian history books. The Wallachs rose up against their Hungarian lords. They had had enough of servitude, they knew their chance had come when the Austrian Army marched past on its way to Arad. They would prove their loyalty to the Habsburg crown and hope for a better deal, at least for bigger plots of land.

"Petronella Rácz, though," I told Julia, "survived the massacre."

"If she had died, too, we wouldn't be here."

⊰ ⊱

We drove on to Alba Julia. It had been Gyulafehérvár for several centuries, while Erdély was Hungarian. Julia liked the new name. And she loved the big Orthodox cathedral, its Byzantine frescoes, pink walls, freshly painted towers, elaborate outer walls, pristine rose gardens and gold-speckled portraits of Michael the Brave and his unprepossessing bride, Stanca. In glamour and wealth, it dwarfs the thirteenth-century Hungarian Catholic cathedral, St. Michael's, just a few feet away from the Orthodox rose gardens.

This is the place of János Hunyadi's tomb. His name has broken off the stone sarcophagus, the Turks chipped at his effigy, and broke off his nose some eighty years after his death when they finally conquered Gyulafehérvár. They took pieces of Hunyadi to ward off evil. The Hunyadis' raven is still holding the Hunyadi ring in its beak over his empty shoulders. Next to him is László.

A few kilometres north, we stopped at a walled church. "Unitarian," the minister told us proudly. "Built in the shape of a cross. Only the apse is left of the thirteenth-century building, the rest was destroyed by the Habsburgs in 1849. They sent a regiment of *labanc*. New white uniforms after Arad. They searched for *kuruc* soldiers in all our houses, shot the priest on the steps there, in front of the church. We had supported Kossuth, you see." He said that with great familiarity, as if Kossuth might still be around, his grave not sunk into the mud near Turin, Italy, where he died in exile on March 20, 1894, more than a hundred years ago.

We spent the night at the Hotel Ambassador in Cluj/Kolozsvár, King Mátyás's town. It had been, for so long, a centre of Erdély culture, the place that the 1920s patriotic song promised "will return" to Hungary. We walked through diesel-reeking streets lined with old, grimy, Baroque buildings and down narrow alleys whose bravely orange and ochre houses reminded me of Buda.

"In 1921," I told Julia, "right after the Treaty of Trianon, the reigning Romanian prime minister told the world that ten years from then, you'd never notice that there had been Hungarians in Cluj." The mayor of Cluj, the man Hungarians called "mad mayor Funar," was now — in 1998 — doing his best to eradicate all traces of Hungary. He ordered the destruction of monuments, the rebuilding of whole areas; he forbade the Hungarian language and set about reinventing history.

There still remains the vast fourteenth-century Catholic church in the centre of Cluj, St. Michael's. Its pillars still curve into a hopeful vaulted ceiling. It is bare of pictures and statues, though the stained walls betray where they had been. There is a hand-carved pulpit with intricate lattice-work, intertwined wooden figurines, that reached some twenty feet above our heads. The altar celebrates St. Michael's victory over the unfortunate dragon.

An old woman in black told us there used to be golden paintings, mosaics from the East, coloured glass windows, and that Erdély's nobles' flags had flown from their own wall standards high near the arches where the light would fall on them on a Sunday morning.

Outside there was still the statue of King Mátyás astride his stalwart bronze stallion, at least fifteen metres tall, flanked by ten Romanian flags flapping comfortably in the April breeze. Julia pointed to a chiselled-off part of the pedestal where the word "Hungarea" had been removed. Perhaps the mayor decided the Hunyadi king was not Hungarian.

"It's nothing like I imagined," Julia told me. And she confessed she had been expecting to see some of Dracula's country, not just tombstones and memorials to lost battles. "What happened to the vampires?"

In the Wallach version, Vlad Drakul, or Vlad the Impaler, was not a vampire but a somewhat eccentric patriot who liked to impale his enemies on wooden stakes and watch them writhe in agony while he ate his meals. There is some debate as to how many people he impaled but none about his bravery. In the fifteenth century, when the Turkish Empire stretched its hands into Eastern Europe, Vlad wanted witnesses to his killing binges, a few who would carry home such frightening tales of savagery that even the Turks would stay away from his lands.

Once when the sultan sent two emissaries to discuss a treaty with the Wallachian prince, Vlad observed that they had not removed their turbans in his presence. He reminded them — politely — that in Wallachia you should be bareheaded when delivering a message to a supreme ruler.

"Simple courtesy," he told them.

In their country, they informed Vlad, you kept your turban on as a mark of respect for Allah. Vlad took that under consideration for a few minutes, then ordered his men to nail the offending turbans to the Turks' heads so they'd always remember to show respect to their god.

When the sultan heard the tale, he was enraged. Yet he waited a few years before sending new armies into Wallachia. The Voivod (the ruler), it seemed, could match him in cruelty.

Vlad disliked the *boyars*, or gentry, of Transylvania almost as much as he disliked Turks, because many of them had failed to recognize his right to be their supreme ruler. They thought he had been imposed on them by a faraway court.

"Let me guess: the Austrians?"

"No, alas, it was the Hungarians. János Hunyadi gave him the job, and he was sorry almost immediately, but too late. Your great-grandfather, Vili, told me that Mátyás took Vlad prisoner once and kept him in Solomon's Tower at Visegrad for over ten years."

"And he let him go?"

"He had to. While Vlad was in the tower, Mátyás's sister used to visit him and they fell in love. They got married. King Mátyás then let him have Transylvania back. Have I told you about his castle?"

"Not yet."

In April 1459, he invited a bunch of *boyars* to a Pentecost celebration at his castle in Târgoviste."

"They didn't go, right?"

"Wrong. They went dressed in their silken finery, wanting to impress Vlad with their own wealth and power. They came from afar, many over several days' journeys, expecting a feast and Vlad Drakul didn't disappoint them. There were whole roast pigs, three hundred hens, pigeons drowned in honey and barrels of fine Eger wine. They ate and drank until dawn. When the *boyars* and their families were sound asleep, Vlad's men took their weapons and their horses.

"In the morning he told them he wished to have a new castle built above Poenari, near the Curtea de Arges, site of an ancient cathedral destroyed by the Turks (*curtea* means "cathedral" in Romanian). He liked the Poenari site for another reason: there were remnants of a thirteenth-century castle nearby. Its stones could be used to build the new walls.

"Vlad gave the *boyars* two choices: build the castle, or be impaled on the long wooden stakes around the periphery of their feast."

"I guess they built the castle."

"They marched up to the top of the mountain above the village of Poenari and began to build Vlad's castle. It took them ten years, their silken finery falling off their backs, their wives and children dying around them, but they succeeded. The stones are still there today. If you climb the one thousand two hundred steps to the top of the mountain, you can see them for yourself."

We took off from the main road at Gyalu and drove up the Bihar Mountains on a dirt track, deep-gouged by wagon wheels. The higher we climbed the cooler the air was. Mountain sheep grazed on blue-green grass as hawks circled overhead. There were long, wooden houses with decorated windows and hand-carved doors. We stopped in Calota to watch a group of boys play soccer, shouting at one another in rough Hungarian. Around here I could imagine what the old Rácz homestead might have felt like; around here it did feel like the place Vili had loved.

Julia said we should come back here one day.

64

M Y M O T H E R A N D I were on one of our trips to Hungary. We went searching for our emotional inheritance, remembering Vili's stories now, with so many layers of later knowledge obscuring the original.

Although her childhood memories of Vili were tinged with anger at his "gallivanting," my mother never stopped loving him, and being awed by him. He was so much grander than anyone she met later, so much more vital, she was even trying to forgive him. "So many of them," she said over wine in the Apostolok. "It's difficult to imagine he remembered who each one was. But he did. On the first of the month everyone was remembered. Some received flowers (he did love sending roses), some got champagne. The lucky ones got money. I think he must have had at least sixteen children apart from us."

"Did everyone know about it?"

"Most people knew. Leah and Sari and I knew all the time we were growing up. And the fights were terrible then. I think that in the twenties mother thought she could change him. Later she gave up."

"They still fought."

"Yes, but they were over the worst of it."

"In many ways," she added later, "you saw the best of him. He was still the dashing storybook hero, but his duelling days were over, and he had no fortune left to squander on starlets. When I was a child, he had little time for magic tricks."

We were on our way to Bácska, a kind of pilgrimage to the place where three generations of the Ráczes had lived, where Vili was born.

My cousin István, Edy's son, and Edy herself decided to come for the journey.

István did the driving. Like all the Rácz men, he is broad-shouldered, square-faced, starting to lose his hair. He is an engineer and spent most of his life in Africa in countries that preferred Russians to Americans. A mathematician, he counted his successes in dams built and railroads completed. István said he came on the journey because his "foreign" cousin would not be able to find the way. But when we arrived in Bácska, I knew that his own reasons for coming were, like my own, rooted in his childhood's stories. His grandfather was Vili's brother Gyula.

The last time I had seen him had been during the final days of the Revolution when his mother, Edy, brought her two boys over to Leah's to say goodbye. She hadn't believed that the Revolution was over. She was going to fight on. The boys stayed with their father while she commanded the defence of the British Embassy. Back then her hair was wild over her shoulders, now it had thinned and whitened. When the Revolution was over, she was arrested, interrogated, condemned to death, had her sentence commuted to life and spent ten years in jail. Now, István was still unsure whether to be proud of her or angry. He and his brother had grown up in a state orphanage.

We crossed the Hungarian border south of Szeged into Serbia. Szeged was once at the centre of Attila's empire, the salt capital of the Huns. After the defeat at Mohács the Turks plundered the city, killed its citizens and made it the centre of their western dominion.

At the border both sets of guards examined our passports with undisguised curiosity.

This was an unusual place for tourism, the war still smoul-
dering in Mostar and Pale, heavy artillery moving out of the
hills overlooking bloodied Sarajevo, but Canadians hadn't
yet joined in the NATO bombardments, and there had been
no ethnic cleansing in Kosovo.

The asphalt was gored and pitted, the houses pockmarked
with bullet holes. The grass faded yellow, puddles of mud in
the fields; it had snowed here a week before.

István has Vili's hazel eyes, and like Vili, he loves this land.
He talked of the black earth of Bácska oozing minerals and
water, land that has been a breadbasket for a thousand years.
He stopped the Skoda to pick up a chunk of hardened mud.
He rolled it around in his thick palms, through his fingers, as
if it were fine silk or flour he was testing for consistency, and
he held it up to my face to smell. Pungent, like rotting leaves.

"It's the best farming earth in the world," he said with
longing.

Edy sat in the back with my mother. She was talking about
her childhood.

When we arrived in Kula, we fell silent. István parked the
car in front of the church.

I was sure this could not be the place. I had imagined the
church would be like a French cathedral, all fractured light
and hushed, upward-reaching, incense-laden air, columns
and arches. It was, instead, a simple white building, symmet-
rical, with three alcoves above the door; only one of them
had a statue: a grey, metal, rusty Saint John wielding a bent
cross in one hand, like a stave. The bell rang for ten o'clock
matins, but no one came. It was dark and cold inside. No
candlelight, no mosaic windows. Huddled in her coat, my
mother led the way, hesitated at the holy-water urn, then
reluctantly dipped in a gloved finger and bobbed toward the
altar in a half-hearted gesture of obeisance.

The church was too small to contain Vili's stories. How their
mother would scold the boys to be quiet, their first-row seat too

close to the altar, the priest stopping his sermon to scowl at the Rácz family stall, my grandfather shoving his smaller brothers onto the marble paving stones, the village boys taking up the snickering as the priest turned his back for the *Agnus Dei*, the silver bells ringing in the Communion. My great-grandmother, Jolán, resplendent in black, her face covered by a thin, black fringe of lace, her big body leaning forward as she knelt in prayer.

My great-grandfather never attended church.

There were two rows of wooden pews; the stone floor was uneven. We approached the communion table at the front of the church, twelve desultory pictures on the stone walls, the Stations of the Cross. The table was covered with a white lace cloth, "handmade," my mother whispered. The altar was white, too, a gold cross in an alcove above the curtain-covered recess where the bread and wine would be kept. The red Eucharist light was on, indicating that Jesus is here, it's OK to pray.

We looked for the front pew where the boys had played. It was hard to see in the oppressive dark. We ran our fingers along the backs of the pews and under the seats; perhaps some memory had remained — a plaque, maybe, or scratched-in names, some sign that the Rácz boys had once cavorted here — but there was nothing. The only light came from the flick-ering red of the Eucharist and the one window to the left.

Now that my eyes had grown used to the darkness, I saw that someone had laid white flowers on the altar and there were unlit candles on either side of the open book.

My mother shivered. "I think we should go," she said in English, distancing herself from the surroundings.

She was pointing to a small, dark figure approaching from behind the altar. Draped in black, it floated toward us silently. Then it made a faint rustling noise just as we started for the doorway, where my cousin István stood with his back toward us, attempting to decipher something on the oak door.

"We can't turn the heating on in November yet," the apparition said in Hungarian, its voice surprisingly human, "but you are welcome."

My mother made a fast recovery. "Good morning, Sister," she said in her best convent-girl intonation. She launched into a long tale about why we had come. It was long because there was no simple explanation for our presence. None of us was sure exactly what we were looking for.

The nun was smaller than my mother. She had to tilt her face up to look into my mother's eyes. She smiled and bent her head again.

"I could switch on the light for you," she said at the end of my mother's tale. "Maybe the painting behind the altar ... It's an old one ... a gift to the church. Before my time."

It was the painting that Vili had described, St. George draped in red cloth, red leather armour like the Huns had worn into battle, kneeling, his legs bare, arms extended as if to say, "Welcome to my house." On either side, kneeling angels, one of them holding his iron sword. In front of them, bigger than all three figures, the dragon, green, shiny, still fearsome in its majesty. Its head is bowed, not in defeat but in sadness, a broken arrow piercing its brave heart. It is a magnificent dragon, long, sturdy — not Carpaccio's puny, dog-like creature in Venice, not the humbled beast dragged onto St. Marco's by the victorious knight. This dragon occupies his painting, and he was looking at me as I approached him.

No wonder Vili's father never came to church — if this was his painting, he was not a real Christian. He was fonder of the dragon than of the knight.

There used to be talk of a dragon in Transylvania, an ancient one that once ruled the dark mountains. Vili had told me a story starring a green-scaled dragon that came out of the night sky to wreak havoc on the Turkish encampment. It was a fire breather, sinewy, bat-winged, silver-necked. It could turn swiftly and silently like a cat, and arrows would bounce off its tail. The pasha sent a parchment note back to the sultan: There is a Hungarian dragon guarding the mountain passes, it killed a regiment of janissaries and burned our tents, its breath was so hot our spears melted.

The sultan didn't believe in dragons, so he had the emissary beheaded. Perhaps all Hungarians breathed fire, he opined, must be the paprika in their diet. He expected Kolozsvár to be taken by the end of the dry season.

The nun showed us the way to the priest's house across from the church. The big courtyard beyond the iron gate had once been an oleander garden, she told us, but the parish needed the space for a basketball court.

Once it had been a great house with gabled windows, four interconnected buildings in a rectangle around the garden designed by a specialist from Budapest. He had placed the plants so that the hardiest protected the more fragile. In the middle there had been a fountain that pumped water even during the winter months.

In 1918 Serb partisans had used the Murillo angels on the spigots for target practice. The rosebushes were trampled during the war. The nuns — there were five back then, now only one — had tried to revive them and plant new ones, but no one understood roses and the garden grew wild. This nun had never seen the fountain, of course — she hadn't been born in 1918 — but she had heard the stories.

Vili had said that ten bay horses took turns drawing water for the fountain. When guests came, the servants dropped colours into the tank changing the water to blue and pink or to red and purple, and lights went on around the black marble pool. His father had brought the marble slabs himself by horse and cart. The fountain was a gift for Petronella, Vili's grandmother, the first of the Ráczes to come to Kula. She had died before Vili was born, but the old men in the village still remembered her. She had been a great beauty.

She was small, dark-haired, like my Aunt Leah. When she

arrived in Kula, her feet were swaddled in a multitude of black socks and stuffed into too-large, brown, polished man's walking shoes. There were bundles of clothes in the cart, a walnut chest with brass fittings and one old, hand-carved oak dresser turned on its side. There were bullets embedded in the dresser's backboard; its mirror split into three jagged pieces still held in place by the frame. The chest was as wide as the cart. It took four men to shift it, and it scraped the wood off the sides of the cart with its brass handles shaped like dragon's tails, thick and scaly. The lock, too, was in the shape of a dragon's head.

Petronella sat straight, shoulders back, on a plank across the front of the cart. She was dressed in black — a long-sleeved blouse, a string of pearls, a wide skirt laid out around her, black cloth gloves. A short, black lambskin coat. She held a small child on her lap. Two broad-hoofed peasant horses pulled the cart. Their flanks were steaming in the chill October air, they whinnied in anticipation as Petronella jumped from her perch, her child still held in her arm, and spread straw on the frozen ground before them. She paid in advance for her room at the guesthouse and boarded her horses with the village blacksmith.

The next morning she went to the cobbler's on the main square. He was surprised when she removed her large man's shoes and rough woollen socks to reveal fine, black silk hose, almost transparent. And he was astonished at the size of her feet, which were smaller even than those of the Austrian ladies who used to come with their husbands to the hussar ball in Nándorfehérvár.

Child's feet, he told her, and I imagine that she smiled just like all the Rácz women smiled when they received this compliment. "You must be careful you're not blown over in the wind," he told her. "Winter's coming, we have fierce winds here on the plains. Not like your Erdély, where the mountains catch the wind. This is tough country, Bácska. Not for the timorous." She looked at him, the smile gone now. She didn't answer. The next day he told the men gathered in the gaming house that one thing this one wasn't was timid.

She ordered black lace-up boots, made of his finest leather. She offered to sell him the man's shoes she was wearing. They were barely worn, the soles still shiny, good craftsmanship. The cobbler made her boots for nothing, accepting the man's shoes as payment.

It was 1849. Nobody asked her any questions.

She walked to the church, her black skirt swishing around her, the women staring from their windows, whispering. She held the child's hand all the way. Like his mother, he was all in black, britches, velvet jacket, wide collar, heavy shoes. He tried to pry open her fingers, he wanted to run, he'd been cooped up too long in the cart. A sturdy little boy, strong for his size. She could barely hold him, stubborn as he was, but she did. She whispered something to him, he whimpered then quietened. His socks had slipped down around his ankles in the struggle, his chubby legs were red from the cold.

She pulled her woollen scarf around her head when she entered the church, dipped her finger into the holy water by the door, genuflected, made a tidy sign of the cross. The child tried to do as she'd done, but he couldn't quite reach the water. When she let go of his hand, he ran to the alcove to see the Christmas crèche. A straw house, painted plaster animals, the Virgin dressed in blue and white muslin.

Even the nuns stopped to watch her as she passed. She went directly to the sacristy and asked where she might find the priest. She was very pale and very young. Her voice was soft, her eyes grey-green, her small face oval; a few strands of back hair had escaped from her shawl. A nun walked with her to show the way to the whitewashed house next to the church, behind the stone column that stands there still.

There are three stone men seated on top of the column, each gazing wistfully in a different direction. One wears a hussar's tunic with buttons and braid, another an open shirt, the third a Roman toga. I couldn't imagine what their significance might be. Perhaps Petronella, too, looked up at them and wondered.

Father Ignác seemed to have been expecting her. He was courteous, offered her coffee and cakes, not in his study where the parishioners came to ask for his advice or to consult about funerals and weddings, but in his formal livingroom, open only for special occasions. The housekeeper bustled about for a while, preparing food, offering sugar with Father Ignác's silver sugar-cube holder, setting out the embroidered holiday napkin squares, asking the boy if he'd like some lemonade. The priest inquired about Petronella's health, she about his. Then he closed the door behind the housekeeper. She heard the murmur of their talk, but she couldn't make out the words.

No one knew what was said, but Petronella was with him for a couple of hours, and the next day the priest came for her in his carriage and took her to a big farmhouse some five kilometres from Kula that had once been the home of a landowner who joined Kossuth's army in 1848 and who died near Kolozsvár. She must have bought the land and the house, furniture and all, from the widow, the priest acting as go-between.

Father Ignác hired two men to carry her big trunk into the house. They said it was so heavy it might have been filled with gold. They lugged the oak dresser into the bedroom and set it up exactly as she had instructed, next to the window, away from the light. She left the gilded Orthodox Madonnas in their niches where the Serb woman who had been married to the Hungarian had placed them for worship. But she had the men take the big, black cross out of the child's room and give it to the nuns.

Petronella hired a hundred men to work her new land, some three thousand acres of the best earth there was in Hungary.

She grew wheat and barley, she planted cherry trees, and a vineyard, she bought dairy cows and ten more horses for the planting season. She had a well dug in back of the house, raised chickens, had a shed built for the cows. She hired a maid, a cook and a washerwoman.

She made no friends in the village. Though she attended church every Sunday, she never stayed to chat on the church green or join in the seasonal celebrations. She declined invitations to luncheons. She received no visitors and, as far as anyone could recall, no letters.

She never replaced the dresser's mirror. It was the only mirror in her bedroom, and she must have gazed at her own fractured reflection every day.

She dressed in black all her life.

Once a year, they said, around Pentecost Sunday, she'd wrap herself up in her shawl and lambskin coat and have her travelling trunk placed on the cart. She would take the reins herself, the child beside her, and they'd set out toward the Carpathian Mountains. They'd be gone a couple of weeks. Though Vili's father was none too exact about where they went, our family's stories were clear that she had come from Tövis, near Arad, and that's where she returned every year.

It was Petronella's husband, my great-great-grandfather, who was shot at his diningroom table near the city of Arad on October 20, 1849.

They had sat at opposite ends of the oak table, a distance of more than ten feet, and more than thirty years. There was a crystal decanter of regional red wine by his right hand. The maid ladled thick soup into their fine china plates. His silver spoon dipped in and out of the broth. Petronella didn't like the gristly chunks of pork the cook prepared for her husband. Except for his joyful slurps, there was no sound — the master didn't wish to have talk while he ate — till the crack of the single shot.

The Catholic priest of Kula seemed unsurprised to meet us, as if every day there were odd visitors from far-off countries looking for signs of their ancestors. He had just come from a funeral service and was in a hurry to give another old parishioner his last rites. He showed us the parish registers for the turn of the century, but he was impatient for us to leave. The register didn't show any Ráczes. The priest knew of no house that had belonged to the family.

The cemetery, he told us, was on the outskirts of town. There was a Rácz family gravestone. "It's expensive to maintain all the old tombstones," he said, "as years go by and no one comes to care for them. We allow the locals to bury their dead in the family plots." What they paid would help keep the ancient memorials in place a little longer. He was unapologetic.

Sari had told me there would be a big, white cross to mark the place, and she was right. There are four stone blocks, one on top of the other — two tall, two square, each narrower than the one beneath, stacked like children's playing blocks. At the top is a cross about four feet tall. The chiselled stone glistened white in the late November sun.

On the big, vertical centre block, the letters announce "The Rácz Family" in deeply etched serifs. One side is given to my great-grandfather György, born in 1846 in Arad, died in May 1909 in Kula. In italics, the script goes on to declare that he was a great landowner, a scholar and an agricultural representative of Bácska. *May he rest in peace.*

So the sturdy little boy accompanying Petronella to Kula must have been three years old.

György was strong like his father, big for his age. Fine, dark hair, his mother's. For awhile he kept close to the farmhouse, helped the cook feed the chickens, collected their eggs in the

mornings, followed his mother into the fields to check the
new shoots in the spring. He skipped stones on the runoff
pond in the summer.

Once winter set in Petronella had the head man clear the
ice for György. He skated on the pond alone, wearing the red
mittens and a red, fringed scarf his mother had knitted him.
He didn't know that the Kula children watched him.

He cut a hole in the ice and hung string into the water for
fish that never came. He tried to tempt a matted stray dog
into friendship. He spoke to the dog in a strange dialect that
the other children didn't understand.

When he was six, Petronella took him to the village school.
She had a new carriage drawn by two young black horses. A
servant in a black jacket with gold braid and gold buttons led
the boy in to meet the nuns. Petronella watched him go but
did not leave her seat. The village children told their parents
that night that she had eyes the colour of storm clouds.

György loved school. Years later he would berate his three
unruly sons about their lack of interest in learning. He was
fluent in Hungarian, Serbian, English, French, Latin and
German. He finished top of his school in 1856, one hundred
years before we left Hungary. Petronella sent him to the
Piarists' school in Budapest, then on to Oxford. When he
returned, she had built a new house, bigger and fancier than
the last: twenty rooms, each with a chandelier, indoor plumb-
ing with running water, porcelain bathtubs and a second
storey with a grand sittingroom where no one ever sat.

On the other side of the Rácz family tombstone, there is
Jolán, my great-grandmother, who died in 1904 in her fifty-
third year, and two children, aged nine and two, both girls. A
boy who died in his twenty-third year in 1889, the year of my
grandfather's birth, gets pride of place on the other side.

István fetched sandwiches from the trunk of his car. We sat
in a row on a white stone bench near the entrance to the
cemetery, drank canned iced tea and ate dark bread and

thick cheese. Only my mother talked. She was disappointed. Somehow, in her mind's eye, the tombstone had become larger, more like a mausoleum, nothing as simple as this grave. Vili had talked of a monument, a marble slab you could see from a mile away, a place guarded by willows near a brook, blackbirds perched on the branches, whispering leaves. It's where he had wanted to be buried. In New Zealand they don't have willows in the cemetery because their shade kills the grass.

A man on a bicycle weaved along the cemetery path, an orange knitted sack hung from his handlebars, a watermelon over his shoulder. He wore a blue cap and jacket, white shirt unbuttoned, dusty shoes. He wobbled when he spotted us, his head turned even as his wheels continued forward.

"Hello," my mother said in Hungarian. She started toward him, her sandwich aloft in her hand. "Are you from these parts?" As if a man on a bike wheeling along with one hand on the handlebar, a melon over his shoulder, could be planning to travel far.

"Oh yes," he said, *igenam*, his accent leaden with the local dialect.

"Do you know where the *tövisi* Rácz house used to be?" she asked.

"*Igenam*," he told her, stopping the bike, but only just, his hand still on the handlebar. "You're the people from afar, looking for your folk, are you?"

My mother told him we had travelled a long way to find the house.

"Not a house," he told her, placing the melon on the seat of the bike, "more of a castle. She, the grandmother, she came from somewhere in the mountains." He pointed over his shoulder to the east. "She had it built just so. As she wanted it. People around here used to call it the Castle. They said she must have come from a place like it. Never fitted in here, she didn't."

"Who?" my mother asked.

"Petronella Rácz. Small, like you, she was. Tiny. Built that thing with turrets and towers. Her son added a courtyard where the carriages circled, the lawn with bushes in the shapes of bears and wild boar, the cellar where they laid down the wine, an icehouse bigger than the churchyard and people coming for parties all spring and summer. Everyone still talks about that place.

"My great-grandfather was overseer of the vineyard. We grew red Soproni grapes, sweeter than the Egri. Those fields there" — he pointed east of the cemetery — "were vines as far as the eye can see."

"What happened to it?"

The man shrugged. "What happened to everything around here. The commune tore out the vines. Bourgeois stuff, wine. They planted hybrid corn. The house is barracks for the army."

"Which army?"

"Whichever army happens by," he said. "In '41 it was the Hungarians and the Germans. In '45 the Russians. Right now it's the Serbs. Don't you know that where you come from?" He'd grown impatient with her questions.

We drove in the direction he'd pointed. The fields were winter brown, the stubble of the previous summer's corn, an oak tree in the distance. The road runs into a gate, a barbed-wire fence on either side. István parked the car near the fence, but not too near. One never knows with soldiers. There was a guardhouse and a young man in green uniform. His machine gun leaned against his knee. He was reading a paperback book. He regarded us with curiosity.

We tried German and English. István advised against Hungarian. In 1941, when the Hungarian Army marched back into Bácska singing patriotic songs about retaking the motherland, there were Serb partisans in the area. With a little help from the Germans, they rounded up some two thousand people and shot them. When the Serbs came back in 1947, they exacted revenge.

There was a time when Russian would have worked here, but now it was hard to tell how the Serbs felt about the Russians. In the end my mother smiled at the guard and pointed over the fields toward the barns, then circled us with her hand and made a walking gesture with her fingers. He nodded and let us pass.

There was mud and manure along the narrow path, the smell of cows near the old barns. A tractor was loading straw into feed bins. Two shaggy Hungarian sheepdogs barked at our approach. In the field past the barns there were a couple of bay horses nibbling at low branches on the aspen lining the path. Looking back over the barbed-wire fence between the aluminum sheds, we could just make out a long, yellow building, slate-grey roof, tall, gabled windows.

I thought of Petronella drawing those windows on a sheet of paper so the builder would know exactly how they should be and of György learning to skate over the pond where the aspen stand, of Jolán sitting in her garden tending her ole-anders somewhere near the yellow house and of young Vili running up this hill in the early morning sunshine when the world was still young, as he used to tell me, never stopping till he reached the fence where his black stallion waited for him to return from school.

EPILOGUE

"LIFE IS," VILI ONCE SAID, "a succession of loose ends, roads leading nowhere in particular, tales unfinished, so many left unexplored, endless possibilities lighting the way you travel. Often we don't even know what happened until the train we should have taken has already passed by. Whatever you do, grab the rail, jump on. Don't live a half-lived life."

It may have been Vili's words that made me start looking for my father. Or, it could have been the timing.

In my early teens, I developed an odd curiosity about him. It started at the Wanganui Sacred Heart Convent school, trying to deal with too many English-speaking strangers and realizing that neither my grandfather nor my mother was going to save me from the next set of unfathomable lessons. I began to tell myself stories about how my father and I would meet, he would instantly recognize me, clutch me to his chest and ask what he could do to make up for his absence throughout my life. I tried to cajole Leah into revealing where he was, and when that didn't work, I played for sympathy with Sari, who was acting deeply religious around then. She had once mentioned that she had heard from him. The addresses she gave me didn't work. My letters all came back "addressee unknown."

I hired a private detective with my first paycheque. I was finishing high school, earning my keep by working as a cleaning woman on what they called the "mental ward" of a Christchurch hospital. The detective reported that my father had lived in Perth, Australia, that he had remarried, and had left for somewhere in the United States. My money ran out before the detective found him there.

Years later, by some quirk of fate, with a whole world to choose from, my father and I both ended up in Canada.

One day in late 1975, when I was no longer even thinking about what might have happened to him, a stranger phoned me. "I saw the article about you in the newspaper, and I'm pretty sure I know your father," he said. At the time I was working at McClelland and Stewart, a Canadian publishing firm. There had been a story about publishing people that included a picture of me. "He has changed his name to Spencer and he lives in Winnipeg, but I'm certain it's him."

The stranger supplied a number of details about my father. He had married another Hungarian woman and lived with her and her two children. He was a social worker. He had dabbled in politics. He played bridge with style, though he was no professional; he was charming and witty; he read voraciously; he had a library that professed to interests in art and film, history and literature. He was a patron of the local theatre. The man on the phone knew him well, and he was sure my father would want to meet me.

"Would you like to meet him?" he asked.

It had been almost thirty years since I had last seen my father and I wasn't sure. In the end, though, I decided to explore what Vili had called the life unlived.

I called the number the man had given me, but couldn't find my voice. I called again, asked to speak to Mr. Spencer and hung up when he came to the phone. When I finally worked out the words to say, they seemed awkward and overly emotional, so I went for flippant when I called him next. We had a clumsy conversation during which I said I was, maybe, his daughter and he said that was impossible. He had no daughters and he had never been to Hungary, he was born Canadian. He sounded like Béla Lugosi in a bad vampire movie, still trying to say "the" and ending up with "de." I wanted to shout at him that it was not just his story, it was mine, too, and we had to end it somehow. But I didn't. I hung up.

A few months later I was in Winnipeg with my boss, the fearless Jack McClelland. It was around ten o'clock at night. We were having drinks at the Fort Garry bar and I told him the story. "Are you sure you want to know this guy?" he asked. I must have said yes, because he picked up the bar phone and called the number I gave him. He told Mr. Spencer that he was a stringer for *Time* magazine, that *Time* was doing a major story about his daughter, the editor in Toronto, and would he please consent to a brief interview.

It was a good lie, and it worked.

After some haggling, they agreed, and Jack handed me the phone. "You can pick it up from here," he said.

I couldn't. The right words still didn't assemble.

So Jack, still playing the part of a *Time* magazine reporter, arranged for us to meet.

The next day, when I finally saw my father, I was amazed at how ordinary he looked, and how much like me. We stood in his Winnipeg livingroom, his coffee table laden with books and magazines. There were photographs of his wife, and a young man and woman I assumed were her children. There was a worn couch, a Persian rug, a window overlooking a park, a TV set. His wife made tea and offered cookies.

I asked him why he had left Australia, and he told me he was still afraid of my grandfather. He had changed his name to escape Vili's ire, settled in Canada so Vili couldn't trace him and demand sixteen years' worth of child support. "Did you know how strong he was?" he asked. "Did you see him angry? Did you know he once ran a man through with his sword and threw a second man out a window ..."

"That was because of Leah. Not child support."

"He was capable of anything," my father said.

He didn't know my grandfather had been dead for eight years. He didn't ask about my mother, or Leah, or Sari. He didn't ask whether I had any children. He kept glancing toward his wife, nervously, anxiously, as if asking her permission to talk with me.

To my great relief, he didn't ask whether there really was a *Time* magazine feature.

I met him once more, when he was dying. He had Parkinson's and was huddled in a big brown armchair in the corner of their apartment. His wife told me how they had met and fallen in love in an Austrian refugee camp and how he had made so much effort to become a real father to her children. "He is a very good man. You should know that," she told me, and then she left us alone for a little.

He spoke haltingly. "There were so many other ways it could have gone," he whispered. "It was the war, you know. Puci and I, we never had a chance. You and I, maybe we could have been friends. Do you think we could have liked each other, in another life, could you have been fond of me? I have thought about you, you know. It's not been easy knowing you were out there."

When I said goodbye, he was crying.

He died in October 1995.

My mother had come to stay in Canada when my daughter Catherine (named after Kati, of course) was born. She had loved New Zealand but her marriage hadn't worked out. It hadn't been hopeless like the one to my father, or necessary like the one to Jenö, this one had been the one for love. But it didn't last.

She listened to the tale my father's wife had told me, the course of their life and their journey. When I finished she asked: "And what did he say about his Russian son?"

"His Russian son?"

"Didn't you know?" she seemed surprised. "I thought Leah would have told you. Or Sari. I thought I was the last to find out. I so often was the last to find out anything about him. Didn't he tell you he had a wife and a son somewhere in Siberia? The Russians encouraged the prisoners to mate."

"They did?"

"Perhaps they thought being married would give them more incentive to work hard. Perhaps they were less likely to escape. I doubt if they were thinking of the prisoners' comfort. But perhaps they were ..."

"How do you know about his other wife?"

She searched for an answer for a while, then admitted defeat. "I don't even know who told me, or how long I've known. It never seemed to matter. Didn't your grandfather tell you?"

"No."

"With all those stories, it's odd he should have left that one out."

When my mother plays bridge with her friends in Toronto, they often talk about "peacetime" and the dances they had enjoyed, and sometimes they talk about the forced marches through the snow on the way to Auschwitz where some of them lost their families. One of her friends rescued her little girl from a train on the way to the camps. She survived the last months of the war scrubbing floors at 60 Andrássy Avenue, then the Arrow Cross headquarters. They hadn't known she was Jewish. Another was in Hungary's Romanian embassy when the war ended and made her way on foot all the way across the Carpathians, then the Hungarian Alps and on to Vienna. Another had been in the Hungarian Army. They argue about whose house was hit first when the Russians came.

They know all the songs of my childhood. And sometimes they tell me stories I have not yet heard.